692.8 SKITMORE 11-99

CONTRACT BIDDING IN CONSTRUCTION.

Contract bidding in construction

Contract bidding in construction: Strategic management and modelling

MARTIN SKITMORE MSc., PhD., FRICS, MCIOB
SENIOR LECTURER
DEPT. CIVIL ENGINEERING
UNIVERSITY OF SALFORD
GR. MANCHESTER M5 4WT, UK

Longman
Scientific &
Technical

Longman Scientific & Technical.
Longman Group UK Limited,
Longman House, Burnt Mill, Harlow,
Essex CM20 2JE, England
and Associated Companies throughout the world.

First published 1989

British Library Cataloguing in Publication Data
Skitmore, R.M. (Ronald Martin)
   Contract bidding in construction
   1. Buildings. Construction. Contracts.
   Bidding
   I. Title
   692.8

ISBN 0-582-01855-2

Produced by Longman Group (FE) Limited
Printed in Hong Kong

To
Anne

If the organism carries a *small scale model* of external reality and of its own possible actions within its head, it is able to carry out various alternatives, conclude which is the best of them, react to future situations before they arise, utilize the knowledge of past events in dealing with the present and in the future, and in every way react in a fuller, safer and more competent manner to the emergencies which face it.

Craik, K. J. W., *The nature of explanation*, Cambridge University Press, 1943

Contents

Preface

It has been claimed that the *raison d'être* of any organisation is defined by its objective and objectives (Kempner 1976: 273) and, therefore, if an organisation fails to achieve its objectives it can be said to have failed as an organisation. In some organisations, however, particularly those established in the distant past, this precept is patently tautologic in that the existence of the organisation is its very objective.

Irrespective of any stated or unstated objectives is the fundamental need for direction, for without such direction the organisation '. . . is like a ship without a rudder, carried on a current of circumstances from crisis to crisis until it encounters a crisis that is too big to handle or that lasts just too long' (Fellows *et al.* 1983: 10). The seafaring analogy of objectives and direction provides some instructive examples. Columbus, for instance, appeared to be quite clear on these matters. Objective – India and the Spice Islands; direction – west. The objective, of course was never achieved by Columbus (although he failed to realise it), but the enterprise was nevertheless still considered to be successful.

Another, rather different, example concerns the Nobel Laureate Dr Fridtjof Nansen who, in 1893, in attempting to reach the North Pole, deliberately embedded his ship *The Fram* in the polar ice cap. In what has been described as the greatest human exploit of the nineteenth century (Cameron 1980: 121), *The Fram* and its intrepid twelve-man Norwegian crew finally re-emerged after a 3000-mile, three-year drift having passed quite close to the Pole en route (Nansen had, of course, taken the natural precaution of conducting some prior investigations into the polar currents and of substantially reinforcing *The Fram's* hull). Though failing to reach his objective, Nansen's exploits were nevertheless adjudged to have been highly successful. As for direction, it would seem that some knowledge of the future movement of the 'terrain' quite adequately compensated for the captain's inability to steer his vessel!

Key elements in these two examples are 'luck' and 'foresight' in the face of some degree of 'uncertainty'. An organisation possessing the quality of perfect luck or perfect foresight or operating under conditions of perfect certainty would seem to be in a very strong position indeed. This is not to say, of course, that the organisation will necessarily be successful even with these exceptional attributes. For the organisation to be successful, two other considerations are necessary. First, events outside the control of the organisation can obstruct its successful progress and, secondly, events within the control of the organisation may be handled badly.

With perfect luck, perfect foresight or in conditions of perfect certainty, events outside the control of the organisation simply constrain its activities. Events within the control of the organisation are a different matter. Perfect luck would suffice, but perfect foresight or conditions of perfect certainty are not sufficient on their own. What these last two qualities bring is a perfect knowledge of the outcome of decisions. The essential problem, it would seem, is to make decisions whose outcome will best ensure the successful progress of the organisation.

The solution to this demands some knowledge of three aspects of the problem: knowledge of what possible decisions could be made, knowledge of the outcome of each possible decision and knowledge of how these outcomes affect the successful progress of the organisation.

This is not the whole story, however: knowledge alone is not the answer – but wisdom in application of knowledge and a positive approach is (Rutland 1984: 17).

The knowledge is not easy to obtain, especially in view of the dynamic nature of the problem. Often action is limited, in these times of accelerating technical, social and economic change, to a business recognising opportunities and threats which could arise and altering course accordingly (Barnard 1981: 21).

Adrian (1973) and others have proposed 'the systems approach', and corporate planning systems in particular, as increasingly becoming a tool that senior management can use to influence the strategic direction of the firm. The development of such systems, however, is not any easy task for, as Bahrami advises:

> The challenge confronting academics and practitioners alike concerns the issue of how to develop corporate planning systems which are likely to cater for the firm's specific needs; how such systems can be used effectively in order to develop strategies

which integrate the firm's major goals, policies and action programmes into a cohesive whole; how this can help marshal and allocate resources which result in the adoption of a viable strategic posture based upon its competences and shortcomings, anticipated changes in the environment and contingent moves by intelligent opponents. (Bahrami 1981: 2, 224)

This is clearly a very ambitious programme indeed and is burdened with many severe difficulties in several dimensions, involving such fundamental questions as what is meant by knowledge, wisdom and successful progress and how can they be measured and acquired? A major issue is the role of information in decision-making, the understanding of which is, according to Young (1978), one of the central problems of management science.

Failure to address these issues has been the reason for the lack of application of many operations research techniques, for instance, often criticised for relying on oversimplified assumptions or the existence of data that are never actually available (Wagner 1971: 1273). The real challenge, according to Wagner, is to conduct substantive and robust analyses of research problems that arise from practical situations to identify the truly pivotal factors involved and enable the assessment of the potential application of formal solution techniques.

Strategic management is about making decisions which affect the future of the whole business enterprise. For construction contractors this means deciding which projects to undertake and, in a competitive environment, the bid levels necessary to secure them. One would expect to obtain guidance on these aspects by reference to books on either strategic management or bidding strategy. Unfortunately, this seems not to be the case.

Strategic management books are aimed primarily at companies providing a specific range of goods or services for clearance in the market-place. Decisions are of the profit/volume type and distributed across the whole range of goods or services. Although there are superficial similarities, some of the factors considered to be trivial in the general literature have major implications in the construction context. The acute lack of information, for instance, has quite far-reaching effects on the company's options and evaluation of options. In many cases the decision-maker will be only dimly aware of the opportunities available, the prices to be charged by competitors or even the likely production costs.

Bidding strategy, on the other hand, totally disregards many salient features of strategic decisions for mathematical convenience.

It is effectively a body of solution techniques looking for a suitable problem. A further difficulty is that, despite over 1000 publications on the subject over the last thirty years, there is as yet no standard text available.

My approach in collecting material for this book has been as purely empirical as humanly possible in simply recording all the evidence, both factual and circumstantial, remotely connected with the bidding decision. The next, and by far the most difficult, step was to attempt to find some theoretical structure which somehow embodied this evidence. This experience took me on a largely fruitless but nevertheless highly educational journey into many subject disciplines – Management Science, Behavioral Science, Economics, Pricing Theory, Decision Theory and Operations Research to name a few. Of all the literature covered at this time, three books were to have a major influence on the final outcome. First, Johnson & Scholes' *Exploring Corporate Strategy* suggested the basic structure of the decision process to be that of option evaluation and selection. From this I was able to develop the idea of strategic option identification as a means of restricting the option set independently of the selection decision. Secondly, Loomba's *Management: A Quantitative Perspective*, in suggesting breaking the problem down into deterministic and non-deterministic approaches, provided the means for separating the aspects caused by uncertainty. And finally, Ansoff's *Strategic Management* showed me the type of model to use and the courage that would be needed to use it.

The general arrangement of the book is in two parts. Part One describes the building of a strategic decision system, first by examination of some reported existing systems and then progressively by a step-by-step introduction of the key elements involved. Part Two is devoted exclusively to the application of statistical models to some aspects of the system.

One of the guiding principles in writing this book has been to avoid the simplification 'first state your objectives' as it is patently clear that, for construction companies at least, this task is no easier than any other decision.

The first chapter identifies bidding as a decision-making process and subject to all the usual problems associated with making decisions – the nature of the decision choice behaviour, motivation, the ability of the decision-maker, the environment and feedback, and group decision-making under conflict – concluding in the consideration of corporate decision-making for policies and strategies. Chapter 2 examines just what constitutes a strategic decision for a construction company and the nature of the decision choice process. The use and lack of use of corporate decision systems by construction companies is tackled next, leading to some proposals relating to the scope, practical needs and design of such systems.

Chapter 3 is the first of three chapters aimed at building up a conceptual model of the project selection/bidding environment. This chapter deals with all the issues associated with the static, deterministic version of the problem – the outcome environment, consisting of people, property and money; and project character-istics, covering the types of work, types of clients, geographical location, and competitors. In recognition of the existence of multiple and conflicting objectives, some recent techniques are described by which a formal approach to the decision can be made. Chapter 4 introduces time-related aspects of the decision. The main effect is to redefine the problem from that of simultaneous to sequential project selection. A modified form of Gottinger's 'sequential machine' model is described in which all the components of the decision appear.

Chapter 5 describes the final stage of the model-building process in which all the remaining non-deterministic aspects of the situation are introduced. Because of the uncertain nature of the factors involved, the informational net must be cast wider for knowledge of likely future events. As far as project opportunities are concerned, this involves considerations of political, economic, social and technological factors. Four separate studies are described which attempt to formalise the project selection procedure and a final conceptual model is presented which incorporates all the major features of the decision.

Chapter 6 completes the specification of the project decision sys-tem by defining the various options available to the decision-maker. Several general decision strategies are considered as possible option identification rules. The need to make future decisions is dealt with by a nested version of Gottinger's machines. Finally, the system is examined in terms of computational load and the major difficulty is found to be in the size of potential option combinations. Some strategies are described which may alleviate the situation.

Part Two describes the various statistical approaches that have been made to aspects of the problem. Models of construction demand and the occurrence of project characteristics are examined together with such aspects of outcomes as cost and estimated cost. Various likely probability distribution types and parameters are described. Statistical models of bidding behaviour, both collective and individual, are also covered in this chapter, together with such topics as collusion, data limitations and suicidally low bids. Finally, an introduction to the probability of entering the lowest bid is made.

I have been extremely fortunate in gaining really high-quality help and guidance in the work that has gone into this book (see footnote). My thanks and gratitude go to the many people who generously gave me their time and energy. Inspiration in the early days came from Professor Ron McCaffer and Brian Fine with moral and intellectual support from my dear and former colleagues Professor Roger Burgess and Dr Ted Traynor. Jonathan Aylen and Professor Milner of the Department of Economics contributed their views on the role of economic theory and models in construction. Professor Kenneth Gee, of the Department of Business and Administration, and Professors Geoff Lockett and Doug White of the Manchester University Business School provided valuable insights into bidding models and the application of multi-attribute theory. Marcel Weverberg of the University of Antwerp volunteered several of his own publications on bidding. My thanks also go to John Laing (North West) plc, Trollope and Colls Ltd and Joe Matthews of Adamson Butterly who, among other construction organisations, provided practical advice on the reality of bidding. Peter Harlow of the Chartered Institute of Building and Mike Patchett of the Salford College of Technology greatly helped in covering the literature. Richard Fellows and Bob Newcombe, both of Brunel University, contributed on aspects of company objectives, as did Peter Lansley of Reading University, who also provided me with a very useful restricted access report and other published material including the translated paper by Dressel (c.1980).

There are many others who contributed in some way and I trust that they will forgive my failing to give them a mention. There are four remaining people that deserve a special mention. Dr Mike Paterfield, recently of the Department of Mathematics, gave me considerable assistance in modelling bids and in developing the multivariate approach. Roy Thomas of my own department has been subjected to the most terrible pestering by myself over the last six years, all of which he has endured both graciously and positively. Without Roy, this book would certainly not exist. Dr Ernest Wilde of the Department of Mathematics has been my guide and mentor over the last five years, offering steadfast encouragement and fatherly advice on all occasions. The developments on the multivariate approach to bid analysis are directly attributable to Ernest's early work on formulating the problem.

Finally, I must thank my wife Anne who not only typed the original manuscript, tolerated the lengthy periods of my time spent in researching and preparing this book, but also played some part in conceiving and developing the concepts involved.

Martin Skitmore
Salford, 1988.

Footnote: most of the preparatory work was undertaken between 1981 and 1986. The author would be grateful to receive any information concerning similar or relevant work since 1986 for possible inclusion in a further edition of the book.

Acknowledgements

We are indebted to the following for permission to reproduce copyright material:

American Society of Civil Engineers for table 7.1 by Gates from table 2, p. 294 of *Journal of Construction* Vol. 97, 102 (1971); Blackwell Scientific Publications Ltd. for figs. 3.1, 3.2 & 3.3 from tables, pp. 311–316 of *Modern Construction Management* (2nd Edition) by Harris & McCaffer (1983); Butterworth Scientific Ltd. for fig. 5.1 from a figure by H. J. Otway and P. D. Pahner in *Futures* Vol. 8, 2 (April 1976); Chartered Institute of Building for table 3.1 by McKenzie and Harris from table 3, pp. 25–29 of *Building Technology and Management* Vol. 22, 5 (1984); Kluwer Academic Publishers (Dordrecht) for fig. 4.1 adapted from a figure by Gottinger in *Coping with Complexity Perspectives for Economics, Management and Social Sciences* (1983); Pergamon Press Plc. for fig. 6.1 by Grinyer from fig. 1, p. 9 of *Operations Research Quarterly* Vol. 24, 2 (1973); University of Bath (School of Management) for fig. 5.2 adapted from 'Long Range Planning and the Construction Industry' – unpublished thesis by M. Foster (1974).

Part One

Strategic management

1

Decision-making

Pricing as a decision-making process

Contract bidding is essentially a commercial activity and is closely related to product pricing. As in product pricing, contract bidding decisions are not made in isolation but are related to other decisions concerning product range, production and marketing. These decisions collectively influence the demand for and sales of products and affect the financial state of the company. Sales also affect and are affected by the demand for products and have a direct influence on financial state (Fig. 1.1).

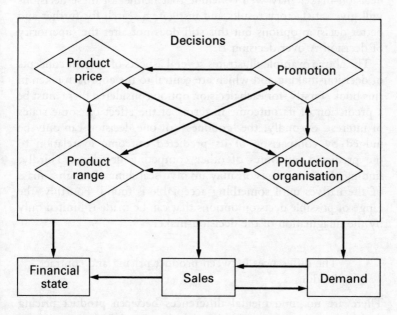

Fig. 1.1 Product pricing

3

The important feature of this system as depicted in Fig. 1.1 is that decisions are seen as the *cause* of outcomes such as demand, sales and financial states. This is not to say, of course, that such states are determined exclusively by company decisions, for clearly other external factors over which the company has no control, such as government policies and the current economic climate, also have an (often considerable) effect. From the point of view of company decision-making, however, the interest lies in the results of its own decisions. Any changes in outcomes caused by external events will, by definition, happen anyway. It follows therefore that the 'goodness' of the company's decisions can only be judged *relative to each other*. For a simple example, if decision A will result in a financial state of £90 000 and decision B will result in a financial state of £70 000 over the same time period under the same external factors, then decision A can be said to be £20 000 'better' than decision B, and decision B £20 000 'worse' than decision A (under the assumption that more money is better than less money!). If we further introduce the fact that the financial state was £100 000 before the decision was made, then we can deduce that the decisions will result in a loss of £10 000 and £30 000, or 10 and 30 per cent, respectively. On this basis the decision-maker may well conclude that neither of these decisions will give satisfactory results and instigate a search for further and better decision options but this still does not alter the superiority of decision A over decision B.

The above example illustrates several aspects of current concepts of decision-making and which are central to the approach taken in this book. Firstly, for each decision option considered there must be a prediction of its outcome in terms of the effect on some states of interest. Secondly, the 'goodness' of one decision can only be judged by comparison of its predicted outcome in relation to the predicted outcomes of other competing decisions. Thirdly, finding the 'best' decision may involve searching through a mass of alternatives until something acceptable is found. Fourthly, the range of possible decision options that can be made is limited only by the imagination of the decision-maker.

The differences between product pricing and contract bidding

There are no fundamental differences between product pricing decisions and contract bidding decisions. All the conceptual elements of the decision process shown in Fig. 1.1 are present in both types of decisions although the names commonly used may be different. The important differences that do exist are of emphasis rather than direct disagreement. These differences fall into three categories – the buyer/seller relationship, the economics of mass production, and the aspects of time and uncertainty.

The buyer/seller relationship

There is a well-established convention that, in the consumer goods industry for instance, the seller is the manufacturer/producer/wholesaler/retailer who places his product on the consumer goods market and the buyer is the consumer who selects and ultimately pays for the goods. Insofar as contracting is concerned, this distinction is not quite as clear-cut. On the one hand the contractor places his goods or services on the contract market (the seller) and the client selects the contractor and ultimately pays for the contractor's goods and services (the buyer). On the other hand the client places his contract on the contract market (the seller) and the contractor selects and ultimately pays for the contract in terms of goods or services (the buyer). The difficulty is, of course, due to the inconsistent interpretation of goods/services and payments. It is equally valid (but unconventional) to refer to a transaction as a process in which producers 'buy' consumers' money and consumers 'sell' their money to producers. The root cause of the problem is in the arbitrary distinction between goods/service and money, which inhibits the analysis of transactions involving the exchange of goods/services alone or money alone, and the assumption that price is a fixed characteristic of the product rather than occurring as a result of market forces.

In contract bidding a more fruitful approach to defining the client/contractor relationship is to consider each as a decision-maker trying to get the 'best deal' for himself. What constitutes a 'best deal' is clearly a matter of judgement for the individual decision-maker, but we can guess that the client will be looking for a contractor to provide the goods or services he needs at a right price, and the contractor will be looking for a contract to provide an opportunity for the provision of goods or services at a right price. This implies for the client the existence of a relationship between each potential contractor and the level of benefits to be received from each and, for the contractor, a relationship between each potential contract and the level of benefits to be received from each. In decision-making terms, the client must complete at least a two-stage decision-making sequence. Firstly, he has to consider the range of contract (specification or framing) options available to him and the likely consequences of each option has to be predicted before making the final decision. Secondly, on receipt of bids for the contract, the client has to consider the range of contractor selection options available to him together with the likely consequences of each option. These second-stage decision options are not, of course, limited to a mere binary selection from the bids received: the possibility of negotiation, rebid, abandon etc. should also be included. The contractor also has to consider a possible two-stage decision-making sequence – whether to bid or not and, if the former, the various bids and alternatives (such as contract duration) he could offer together with the likely consequences of each decision option.

The economics of mass production

There is a virtually obsessional treatment in the literature of the economics of mass production of consumer goods in the form of product mix strategies based on the so-called price mechanism. Contracting companies, on the other hand, display a seemingly indifferent attitude to product mix problems.

Three major factors exist to explain this indifference, certainly in the construction industry. Firstly, the price of construction work generally has little, if any, affect on the overall demand for construction. Secondly, there is no mass market for individual contracts. Thirdly, the flexibility of production enabled by the common and wide-ranging craft skills available to the company, either internally or by means of sub-contracting, enables many types of contracts to be undertaken without the need for retooling or reskilling. This does not mean that the range of contracts is not an important issue. It simply means that the usual economic approaches to product mixing by optimising on price/demand curves are inappropriate in this kind of situation. For contracting companies the major concern is to make any sales at all. These companies operate in a very competitive world where, because of the contracting situation, product differentiation is virtually non-existent. Here product mixing is seen to occur as a result of moving into less competitive markets rather than as a resourcing problem.

Time and uncertainty

Unlike the usual view of product pricing as a static situation in which production/pricing/sales are assumed to occur virtually simultaneously, in construction work this process takes relatively far longer and involves many contract overlaps. This means that the situation must be viewed as a flow process in which events need to be considered over a continuous time period.

It is also clear that, unlike the economists' world of mass production where repetitive production costs and price levels are assumed to be accurately known, the construction contracting situation demands that estimates be made of the price level and future production costs for a product and in an environment only loosely resembling previous products and environments. This means that the situation must be viewed as non-deterministic in which events need to be considered in terms of their probability of occurrence.

The structure of decision-making

Although decision-making is one of the most common forms of mental activity known to man, there does not appear to be any complete theoretical basis which adequately describes or models the processes involved. Decision-making, however, must, by definition, involve some choice among alternatives for there to be any decision at all.

In human decision-making the relationship between alternatives and choices can be quite complicated. An approach often prescribed is to first assemble all the possible alternatives (decision options) that are available and then to choose the most favourable-looking option. The alternative is to first postulate a decision that would be favourable and then to find out if such a decision is really available. A little thought soon reveals that the second approach would be unnecessary if a truly exhaustive set of alternatives could be assembled. While it is theoretically possible to assemble a set of this nature, it is clear that the cost of such a procedure will often be prohibitive. What is needed is an *efficiently reduced set of options*. It follows from the foregoing argument that the efficiency of this reduced set will be determined by the trade-off between the cost of finding some options and the probability of overlooking a better option – a kind of Pareto optimality. In cost terms, conservatism or 'stick with the knitting' policies are seen as low-cost option derivation procedures. The existence of an 'opportunity set', in which decision options are provided by some external agency, also falls into this category. Thorough investigations, such as feasibility studies and market research, on the other hand, are seen as relatively high-cost option derivation procedures.

7

The precise way in which decision choices are made is the subject of a great deal of controversy and many competing models have been proposed. These models can be divided into either option-oriented or outcome-oriented decision choices. Option-oriented choices are usually associated with simple gambling policies such as always choosing the same option (e.g. backing top-weight horses) or purely random choices (e.g. selecting bets with a 'pin'). The essential feature of option-oriented choices is that no attempt is made to evaluate the outcome of the options available. Here the decision-maker is simply applying some formula or *policy* to the choice of options, as a result perhaps of some previous analysis, in the hope that a favourable outcome will result. Outcome-oriented choice processes attempt to relate each decision option with the anticipated outcome of that option. The decision-maker then chooses between outcomes which will then determine the appropriate decision option. As with option-oriented choices, some formula or *strategy* may be applied, but in this case the formula will provide a means of choosing among outcomes rather than decision options. The different use of the terms 'policy' and 'strategy' here is deliberate in that *policies are viewed as a means of governing decisions by directly dictating the choice among decision options while strategies are viewed as a means of governing decisions indirectly by dictating the choice among anticipated decision outcomes.* There is also a cost implication associated with policies and strategies. In general terms, policies should provide low-cost decisions while strategies, requiring some knowledge of outcomes, will entail relatively higher-cost decisions. Also in general terms, the use of strategies is more likely to provide more favourable outcomes than policies as strategies utilise more knowledge. Again, an efficient procedure seems to be needed in trading-off the costs and results associated with the use of policies or strategies.

Different types of policies and strategies are distinguished by the *techniques* employed. These techniques range from purely fixed to purely random. In the betting analogy, these are, for policies, equivalent to the 'always bet on top weight' (fixed) and 'select with a pin' (random). In the same analogy, for strategies, the equivalents are 'always bet on the horse with the greatest probability of winning' (fixed) and 'select a real number between zero and unity with a pin and match it to the horse with the nearest probability of winning nearest this number' (random). Policies and strategies employing purely random techniques clearly result in identical decisions, the only difference being that random strategies, by the definition used here, require some prior knowledge of likely outcomes and are, therefore, generally the more inefficient of the two procedures. Fixed policies and strategies come in many, sometimes very complex, forms. In general, the use of techniques of greater complexity is more likely to provide more favourable outcomes than simpler techniques as complex techniques utilise more knowledge, but at a greater cost. Once more, an efficient procedure is needed in trading-off costs and results associated with the use of different techniques.

From the above analysis it can be seen that the structure of decision-making involves three distinct sub-decisions to be made: firstly, the decision options to be considered; secondly, whether the decision will be governed by a policy or a strategy; and thirdly, the type of policy or strategy to be employed. All these sub-decisions are concerned with trade-offs between knowledge (of the main decision options available and their associated outcomes) and the costs involved in the acquisition and application of this knowledge. Quite *what* sub-decisions are made depends on the context of the decision-making situation and the decision-maker himself.

Decision choice behaviour

It is possible to conceive of all kinds of life forms as decision-makers in some sense. Even 'unthinking' forms such as plants could be treated in some sense conceptually as decision-making mechanisms in that they 'decide' when to germinate, flower, reproduce, etc., or 'how' to adapt to changing environmental conditions. What prevents us from seriously regarding plants as decision-makers is that we are reluctant to accept the proposition that plants are in any way aware of alternative courses of action that may be available. In other words, we do not consider a plant capable of undertaking our first sub-decision, i.e. assembling a decision option set. Applying this same argument to animals, however, makes it less easy to dismiss the notion that some processes more closely resembling decision-making may be possible.

Battalio *et al.* (1986) describes a series of experiments in which some rats were allowed a choice between food and a 1 per cent sodium saccharine solution and some pigeons were allowed a choice between food and not working ('leisure'). The object of the experiments was to examine the animals' behaviour in relation to four competing hypotheses concerning the basis of the 'behavioral allocation rules' involved. The first of these hypotheses was that essentially random behaviour controls choice, the most prominently cited example of this being Becker's (1962) economic irrational choice model. This hypothesis seems, according to Battalio, particularly appropriate for organising animals' choices given their limited cognitive capacities. The second hypothesis was Herrnstein's (1961, 1970) 'matching law'. The matching law is the leading quantitative choice model employed by psychologists for describing choices between concurrently available choices, primarily with respect to time-based activities. Under this hypothesis the relative amount of time spent on an activity is proportional to the relative reinforcement obtained from that activity. The third hypothesis was Staddon's (1979) 'minimum distance' hypothesis under which behaviour is conceived as being organised by attempts to achieve a preferred distribution of activities, and that when faced with constraints on their activities, organisms choose a distribution which minimises deviations from the preferred point. The fourth hypothesis was the 'generalised CES utility function', prevalent in much of the economics literature. This hypothesis is the antithesis of the minimum distance hypothesis in that choice behaviour is regarded as being a motivational process in which individuals have minimum consumption requirements, either necessary for survival or psychologically determined, which must be met prior to having any discretionary choice over expenditures.

In the experiments with the rats, two levers were available. One lever delivered food pellets in predetermined amounts, and the other delivered a 1 per cent sodium saccharine solution in predetermined cupfuls. Two variables were systematically manipulated – the number of total allowable lever presses and the size of the sodium saccharine cup. All other variables, such as the level of hunger and thirst of the rats, were held constant experimentally. The data obtained from observing the two rats involved were examined against the four hypotheses resulting in the conclusion that the fourth one, the generalised minimum needs hypothesis, was generally the most appropriate, the other three competing hypotheses having a probability of less than 0.001 of being correct. Significant differences were, however, found between the observed behaviour of the two rats leading to the conclusion that consistent aggregation across individual subjects would be somewhat problematical.

In the other experiments, the job task consisted of pigeons pecking a response key for access to a food hopper containing mixed pigeon grains. In this case the variable systematically manipulated was the number of responses required per payoff of food. Other variables, including the amount of 'free' and 'earned' food available, the overall and hopper access time allowed, audio distractions, and the pigeons' hunger and thirst levels, were held constant experimentally. Identical results to the rats' experiment were found, that is, the generalised minimum needs hypothesis applied and significant differences existed between the four pigeons involved.

These experiments serve to illustrate some of the problems involved in the analysis of decision-making and psychological processes generally. We will, however, restrict our considerations to the experiments in terms of the structure of decision-making.

1. The experimental procedure was designed to severely restrict the set of decision options available to the animals by providing an 'opportunity set' of feeding alternatives. Whether the animals were able to expand this experimental set to include further alternatives of their own was not recorded. The assumption was, of course, that the desire to feed would distract the animals from all other considerations. It is, however, quite common for animals to inconveniently pursue other matters during the course of experiments of this nature, indicating that other options have not been entirely eliminated.

2. It is not clear whether the animals were making decisions as a matter of policy or strategy in these experiments. In other words, were they pressing the response key simply because pressing response keys was a good thing to do irrespective of what might happen (policy), or because they wished to obtain some food (strategy)? The distinction is not quite as fatuous as it may seem. Policy presses can be induced by a conditional reflex, for instance where 'decisions' appear to follow from training or previous experience and quite independent of outcomes. Again, no details are recorded of the animals' background to assess this factor, nor of any evidence of learned behaviour during the experiments. It must be assumed, however, that a researcher of Battalio's experience would carefully control this aspect of the investigation.

3. The object of the experiments was to ascertain the technique used by the animals in arriving at their decision choice, described by Battalio *et al.* as the motivational forces underlying individual subject behaviour. The result of this, the generalised minimum needs model, is significant in that

it suggests the animals were applying some *survival* mechanism to the task. The other result reported by Battalio, that individual 'subjects' seemed to exhibit different choice behaviour, is also very significant in suggesting that, even with life forms of these very limited cognitive capacities, no one single policy or strategy model exists to explain the actions of all the 'decision-makers' studied.

Battalio *et al's* view of decision choice behaviour as being in some way related to motivational forces is a view shared by many in the decision-making field. Motivation, dealing with both arousal to action and the direction and persistence of that action, can be defined as a label for the determinants of (a) the choice to initiate effort on a certain task, (b) the choice to expend a certain amount of effort, and (c) the choice to persist in expending effort over a period of time. That is, motivation has to do with a set of independent/dependent variable relationships that explain the direction, amplitude and persistence of an individual's behaviour, holding constant the effects of aptitude, skill and understanding of the task, and the constraints operating in the environment (Campbell and Pritchard 1976: 65).

This definition supports the view that motivation is an important factor in decision choice behaviour, but also highlights the necessity to consider other, perhaps equally important aspects, such as the ability of the decision-maker, his knowledge of the task, and the impact of the environment. In animal experiments such as described by Battalio *et al.*, these other aspects can be kept to a minimum experimentally (by controlling the environment) and by suitable choice of 'subjects' (life forms of limited cognitive ability and understanding). Human decision choice behaviour in the 'real world' is much more complex and involves the consideration of all these varied and interrelated aspects of motivation, ability, understanding and environment.

Motivation

Like decision-making generally, there is no single theory of motivation. The many theories that have been proposed can be broadly divided into two classes: content theories, which are concerned with the identification of those variables that influence behaviour and pay little attention to the means by which that influence is achieved; and process theories, which focus on the mechanisms by which desires are translated into action. Both classes of theories are rather narrow in their outlook, however, being rather like the blind man describing the elephant, with each focusing only on a part of a more complex overall picture (Filer 1986: 268). In terms of our model of decision-making, content theories deal with the type of outcomes that are likely to be of interest to the decision-maker while process theories deal with the techniques that decision-makers use. Some of these theories are reviewed below.

Content theories of motivation

Most content theories are some form of 'need'-based theory of motivation. As such, they are derived from the concept of needs as presented by Murray (1938) and in which he hypothesised, based on clinical observations, the existence of over twenty specific needs that human beings attempt to satisfy with their actions. Motivation to undertake an action is said to occur because the taking of that action can at least partially meet one or more of these needs.

In 1954, Maslow postulated that human needs fall into a well-ordered hierarchy of several levels. He believed that needs at one level must be largely satisfied or met before the individual would attend to those at a higher level. Thus the difference between the needs of individuals and the difference between an individual's needs over time may be attributed to the difference between the individuals' and individual places on the hierarchy.

The hierarchy proposed by Maslow contains five categories which are, in order of decreasing potency:

1. *Physiological needs*, or the need for food, water, sex, etc.
2. *Safety needs*, or the need for security and freedom from bodily threat.
3. *Social needs*, or the need for belonging, friendship, affection and love.
4. *Esteem needs*, or the need for both self-respect and the respect of others.
5. *Self-actualisation needs*, or the drive to achieve fulfilment of one's goals and potential.

Alderfer (1972) reformulated Maslow's hierarchy into three basic categories called existence needs, relatedness needs, and growth needs (ERG model). In Maslow terms, existence needs are similar to physiological needs in pertaining to needs for physical substances that are in limited supply, such as food, clothing or shelter. Relatedness needs involve the social aspects of human intercourse such as love and communication. Growth needs are similar to Maslow's self-actualisation needs. Although the ERG need categories are similar to Maslow's, Alderfer places less emphasis on the hierarchical aspect of the categories, believing that all three categories must be met for an individual to be content with his/her environment.

Georgescu-Roegen (1966) has also considered hierarchical structures in his dialectic laws of consumer behaviour. The most important law is that needs are arranged in a hierarchy with three distinct layers: biological needs, with the same hierarchy for all human beings; social needs, with the same hierarchy for all members of the same society; and personal needs, with no uniform hierarchy.

Akin to the work of Maslow and Alderfer is that of both McGregor (1960) and Argyris (1957). McGregor divides human beings into two broad types: those who are primarily motivated by a desire to satisfy lower-level needs (Type X) and those who are self-motivated and seek self-actualisation (Type Y). Argyris further postulates that the natural course of human development is to progress toward 'maturation', defined as increased activity, independence, awareness of and control over self, aspiration for superior (or at least equal) position, and the development of long-range perspectives. Here, the inherent needs hierarchy of Maslow is reasserted but with the implication, in Argyris' model, of some continuum of human 'development' or development states.

In the decision-making environment, need-based motivation theories imply that an individual's decisions are determined in part by how well the anticipated outcomes of decisions are perceived to satisfy the needs that are uppermost in his/her attention at that time. This implication equally applies in situations where the decision-makers and decision recipients are separated. Thus an employer's decisions will be influenced to some extent by his/her own need status together with the need status of the employees. Individuals who are still primarily dealing with lower-level needs might best be served by the provision of increased money (with which they could buy food or housing), but those for whom these needs had already been met would be better served by recognition and the chance for accomplishment (thus bolstering their self-esteem and self-actualisation).

To the extent that the individual and society associate self-worth with income, added monetary rewards may also help to satisfy

14

these needs. Perhaps this helps to explain the extensive reliance on money as a motivator. Money alone, among all possible types of outcomes, can contribute toward the satisfaction of all levels of needs, thereby at least reducing the importance of correctly identifying an employee's current need status (Filer 1986: 271). Filer, in support of this statement, cites Guzzo and Bondy's (1983) survey of productivity-enhancing experiments in the USA where it was found that financial compensation was an effective way of elevating productivity in a wide variety of situations, including several where it might be assumed that workers' lower-level needs had been largely satisfied. There is a flaw in this argument, however, in that Filer implicitly assumes a one-to-one correspondence between productivity and motivation/needs, thereby compounding the already uncertain validity of the needs-based theories of motivation. On the evidence presented by Filer, it is by no means proven that changes in productivity associated with changes in remuneration are necessarily exclusively related to needs status.

Although the concept of need hierarchies has met with wide acceptance among practising managers, it seems to have lost favour among theorists in recent years. In part this may be due to difficulties in obtaining empirical support for these theories. Another factor is that the structure of needs seems to differ across individuals and groups in ways beyond simple differences in the extent to which higher-level needs have been called into play by the satisfaction of lower-level ones (see Friedlander 1965, for instance).

Process theories of motivation

Process theories, sometimes known as cognitive theories, of motivation tend to focus on the expectations people have regarding the outcomes associated with different courses of action. Thus individuals will make choices based on the attractiveness of possible outcomes and their relative probability of occurrence. This idea forms the basis for what is currently the most influential theory of motivation – expectancy or VIE theory.

Expectancy theory, as outlined by Vroom (1964), maintains that choices are based on two factors: the valence or attractiveness of possible specific outcomes and the expectancy or belief that a behaviour (chosen task or decision) will lead to these possible specific outcomes. In between actual task performance and eventual outcomes may lie intervening or intermediate outcomes, called 'instruments'. The relationship between these instruments and the final, desired outcomes is termed 'instrumentality'. For instance, an individual may believe that by increasing effort he/she may increase his/her productivity and that this will lead to two results. First, the increase in productivity may lead to a greater remuneration from an employer. Second, his/her colleagues may see this behaviour as anti-social and shun him/her during break times. The eventual decision about whether or not to increase effort will depend on the perceived value of added remuneration relative to the experienced 'pain' of colleague resentment (the relative valences), the perceived probabilities that each of these would result from increased productivity (that is, how likely are both the employer and colleagues to notice and respond to the added output – the expectancies) and, finally, the extent to which added effort can produce added productivity (instrumentality).

This formulation of motivational theory leads to the conception of a decision tree in which there are several possible, mutually exclusive courses of action. Each action is expected to lead with some probability to each of several possible outcomes which will, in turn, lead with some probability to desired rewards or undesired punishments. By attaching numerical values to each of the possible rewards and punishments, and numerical combinations, it should be possible to calculate the course of action with the highest satisfaction value attached to its expected outcome(s). Quite how these values are quantified, however, is not addressed by the theory, as formulated by Vroom. They are simply taken as given, although Vroom has commented that if the perceived valences of a number of outcomes are highly correlated and an individual responds similarly to all of them, they might be regarded as needs.

Porter and Lawler (1968) modified Vroom's basic theory by considering the dynamical effects of the motivational process in terms of feedback loops. In their model, individuals are assumed to alter their anticipated effort/reward contingencies as a result of experience of actual outcomes. Thus, in behavioural psychology terms, reinforcement affects cognition, a process we might call learning. This involves the consideration of the effects on anticipated satisfaction that would be derived from a particular reward by past satisfaction of that reward. If this relationship is negative, we are in a world where satisfaction of a need reduces its importance as a motivator (as with Maslow's theory). On the other hand, it is possible that experience with certain rewards increase their valence (habit or addiction).

There is also some evidence (Atkinson 1957, for example) to

suggest that the degree of motivation rises with the probability that increased effort will lead to desired rewards until a certain point where the task becomes so 'easy' that it ceases to be a challenge and reward achievement seems almost a certainty. This implies the existence of two further factors affecting motivation: firstly, a desire to learn and improve skill levels; secondly, the need for stimulation provided by an uncertain and risky environment.

Another addition to the basic expectancy theory model involves the influence of relative rewards. Called equity theory (from Adams 1963), the dominant principle is that we are motivated to maintain equality in the ratio between the amount of effort we exert and the outcomes it generates and the effort and outcomes of 'others' who we feel are a relevant comparison group. The evidence suggests that those who feel themselves underpaid, relative to others, tend to reduce their efforts accordingly, while those who are overpaid tend to believe they deserve their overpayment!

There is an extensive literature that attempts to verify process models of motivation empirically. These studies have been undertaken in a variety of settings (laboratory and field), using a variety of methods (manipulation and correlation) and a variety of measures of dependent variables (including job preference, rated effort, performance and satisfaction). In general the results of these studies are not as positive as the widespread acceptance of the framework might lead one to believe they would be. There are, however, according to Filer (1986: 276), sufficient problems with the studies (limitations in the data, etc.) to make it unwise at present to contemplate any fundamental changes in process theory. One important factor is that, although the theory is formulated in terms of *intra* individual behaviour, most of the empirical work has been done using variations *across* individuals. Thus, without it being explicitly stated, an additional condition that all individuals behave in an identical manner has been imposed.

The ability of the decision-maker

The ability of the decision-maker, when considered in isolation from any underlying motivations or environmental constraints, is judged by his/her competence to execute the three sub-decisions contained in our model – the assembly of decision options, and the choice and application of policies or strategies. Viewed in these terms, such a competence seems to rely on rather straightforward technical abilities involving a minimal amount of judgemental expertise. In many cases, decision-makers do perceive their (and others) tasks to be limited in this way. Professional administrators, for example, can often fall into this category. It is clear, however, that decision-making offers a very wide range of opportunities for the decision-maker to display and exercise decision-making skills. In terms of the assembly of decision options, for instance, the range of options is said to be limited only by the imagination of the decision-maker himself. Similarly, forecasting outcomes associated with each decision option would seem to require an extraordinary ability to see into the future.

The study of decision-making ability is essentially a study of the psychological processes of the decision-maker. Unfortunately, as with most aspects of decision-making, no one generally accepted theory or set of rules has yet been proposed to account for the whole of psychological phenomena. From the preceding discussion, it seems that *perception* is likely to be an important factor in distinguishing decision-making abilities – perception of the decision options available, and perception of the likely outcomes arising from each option are two obvious examples.

There is a vast literature, both theoretical and empirical, on how individuals perceive the world (e.g. Bruner 1957; Kelly 1955) that can be applied to decision-making ability. These contributions suggest that *cognitive sets* determine, to a large degree, one's perceptions and behaviour. The notion of cognitive sets is derived from the cognitive psychologist's model of behaviour, in which an individual is viewed as an *information processor* and therefore his/her decision-making ability is determined by the way he/she uses information to make decisions. The model implies that information is obtained from an individual's environment and is interpreted through the individual's 'cognitive image' of the environment. The cognitive image or set provides a representation of the environment based on past experiences and essentially predisposes the person to respond to information in predictable ways. These patterns are represented by an individual's policies or beliefs about the environment (Brunswik, cited in Hammond 1965). Human decisions are based then upon one's often incorrect interpretation of available information. This leads to judgements considered as probability statements about one's environment and how one reacts to it. This conclusion leads to the human judgement process, and hence decision-making ability, being inherently limited.

The nature of these limitations can be considered in terms of *bias* and *inconsistency*, where bias is a measure of the average error of judgement and inconsistency is a measure of range of departures from this average. In statistical parlance, bias may be represented by the mean error, and inconsistency may be represented by the standard deviation of errors around that mean. We shall, however, retain the psychological terminology in examining these two limiting characteristics of decision-making ability.

Biases in decision-making

The leading research in judgemental biases is that of Amos Tversky and Daniel Kahneman. These two research psychologists have identified a limited number of factors (termed heuristics) which seem to guide human behaviour in performing complex information-processing tasks. In many cases these heuristics appear to result in reasonable judgements but they can often lead to distorted and systematically erroneous decisions. The three fundamental heuristics involved in making probabilistic judgements are: representativeness, availability, and anchoring and adjustment.

Representativeness

Many of the probabilistic questions with which people are concerned belong to one of the following types: What is the probability that object A belongs to class B? What is the probability that process B will generate event A? In answering such questions, people typically rely on the representativeness heuristic, in which probabilities are estimated by the degree to which A is representative of B, that is, the degree to which A resembles B. An illustration is provided by Kahneman and Tversky in which an individual has been described by a former neighbour as 'Steve is very shy and withdrawn, invariably helpful, but with little interest in people, or in the world of reality. A meek and tidy soul, he has a need for order and structure, and a passion for detail.' The question is how people assess the probability that Steve is engaged in a particular occupation from a list of possibilities (e.g. farmer, salesman, airline pilot, librarian or physician)? In the representative heuristic, the probability that Steve is a librarian, for example, is assessed by the degree to which he is representative of, or similar to, the perceived stereotype of a librarian. Indeed, research with problems of this type has shown that people order the occupations by probability and by similarity in exactly the same way (Kahneman and Tversky 1973). This approach to the judgement of probabilities leads to serious errors, because similarity, or representativeness, is not influenced by several factors that should affect judgements of probability. Six factors have been identified in this respect.

The first factor is *base-rate frequencies*, or prior probabilities. In the case of Steve, for example, the fact that there are many more farmers than librarians in the population should enter into any reasonable estimate of the probability that Steve is a librarian rather than a farmer. Kahneman and Tversky's work indicates that such facts tend to be ignored in these situations. In their experiments, subjects were shown brief personality descriptions of several individuals, allegedly sampled at random from a group of 100 professionals – engineers and lawyers. The subjects were asked to assess, for each description, the probability that it belonged to an engineer rather than a lawyer. In one experimental condition, subjects were told that the group from which the descriptions had been drawn consisted of 70 engineers and 30 lawyers. In another condition, they were told that the group consisted of 30 engineers and 70 lawyers. Despite the odds that any particular description belongs to an engineer rather than a lawyer should be higher in the first condition, the subjects involved in the two conditions produced essentially the same probability judgements, with little or no regard for the base-rate frequency information.

On the other hand, people were found to use prior probability information correctly when they had no other information. In the absence of a personality sketch, subjects judged the probability that an unknown individual is an engineer to be 0.7 and 0.3 respectively in the two conditions. However, prior probabilities were effectively ignored when a description was introduced, even when this description was totally uninformative.

The second factor is the *insensitivity to sample size*. This phenomenon has been regularly observed where, for instance, estimates of population averages are made from the averages of samples of different size. Apparently, equal confidence is placed on estimates based on small and large sample sizes, although clearly more confidence should be attached to those based on larger samples. These misconceptions have been particularly prevalent when the representative heuristic is being used. This underutilisation of evidence have been observed repeatedly in situations of this type, and has been termed 'conservatism' (Tversky and Kahneman 1974: 42).

The third factor involves the *misconceptions of chance*. People expect that a sequence of events generated by a random process will represent the essential characteristics of that process even when the sequence is short. In considering the tosses of a coin for heads or tails, for example, people generally regard the sequence H–T–H–T–T–H to be more likely than the sequence H–H–H–T–T–T, which does not appear to be random, and also more likely than the sequence H–H–H–H–T–H, which does not represent the fairness of the coin (Kahneman and Tversky 1972). This intuition does not correspond with the mathematical concept of true randomness which implies that each event is independent of the last one – 'the coin has no memory'. One consequence of this belief is the well-known gambler's fallacy where, after observing a long run of red on the roulette wheel, for example, most people erroneously believe that black is now due. In fact a better policy in this situation would be to bet on red, on the grounds that the wheel may be biased in some way towards the red numbers. Misconceptions of chance have also been found to exist even with experienced researchers (Tversky and Kahneman 1971) where, as a consequence, too much faith was placed in the results of small samples. In the actual conduct of research, this bias leads to the selection of samples of inadequate size and to overinterpretation of findings.

The fourth factor, *insensitivity to predictability*, concerns situations where people are called upon to make such numerical predictions as the future value of a stock, the demand for a commodity, or the outcome of a football game. Such predictions, it is claimed, are often made by representativeness. An example is given by Kahneman and Tversky where one is given a description of a company and is asked to predict its future profit. If the description is very favourable, a very high profit will appear to be most representative of that description; if the description is mediocre, a mediocre performance will appear most representative. The degree to which the description is favourable is unaffected by the reliability of that description or by the degree to which it permits accurate prediction. Hence, if people predict solely in terms of the favourableness of the description, their predictions will be insensitive to the reliability of the evidence and to the expected accuracy of the prediction.

This mode of judgement violates the normative statistical theory in which the extremeness and the range of predictions are controlled by considerations of predictability. When predictability is nil, the same prediction should be made in all cases. For example, if the descriptions of companies provide no information relevant to profit, then the same value (such as average profit) should be predicted for all companies. If predictability is perfect, of course, the values predicted will match the actual values and the range of predictions will equal the range of outcomes. In general, the higher the predictability, the wider the range of predicted values. Several studies of numerical prediction have demonstrated that intuitive predictions violate this rule, and that subjects show little or no regard for considerations of predictability (Kahneman and Tversky 1973).

The fifth factor concerns *the illusion of validity*, that is the unwarranted confidence placed in predictions based on high degrees of representativeness. This illusion persists even when the judge is aware of the factors that limit the accuracy of his predictions. Also the consistency of a pattern of inputs is a major determinant of one's confidence in predictions based on these inputs. For example, people express more confidence in predicting the final-year grade-point average of a student whose first-year record consists entirely of Bs than in predicting the grade-point average of a student whose first-year record includes many As and Cs.

The sixth factor, *misconceptions of regression*, concerns the lack of understanding that people have towards the occurrence of chance events about some mean. An interesting illustration of this is provided by Kahneman and Tversky (1973) where, in a discussion of flight training, experienced instructors noted that praise for an exceptionally smooth landing is typically followed by a poorer landing on the next try, while harsh criticism after a rough landing is usually followed by an improvement on the next try. The instructors concluded that verbal rewards are detrimental to learning, while verbal punishments are beneficial, contrary to accepted psychological doctrine. The explanation offered for this phenomenon is that all good performances are followed by relatively poor performances, and vice versa, in the process of regressing to a mean. The point is that the quality of these performances is a random variable and changes are occurring irrespective of the instructors' action. Because the instructors attributed changes in performance to their actions, they reached the erroneous and potentially harmful conclusion that punishment is more effective than reward. Thus, the failure to understand the effect of regression leads one to overestimate the effectiveness of punishment and to underestimate the effectiveness of reward.

Availability
There are situations in which people assess the frequency of a class or the probability of an event by the ease with which instances or

22

occurrences can be brought to mind. For example, one may assess the risk of heart attack among middle-aged people by recalling such occurrences among one's acquaintances. Similarly, one may estimate the probability that a given business venture will fail by imagining various difficulties it could encounter. This judgement heuristic is called availability (Kahneman and Tversky 1973). Availability is a useful clue for assessing frequency or probability, because instances of large classes are usually recalled better and faster than instances of less frequent classes. However, availability is affected by factors other than frequency and probability and, consequently, the reliance on availability leads to predictable types of biases, four of which are illustrated below.

The first type of bias is attributed to *the retrievableness of instances*, by which a class whose instances are easily mentally retrieved will appear to be more numerous than a class of equal frequency whose instances are less retrievable. In an elementary demonstration of this effect, subjects heard a list of well-known personalities of both sexes and were subsequently asked to judge whether the list contained more names of men than women. Different lists were presented to different groups of subjects. In some of the lists the men were relatively more famous than the women, and in others the women were relatively more famous than the men. In each of the lists, the subjects erroneously judged that the class (sex) that had the more famous personalities was the more numerous (Kahneman and Tversky 1973).

The second type of bias is attributed to *the effectiveness of the search set*. In response to the question 'do more words in the English language start with the letter r or have the letter r in the third position?', it was found that people approach the problem by recalling words that begin with r (road) and words that have r in the third position (car) and assess the relative frequency by the ease with which words of the two types come to mind. Because it is much easier to search for words by their first letter than by their third letter, most people judge words that begin with a given consonant to be more numerous than words in which the same consonant appears in the third position. They do so even for consonants, such as r or k, that are more frequent in the third position than in the first (Tversky and Kahneman 1973).

The third type of bias is *imaginability*, found when one has to assess the frequency of a class whose instances are not stored in memory but can be generated according to a given rule. In such situations, one typically generates several instances and evaluates frequency or probability by the ease with which the relevant instances can be constructed. However, the ease of constructing instances does not always reflect their actual frequency, and this mode of estimation is prone to biases. For example, subjects were asked to consider a group of ten people who formed committees of k members, $2 \leqslant k \leqslant 8$. When asked to estimate the number of distinct committees of various sizes, their estimates were a decreasing monotonic function of committee size (Tversky and Kahneman 1973). For example, the median estimate of the number of committees of two members was 70, while the estimate for committees of eight members was 20 (the correct answer is 45 in both cases).

Imaginability plays an important role in the estimation of probabilities in real-life situations. The risk involved in an adventurous expedition, for example, is estimated by imagining contingencies with which the expedition is not equipped to cope. If many such difficulties are vividly portrayed, the expedition can be made to appear exceedingly dangerous, although the ease with which disasters are imagined need not reflect the actual likelihood. Conversely, the risk involved in an undertaking may be grossly underestimated if some possible dangers are either difficult to conceive of or simply do not come to mind (Tversky and Kahneman 1974).

The fourth type of availability bias is that of *illusory correlation*. An interesting instance of this bias is provided by Chapman and Chapman (1967) in which non-expert subjects were asked to match sketches of mental patients' faces with a variety of possible diagnoses of condition (such as paranoia or suspiciousness). The subjects markedly overestimated the frequency of co-occurrence of natural associates, such as suspiciousness and peculiar eyes. This effect was labelled illusory correlation. In the erroneous judgements of the data to which they had been exposed, the subjects 'rediscovered' much of the common, but unfounded, clinical lore concerning the interpretation of the draw-a-person test. The illusory correlation effect was extremely resistant to contradictory data. It persisted even when the correlation between symptom and diagnosis was actually negative, and it prevented the judges from detecting relationships that were in fact present.

Adjustment and anchoring
In many situations, people make estimates by starting from an initial value that is adjusted to yield the final answer. These adjustments are typically insufficient (Slovic and Lichtenstein

24

1971), a phenomenon termed anchoring. In a demonstration of the anchoring effect, subjects were asked to estimate various quantities, stated in percentages (e.g. the percentage of African countries in the United Nations). For each quantity, a number between 0 and 100 was determined by spinning a wheel of fortune in the subjects' presence. The subjects were invited to indicate, first, whether the number was higher or lower than the value of the quantity, and then to estimate the value of the quantity by moving upward or downward from the given number. Different groups were given different numbers for each quantity, and these arbitrary numbers had a marked effect on estimates. For example, the median estimates of the percentage of African countries in the United Nations were 25 and 45 for groups that received 10 and 65, respectively, as starting points. Payoffs for accuracy did not reduce the anchoring effect. Similar results were obtained when subjects based their estimates on the results of some incomplete computations.

Systematic anchoring biases have also been found in estimating the probability associated with compound events. The successful completion of an undertaking, such as the development of a new product, is a particular instance. For the undertaking to succeed, each of a series of events must occur. Even when each of these events is very likely, the overall probability of success can be quite low if the number of events is large. There is a general tendency to overestimate the final probability in such situations, leading to unwarranted optimism in the estimation of the likelihood that a plan will succeed or that a project will be completed on time.

Further anchoring biases are found in the assessment of subjective probability distributions. In decision analysis, for example, experts are often required to express their beliefs about a quantity in the form of a probability distribution. Such a distribution is usually constructed by asking the person to select values of the quantity that correspond to specified percentiles of his/her subjective probability distribution. By collecting subjective probability distributions for many different quantities, it is possible to test the judge for proper calibration. Several investigators (Alpert and Raiffa 1969; von Holstein 1971; Winkler 1967) have done this and found large and systematic departures from proper calibration. In most studies, the subjects state overly narrow confidence intervals which reflect more certainty than is justified by their knowledge about the assessed quantities. This bias is common to expert and non-expert subjects, and is not eliminated by introducing proper scoring rules, which provide incentives for correct calibration.

Inconsistencies in decision-making

Inconsistency in decision-making means that identical circumstances do not always lead to identical decisions. When decisions made by one individual are noticed as being inconsistent by another, the observer may conclude that the individual making decisions is either incompetent or has hidden motives. Motivational explanations have assumed that the individual's inconsistency arises from his or her self-serving behaviour; however, the psychological theory of human judgement described by Brunswik finds such assumptions unnecessary. Judgement is inconsistent because human judgement is not a fully analytical and controlled process; therefore, inconsistency is an inherent characteristic.

In contrast with biases, studies of inconsistencies in decision-making are extremely rare. While we may postulate that each of the systematic biases described above may be in some way related to systematic inconsistency, no analysis as yet has attempted to link the two together. Indeed, the lack of bias cannot necessarily imply any consistency, as people may well be 'correct' on average but still wildly incorrect in each attempt. In such a case, the result can be far from trivial because the result of individual (especially commercial) decisions is usually much more important than the average over time.

The decision-making environment

Commercial decisions take place in a continuously changing environment. There is nothing more certain that, whatever the state of the environment at one moment in time, it will be different in some ways at the next moment. Insofar as decision-making is concerned, we are interested in how the environment changes in different ways as a result of different decisions. These anticipated decision-induced environmental changes (termed *outcomes*) are, as we have seen, of vital importance in strategic decision-making as they determine the decision choice. From a motivational point of view, the outcomes of interest are essentially concerned with wellbeing. From a psychological point of view, consideration of the environmental aspects of decision-making leads to a fuller and more richer understanding of the abilities of the decision-maker. Following Hogarth (1981), the impact of environmental considerations on human decision-making abilities will be considered in two parts. First, the role of feedback in continuous processes is examined.

26

Secondly, Kahneman and Tversky's work in judgemental biases will be re-evaluated in terms of processes operating in a continuous environment.

The importance of feedback in continuous processes

The environment can be considered to be complex and distinguished by uncertain (probabilistic) relations. However, it also contains considerable redundancy in the form of intercorrelation between cues. The human information-processing system that has evolved to cope with the environment is characterised by essentially sequential processing, limited memory, selective perception, and reliance on cognitive simplification mechanisms (heuristics). Central to these means is the facility to adapt to changing environments and the role played by feedback.

It is important to emphasise that, psychologically, judgement is primarily exercised to facilitate action (Einhorn and Hogarth 1978), and most actions induce feedback that is often immediately available. A simple example, such as walking along a corridor, involves a series of incremental judgement–action–feedback loops monitoring progress during the activity of walking. Similarly, judgements made in social interaction also involve judgement–action–feedback loops; for instance, a smile induces a smile, or the judgement to make a particular comment provokes a reaction that is interpreted before responding in turn.

Receiving and acting on feedback in continuous fashion increases the number of cues and responses available to the organism and thus their substitutability, enabling different sets of probabilistic cues to be used to predict the same criterion in a manner analogous to von Neumann's *principle of redundancy* (by which reliable systems can be established from large combinations of components, each of which is relatively unreliable). Continuous processing is therefore not only consistent with the characteristics of the human information-processing system, it is functional for the organism to treat tasks in this manner.

The role of feedback highlights several issues: the level of predictive accuracy required in dealing with a complex environment; the degree of commitment implied by choice; the importance of learning and the acquisition of judgmental expertise; and the nature of cue–criterion relations.

Judgemental accuracy
Judgement can be likened to aiming at a target, in which case

the choice is the selection of a particular trajectory. Consider four types of environment:

1. static without feedback
2. static with feedback
3. dynamic without feedback, and
4. dynamic with feedback

In the first type of environment, the choice of trajectory is essentially 'one off', and accuracy of judgement is measured as the distance of the released projectile from the target. In the absence of feedback, it is unlikely that accuracy can be improved no matter how many shots are fired. Such an environment is typical of many of the heuristic bias studies outlined in the previous section.

In the second type of environment, the provision of feedback should provide sufficient information to enable some corrective measures to be taken to improve accuracy. Research in heuristic biases seems to indicate that this is not necessarily the case as the biases are so strong that feedback information tends to be disregarded.

In the third type of environment, we can envisage the marksman gradually moving towards the target (or vice versa). The closer he approaches the target then, using the same trajectory, the more accurate he should become. Thus, for instance, the probability of accurately predicting an economic variable or level of job success increases as one approaches the target date.

In the fourth type of environment, both the advantages of an approaching target and feedback should enable further improvements in accuracy to be achieved. Continuous processing, necessitating the receipt of feedback between the starting point and the target, clearly takes place in this type of environment. When available, such feedback could be sampled occasionally at the will of the organism; alternatively, it could be received periodically in the form of outcomes of a temporal sequence of actions (as in dynamic decision theory).

The target analogy highlights two critical dimensions of judgemental achievement: the degree of commitment implied by particular actions, and the availability and interpretation of feedback are often more important than predictive ability *per se*.

Commitment
Feedback plays a crucial role in the organism's capacity to make adaptive responses by reducing the commitment implied by a

particular action. In continuous processing, outcome (negative) feedback can become corrective in that it permits adjustments to the general direction of judgement. In particular, corrective feedback allows the organism to appear as though complex sequences of behaviour had been planned in detail when, in fact, only relatively simple actions need to be co-ordinated across time. An everyday example is in the context of clipping an overgrown hedge. One does not make complex, *a priori* calculations involving, for instance, the cantilever characteristics of branches or differential weights of various woods. Rather, one proceeds incrementally, snipping and observing, thereby reducing the level of commitment implied by particular actions as compared with a more discrete analytical approach.

The hedge-clipping example highlights the importance of feedback in comparison with other variables, such as amounts of information, redundancy and task familiarity, more normally associated with task complexity insofar as feedback affects the commitments implied by particular actions. Indeed, from a continuous perspective, conditions concerning feedback largely determine task complexity.

Judgement can also be used to delay the commitment implied by choice. For example, consider the various strategies one can use when faced with a choice between two jobs at a particular time. The anticipated commitment frequently induces conflict that can be confronted directly or avoided by adopting a non-confronting perspective on the problem (e.g. by choosing an alternative simply to escape the conflict implied by the choice situation itself). Alternatively, one can delay choice. This judgement, however, will involve neither commitment nor conflict unless the failure to choose also closes one's options. Thus choice is often delayed until information reduces the level of uncertainty below a certain threshold. In more general terms, mechanisms that reduce the psychological regret associated with taking the wrong decision will induce action.

Learning and expertise

Learning involves the use of feedback to generate, modify, maintain or abandon hypotheses, a process that occurs across time. An important aspect of both judgement and learning concerns the meaning of inconsistency observed in judgemental strategies. Whereas inconsistency is dysfunctional in that it reduces achievement in the form of predictive accuracy, emphasis on prediction hides the fact that in adapting to the environment, it is the identification of relevant variables that is of paramount importance. Indeed, random variation (observed inconsistencies in judgement) and selective retention (of cues that have been useful) is not only the basic model of natural selection but is inherent in the trial–and–error nature of much human perception, learning and creative thought. From one individual's viewpoint, there is always an unexpected element in the environment (e.g. the reactions of others in a social context). Thus, willingness to deviate from a consistent policy may well both facilitate learning and be adaptive in responding to the unexpected.

Feedback is also central to the learning of expertise. There is evidence to suggest that both physical and conceptual expertise development is characterised by continuous feedback. Weather forecasters, for example, have been shown to be quite accurate (Slovic et al. 1977), an ability attributed to their activities taking place in conditions characterised by accurate feedback received frequently and often shortly after making forecasts.

Feedback, however, is not necessarily corrective. It can be ambiguous, misleading and difficult to discern. There is often confusion, for example, in attributing outcomes to chance or skill, the variables selected for judgement, the weights assigned to variables, or the policies or strategies used. Furthermore, depending on task characteristics such as levels of base rates and selection ratios, or the inability to see outcomes of actions not selected, feedback may even reinforce inappropriate behaviour. Judgement may also induce 'self-fulfilling prophecies' of which the individual is unaware. Whereas the task environments of weather forecasters are relatively simple to interpret in terms of these variables (e.g. there can be no self-fulfilling prophecies), this is not the case in many other situations.

Cue-criterion relations

Imagine a sensitive interview where one would not want to pose the direct question of interest before acquiring a more complete appreciation of the situation. The acquisition of this first-stage information places the interviewer in a position analogous to the target example. The information effectively moves the interviewer one step nearer to the target, thereby increasing his chances of success. Of course, it is not clear that as a person moves towards a target, he/she would continue to rely on the same cues. In an interview, for instance, one formulates new questions as a result of prior feedback. Action (movement), therefore, not only affects the base rate of predictive judgement but also the validity of cues used in judgement.

Discrete assumptions and continuous environments

Research documenting the existence of judgemental heuristics in discrete incidents has acknowledged that these may only apply in specific contexts. Hogarth (1981) argues that several biases revealed through such discrete evaluations are, in fact, indicative of mechanisms that are not biased at all in more familiar continuous environments. Hogarth's observations concern five assumptions implicit in the discrete incidents model: the existence of a finite horizon at which the consequences of decisions can be estimated; the modelling of task uncertainty by stationary probabilistic processes; the requirement of stable preferences or goals; treating the effects of judgement as conditionally independent of outcomes; and abstraction from competitive aspects of behaviour.

Fixed decision horizons

One cannot determine the optimal solution to a decision problem, only the optimal solution to a *model*, or 'small world', of that situation. The use of an optimal decision model necessitates creating discontinuities in continuous processes. For example, consider whether one should invest in a property development venture. The wisdom of the action depends on both the price at the time of development and its estimated value at a specific future date. Since actions have consequences beyond small worlds (e.g. the investment could limit future possibilities or leave one vulnerable to emergencies), one would often wish to act to gain advantage through immediate action yet seek to achieve a position facilitating future actions.

Evidence reveals two mechanisms suited to continuous processing. First, judgements and choices are made relative to momentary reference points; that is, evaluations of choice options are better described by considering differences between potential gains and losses relative to a reference point rather than normatively appropriate comparison of 'terminal wealth states' (Kahneman and Tversky 1979). There is evidence that losses are weighted more heavily than gains, for instance, and that whether something is seen as a loss or a gain depends on the reference point (e.g. is a tax cut a gain or less of a loss?). The second mechanism is the use of aspiration levels to evaluate future positions implied by actions (Simon 1955, 1959). For example, consider whether a person should stick to a long-term career plan. The use of intermediate aspiration levels to handle this complex task not only reduces information processing to within feasible limits but prepares the person to anticipate what can reasonably be expected. By this mechanism there is no need to specify the implications of all possible paths several stages ahead; rather, one makes a rough first estimate (of small world consequences) and then simply handles the details of paths subsequently encountered.

This proclivity for people to decompose decisions into sequential form is also revealed in tendencies to think in terms of incremental gains leading to positions more favourable to future actions. Ronen's (1973) analysis of choice behaviour between two mutually exclusive actions involving identical (positive) payoffs and probabilities of success, preceded by an earlier stage involving different probabilities, found that most subjects favoured the action with the larger first-stage probability. The conclusion suggested by these results is that people are used to functioning in a manner where the immediate goal is to reach a better position from which the ultimate target can be reached. Also, people accustomed to environments changing across time have understandably less confidence in the second-stage probabilities than those provided for the first stage.

A recurring feature of discrete incident research, as typified by Kahneman and Tversky, is that the temporal horizon is reduced to such an extent that the organism is prevented from receiving any feedback at all. When this restriction is relaxed, however, the dysfunctional effects of two well-publicised heuristics – availability and adjustment/anchoring - take on a different perspective. The adjustment/anchoring heuristic is particularly vulnerable in this respect for, in continuous environments, this heuristic essentially provides the basic mode of judgement. Consider, for instance, how one forms impressions of strangers through interaction. That is, in discrete incidents a single (possibly inaccurate) judgement is made. In continuous processing, however, a series of adjustment and anchoring responses, all of which may be relatively inaccurate, takes one progressively to the target. People are not used to considering the probabilities associated with sequences of several future events and often progress incrementally conditional on a current 'best guess', knowing that it can be corrected over time.

A further well-documented bias is the conservatism effect, where opinion, for example, has regularly been found to change slower than the optimal prescription. The conservatism effect is particularly and disproportionally noticeable when large changes are required. The human tendency to resist sudden, dramatic changes, however, may well be appropriate in continuous environments. In particular, if one has imperfect understanding of the task environment, dramatic as opposed to incremental changes can have large, unanticipated and dysfunctional consequences (cf. Lindblom 1959).

Stationary probabilistic processes

In small worlds, the calculation of optimal responses tends to assume specific probabilistic models, the parameters of which do not change across time. In dealing with naturally occurring phenomena, however, people have to face many different types of processes. For example, observations can increase or decrease linearly across time, exhibit random fluctuations around a mean level, follow patterns and/or cycles, change their characteristics, or even be random. Moreover, although the detection of patterns is crucial for prediction, there is no certainty that observations do follow a particular pattern. In the final analysis, this lack of certainty must hold for the whole of human knowledge. There are, however, sufficient examples of small worlds that do seem to explain and predict observed phenomena to encourage this approach, especially as no other approaches are available to perform this function. Until alternative approaches (as yet unimaginable) are devised, the most that can be expected is that patterns may be induced through experience and the application of generally accepted techniques. It follows, therefore, that if different patterns are detected by different people observing the same phenomena, the only measure of correctness available is that of departure from the consensus view. This measure is, in most cases, likely to be a reasonable approximation to the truth. It is well to remember though that history records many incidents where such a measure has been shown to be notoriously inaccurate (Gallileo and Darwin are two obvious examples).

In applying these thoughts to heuristic biases, the regression fallacy provides a particular instance. Whereas extreme observations can be generated by stable processes (although, by definition, rarely), they can also signal changes in the underlying process. When advising 'trapped administrators' how to make successful interventions, for example, Campbell (1969) has suggested that they pick the very worst year and the very worst social unit so that if there is inherent instability, there is nowhere to go but up, for the average case at least. However, the validity of this advice depends on the observed instability being generated by a stationary process, and in many cases it is not evident that this is the case. In fact 'the worst unit' could well subsequently exhibit both instability and a sharp downward trend, thus exacerbating the administrator's position.

From a continuous perspective, much judgemental activity can be likened to extrapolation of multiple time series. It has been found that simple statistical models are, in many situations, preferable to more complex versions. These results are significant in that the simple models require neither much computational ability nor memory capacity and, in this respect, are potentially within human capabilities. The simple models are based on only a few values, such as predicting the next period by the most recent observation. Like judgement in continuous situations, these models rely on the relative inertia of most processes which induce high correlations between successive observations. Since the immediate future is usually similar to the present, minor adjustments effected at frequent intervals can keep one on course. Many anticipations of this kind are exhibited in tracking, for instance, a task in which people can develop a high degree of skill.

Stable preferences

In small worlds, preferences are always assumed to be stable. Motivational considerations lead us to believe that this assumption cannot be justified as the needs behind motivations are, like the environment, constantly changing. The psychological implications have been elaborated by March (1978): choices made at present involve guesses about future preferences; people often experiment and determine preferences through actions; ambiguity in preference is the rule rather than the exception; also ambiguity, and inconsistency, can be functional both from the personal viewpoint (permitting a wider range of experiences) and in social interaction where it is often not advantageous to reveal true preferences (e.g. in negotiations). Furthermore, the mental effort required to imagine and delineate future preferences is considerable. Thus, if people believe environments and preferences to be unpredictable, expending mental energy an such activity will be deemed unproductive.

People manage possible changes in preferences by *reactive* and *proactive* mechanisms. The former mechanism involves the avoidance of precise preferences and letting these adapt to changing circumstances (e.g. through the use of aspiration levels). The latter mechanism involves taking action to inhibit possible future changes by, for instance, the use of decision policies or strategies that are fixed over time.

Conditional independence between judgements and outcomes

Discrete incident research assumes that judgements are conditionally independent of outcomes. The continuous processing model invalidates this assumption as possibilities exist for corrective action in response to outcomes. Depending on task structure, the presence of such treatment effects can complicate the learning of predictive relations, contribute to illusions (e.g. overconfidence), and render problematic the evaluation of judgements and actions. In economics, for example, theorists now recognise that government announcements can affect, and even offset, the policies they are supposed to foster.

Abstraction from competitive behaviour

An important ecological dimension missing from most research on judgement and choice is that decisions are often made in competitive and other social situations. Two instances have already been mentioned: inconsistency in behaviour can be important in competitive situations where it pays to be unpredictable; ambiguity in the expression of preferences preserves greater freedom of action.

Concern with competitive behaviour also helps to define standards to evaluate actions in complex environments. In competitive situations, optimal responses are not necessary for survival. Instead, responses only have to be better than those of competitors or sufficiently differentiated.

Group decision-making

The main vehicle for studying group decision-making is that of Social Judgement Theory (SJT), adapted from Brunswik's (1952) probabilistic functionalism by Hammond *et al.* (1975) to the task of analysing human judgement and decision-making in the cognitive (information processing) tradition. SJT adopts the basic tenet that decision-making processes are covert, that is to say, although people may be able to make judgements, they may nevertheless not be able to report on how they actually arrived at them (Brehmer 1984). The covert nature of the process is the source of three kinds of problems: it is impossible to ascertain whether or not a person has taken a certain factor into account or not; it is difficult to teach judgement; and conflicts are hard to resolve.

SJT attempts to solve these problems by developing mathematical models relating judgement to the information available to the decision-maker. The aim is to find a model which, when given the same information as a person, will produce the same judgements as the person. It is then possible to inspect the model and find out how it works, hopefully leading to some insights into the system being modelled.

SJT theorists have generally used linear models of the form

$$J = b_0 + b_1x_1 + b_2x_2 + \ldots + b_nx_n$$

where J is a judgement described as a weighted sum of the cues $x_1 \ldots x_n$, and $b_1 \ldots b_n$ are the weights determined by fitting the model to the judgements.

The judgement processes of a variety of experts, including quantity surveyors, stockbrokers, clinical psychologists, radiologists and physicists, have been modelled in this manner, with similar results in all cases. Four basis factors appear to have emerged: the judgement process is simple; the process is inconsistent; there is considerable disagreement; and subjects lack insight into their own rules.

The judgement process is simple

Judges seem to rely on very little information. Thus, a judge may ask for a lot of information, say ten or more cues, but is usually found to use no more than three or four. Also, the process is simple in that it usually follows a simple linear model. If deviations from additivity are found, they are usually small and have little systematic importance.

The process is inconsistent

A typical finding in these analyses is that judges are inconsistent. At least two characteristics are known to affect consistency. One of these is that the more complex the task, in terms of number of cues, the lower is the consistency. Similarly, when the task requires the use of non-linear rules rather than linear rules, consistency is lower. Secondly, lower consistency has been found in situations of increasing uncertainty. As the predictability of the task decreases, so does consistency. This result has been obtained in a wide variety of circumstances both in laboratory studies of learning and conflict, and in studies of clinical judgement. The explanation of these results is not clear although it is felt to be a manifestation of Tversky and Kahneman's (1971) 'belief in the law of small numbers', or the belief that the characteristics of the task can be inferred from small samples. Because the judges rely on small samples, their rules change and they become inconsistent, and more so the greater the complexity and uncertainty of the task.

There is considerable disagreement

Disagreement exists between experts who are making the kinds of judgements they usually make. Disagreement also follows from the fact that people are inconsistent. If two people are inconsistent, their judgements cannot be perfectly correlated, even if they use the same rules for making their judgements. Systematic differences also exist between experts such as physicians who are found not only to rely on different symptoms, but also to give different weights to the same symptoms and, occasionally, to use different rules for combining the information from different symptoms. Thus, the hypotheses that people bring to the task are at least as important as the information available. In learning from experience, there is no guarantee that people will learn the correct rules from a given task, or even that they will learn the same rules.

Subjects lack insight into their own rules

In many cases, investigators have collected not only judgements from their subjects but also subjective descriptions of how they have been making these judgements. From these descriptions, it has then been possible to construct models of the judgement process, and these models have then been compared to the models fitted to the actual judgements. The extent to which these models agree gives a measure of the degree of insight people have into their own judgement processes. The results of these studies show that subjects do not have very good insight into their judgement processes.

One particularly striking feature of these results is that the objective models fitted to the actual judgements tend to be simpler than the subjective models. This may be because the objective models oversimplify the situation or people believe their judgement processes are more complex than they actually are. There is some, albeit rather limited, evidence in support of the latter conclusion in that lack of cognitive skill may prevent a person from actually following the rule he/she intends to use. Specifically, it seems that even when people are trying to follow a configural model, and believe that they are following such a model, their judgements nevertheless fail to exhibit configural properties. That is, they are simply unable to follow the model they intend to follow. (Brehmer 1984).

In summary, the results from studies on judgement indicate that judgement processes are simple and inconsistent and that people have limited insight into them. Such processes have been termed *quasi-rational* processes (Hammond and Brehmer 1973) in that their characteristics stem from their being midway between analytical and intuitive thinking. Basically, a quasi-rational process is seen as one that is partially rule-bound (analytical thinking) and partly relying on specific experience (intuitive thinking). Thus people may have rules for making judgements, but the judgements derived by these rules are checked against specific experience from cases similar to that at hand. If a rule-derived judgement does not agree with whatever specific case that a person happens to remember, the judgement is modified. As a consequence, the process is not completely determined by the rules and is inconsistent, a conclusion that is particularly important in the analysis of human social interaction and conflict.

Conflict in small decision-making groups

Within the SJT framework, differences in expertise are interpreted in terms of differences in how cues in a judgement task are used. Thus one expert may know how to use some cues, while another may know how to use some others. These experts may then need to co-operate to produce an optimal decision for a decision problem which requires the use of both sets of cues. This will entail reconciling, or integrating, judgemental differences which stem from differences in how the cues are used. Such a reconciliation will, of course, often imply a change in judgemental strategies.

However, judgemental differences may also occur in the absence of any real differences in expertise. Experts may also differ within their area of expertise, especially when the expertise is derived from their own experience, either because they have learned different rules from experience or because they are inconsistent. Both cases, that involving people with different expertise and that involving people with the same kind of expertise, contribute to conflict caused by judgemental differences.

The methodology for studying interpersonal conflict involves a training stage and a conflict stage. The training stage serves to create, or assess, the relations between the cognitive systems of the people involved. In most laboratory studies, this first stage involves training two or more people to have the judgemental policies or strategies required for the experiment. Alternatively, subjects are selected whose policies/strategies differ as a consequence of their pre-experimental experience. In the conflict stage, pairs of subjects are brought together to work on a new task for which their policies/strategies are only partly relevant. This may be arranged in different ways. One approach, used in many experiments, is to train subjects to use different cues and then put them together in a situation requiring the use of all of them. Subjects are given a series of problems of the same kind. For example, they may receive a series of twenty different countries, each described in terms of the same economic indices, and asked to predict the future economic growth for each. In those cases about which the subjects disagree, they are asked to discuss their differences until they can reach a joint answer agreeable to both of them. The trial then usually ends with a feedback, when the subjects are informed of the correct answer for the trial.

The early results obtained by the method were surprising in that they yielded no evidence of conflict reduction over a twenty-trial conflict sequence – it seemed that people were unable to change their policies. Closer analysis, however, revealed that, although there was little reduction in surface conflict, there was a radical change in the structure of the conflict. Systematic differences between the subjects' policies/strategies decreased rapidly but, at the same time, their consistency also decreased. Further analysis also showed that the decrease in consistency was due to the manner in which the subjects changed their policies/strategies as a consequence of their interaction with each other and with the task. Thus, contrary to expectation, the subjects changed their policies/strategies faster than they learned new ones and, as a consequence, their consistency decreased.

The adverse effects of inconsistency are also obtained when the subjects start with similar policies/strategies, but are required to change because they are not optimal for the task at hand. Under these circumstances, inconsistency causes people who start out with near perfect agreement to disagree more and more as they change their policies/strategies, even though they do not develop any systematic differences. These results have led to the general conclusion that inconsistency will prevent people from realising the true nature of their conflict, attributing differences instead to motivational rather than cognitive factors. As a consequence, they not only fail to resolve their conflict, but attempts to resolve it may actually lead to exacerbation when the subjects start searching for the motives that will explain their differences.

Together with consistency, the characteristics of the task have also been found to have a significant influence on the degree of conflict arising in judgemental situations. Policies/strategies in the conflict stage change to cope with the task in that stage, thus affecting the consistency of the policies/strategies. Disagreement is greater when task predictability is lower because the subjects' policies/strategies are then less consistent. Similarly, complex non-linear tasks also lead to higher conflict because of lower consistency.

These results suggest that it is important to develop new methods of communication to help resolve conflict. A first step in this direction was taken by Hammond and Brehmer (1973). Their computer graphics system presents cases for judgement, accepts judgements via a keyboard, performs a linear judgement analysis, and displays the results graphically so that the parties to the conflict can see what their differences actually are with respect to the cues used, which weights are given to these cues, the functional relations between each cue and the judgements, and their consistency, thus relieving the persons of having to rely on their limited insight and the imprecise medium of words for communicating their policies/strategies.

Corporate decision-making

In a commercial organisation, the type of policies and strategies to be used in decision-making may be laid down by the company's corporate 'rules', dictates or procedures. Such policies/strategies can determine the number and type of decision options in addition to the mode of selection. Different organisations have different corporate rules, which may be explicitly or implicitly applied. There are also differing degrees of tolerance regarding rule-breaking or 'bending' by decision-makers.

Systematic differences between organisations can be detected in the three stages of corporate evolution known as entrepreneurial, mechanistic and dynamic (Blake *et al.* 1966). This taxonomy, called corporate Darwinism, holds that the entrepreneurial corporation is dominated by the drive and determination of a single entrepreneur who plans, directs and controls the activities of subordinates bound to him by fear and loyalty. While the entrepreneurial company may achieve success and grow, its expansion potential is restricted by the entrepreneur's generally limited ability to personally direct and control a large and growing organisation. Thus, unless the organisation can take on a mechanistic character, the company's growth will peter out.

The mechanistic stage is reached when the corporation introduces systematic business practices, involving such things as budgeting, job descriptions, formal organisational charts, procedures manuals, forecasting, etc., to achieve greater order, predictability and control. The mechanistic corporation is typified by one which applies the principles of bureaucracy in order to achieve rational efficiency, continuity of operation, speed, precision and calculation of results (Gerth and Mills 1958: 49). The key element is the formal organisation structure or organisation chart, which represents the intended rational strategy of the organisation in an attempt to create a logically ordered world. Among the common principles used as a guide in designing the hierarchy of authority are specialisation, unity of command and span of control. When a large group of workers is necessary to accomplish a task, the task inevitably will be divided up into sub-tasks, which will be assigned to individuals or groups specialising in these functions. To accomplish the task, the sub-tasks must be co-ordinated with each other using integrative mechanisms (or policies) which, in many cases, do not allow for face-to-face communication. In co-ordinating interdependent sub-tasks, the simplest method is to specify the necessary behaviour in advance of their execution in the form of rules or programmes. If everyone adopts the appropriate behaviour, the resultant aggregate response is an integrated or co-ordinated pattern of behaviour without further communication (Galbraith 1973: 10).

When an organisation encounters new situations (creating task uncertainty), the old rules and programmes are likely to be unsatisfactory; thus there is a need for additional integrating devices. A satisfactory response to the new situation must consider all the affected sub-tasks, and this involves a substantial information-collecting and problem-solving activity (greater task complexity). Hierarchy emerges when sub-task managerial positions are created to handle these information-collection and decision-making tasks necessitated by uncertainty, and still higher positions are created to handle those aspects that cannot be handled at the lowest managerial level. Thus the components of decision-making are distributed hierarchically throughout the organisation by means of the power vested in the various managerial levels in an attempt to maintain control and provide an efficient use of expertise.

While these systematic practices do introduce elements of efficacy and control that seem to be necessary in large corporations, they also cause problems to the extent that the 'system' saps rather than taps human energies, leading to frustrations, tensions, strife, sacrificed creativity, and reduction of meaningful accomplishment. Because of these problems, some corporations have looked for ways to break out of the mechanistic stage into the dynamic stage. In the dynamic stage of corporate evolution, systematic business practices are retained, even strengthened, but initiative and vigour are restored to the very heart of the organisation – its people (Blake *et al.* 1966: 12). The problems of the mechanistic corporation that keep performance below potential are inherent in the use of hierarchy and 'scientific management' generally. First, its emphasis on the system operating like a well-oiled machine leaves the individual in the position of a cog on the machine and feeling uninvigorated, to say the least. Second, the simple, straightforward application of hierarchy and scientific management fails to achieve potential performance when novelty and uncertainty are high, since its integrating mechanisms will be inadequate for the magnitude of information processing and problem-solving involved. Third, the mechanistic organisation may fail to achieve potential performance because there is a lack of fit between the organisation and its members' attributes. In other words, the dynamic corporation is superior to the mechanistic one along three dimensions: the psychological, the structural and the individual (Tomer 1986).

The psychological dimension

In Argyris's (1960) view, motivation is lower than potential in a mechanistic organisation, and the same is true for productivity; it is simply impossible to say that motivation resides 'in' the individual or 'in' the organisation . . . The motivation of the participant is best understood as a resultant of the *transactions* between the individual and the organisation. When the organisation enables a member to satisfy his or her higher needs, especially the need for self-actualisation, the amount of psychological energy available for organisation tasks will be considerably higher. Moreover, there is reason to believe that members' decision-making effectiveness, creativity and ability to play an effective role in groups are also very much related to their ability to satisfy their needs in the organisation.

42

Becoming a dynamic organisation in this psychological sense requires not the elimination of hierarchy but the creation of conditions under which healthy individuals have high motivation (and psychological energy) because of their ability to satisfy their needs while working towards the organisation's purposes.

Transforming an organisation in this sense has been called organisational development (OD), which involves two main themes: helping organisations to build more effective teams; and helping organisations find new and better means of managing interpersonal and intergroup conflict.

The structural dimension

When uncertainty is high, the mechanistic organisation will tend to fail to achieve potential performance because its information-processing capacity will be inadequate to meet the demands on it. Uncertainty derives from the degree of predictability of the work tasks, the stability or rate of change of the work environment, and the degree to which different task elements making up the larger task are interdependent on each other. In the presence of greater uncertainty, more information processing and problem-solving must be done to ensure the successful completion of tasks. Given the organisation of the basic work units and their internal relationships, dealing with uncertainty means either (1) developing co-ordination and control mechanisms so that the organisation's information-processing capacity meets its requirements, or (2) reducing its information-processing needs by (a) manipulating its external environment or (b) settling for lower performance. The approach of the dynamic organisation is to create new self-contained units that contain all the resources, including types of personnel, necessary for task accomplishment, thereby eliminating interdependency (and some of the information-processing need) between hierarchical levels and other units. An example of this is the change from a functional organisation form to more or less independent groups based on product lines or geographical areas or markets (Galbraith 1973: 16), as is done in multidivisional corporations.

The effect of restructuring in this way is to enable the organisation to survive, grow and be efficient in industries and environments characterised by high uncertainty and novelty. Another effect is to provide work that is much more motivating and satisfying for healthy, mature individuals when jobs are characterised by more variety, higher skill requirements, more autonomy, and more performance feedback to the worker and when the job is a more meaningful whole (Nadler *et al.* 1979: ch. 5).

The individual dimension

Changes in either organisational climate or organisational structure can cause changes in individual attributes. On-the-job or in-the-organisation training, for instance, supplies facts, framework for thinking, teaches 'approved' solutions or indoctrinated values (Simon 1957: 170). Training within the firm is part of a larger process known as socialisation. Whereas training tends to be a formal process, much of socialisation consists of informal social interactions through which members acquire new expectations, beliefs, attitudes and learn about group norms. This is social learning contrasted with technical learning. In this process of 'learning the ropes', the organisation makes demands on the individual, and typically a counter-process, individualisation, occurs in which a member attempts to exert influence on the organisation.

According to Schein (Porter *et al.* 1975: 162), organisational effectiveness depends on socialisation. This can be 'managed' in the joining-up process when new employees are brought into the organisation, and in the systematic selection of certain desired 'types' of people. Well-managed joining-up gives generally higher job satisfaction, higher performance and longer tenure than when joining-up results in mismatches in expectations (Kotter 1973).

Another approach is to use special types of experiental or other training outside the firm with the idea that, when the member 'returns' to the organisation, his attitudes, beliefs and values will be closer to what it desires.

In summary, the role of corporate decisions is to formulate certain rules to aid the decision-making processes of people in the organisation. As the company increases in size and organisational skill, there is a tendency to reduce the stringency of its corporate rules and allow decision-makers an increasing freedom to devise their own strategies and policies. In all cases the essentials of the decision process are present. The difference lies in the distribution of the components of the process.

Conclusions

Contract bidding, like all other forms of pricing, is essentially about decision-making. The important differences that do exist between

44

contract and product pricing are, when viewed in decision-making terms, differences of emphasis and complexity rather than matters of direct disagreement. The client/contractor relationship, for example, is more complicated than the usual buyer/seller situation in that the client and contractor have each to make decisions in two stages over time and in uncertain conditions. For these and many other reasons, decision analysis, in contrast with standard economic analysis, currently offers a far more suitable and powerful basis for examining contract bidding problems.

In turning to decision analysis, it is immediately apparent that the subject, unlike economic analysis, is seriously lacking any generally accepted theoretical foundations. A major advantage, however, is the existence of a wealth of empirical evidence. Although much of this evidence relates to human fallibility in decision-making, it does at least encourage the view that decision analysis, again unlike its economic equivalent, is somehow more realistic in its treatment of judgemental phenomena.

The main contribution of this chapter has been to make the distinction between 'policy' and 'strategic' decisions as the means by which decision options are selected. Decision policies are defined here as rules dictating the choice between options *per se*, without regard to outcomes, and decision strategies are defined as rules dictating the choice between options in consideration of outcomes. For practical purposes, policies/strategies are also needed to identify the set of options to be considered, in addition to making the final selection. This line of reasoning leads to several operational questions: What policies/strategies are used? When are they used? How are they used? and Who uses them?

Research into decision-making has addressed the first question in terms of 'why are they used?', and the general answer seems to be 'motivation', usually expressed in some form of needs/drives hierarchy. The only satisfactory answer to 'what' we can offer at this stage is that some form of technique is employed. Quite what technique depends on the context of the decision-making situation ('when') and the decision-maker himself ('who'). There is a voluminous literature (operations research, for instance) concerning what technique *should* be used, but these prescriptions are necessarily based on some simplifying assumptions about the problem. We shall, therefore, defer considerations of this nature until later, when a fuller description of the 'problem' is available.

'When' and 'how' questions have been examined in some detail in this chapter. The clear conclusion is that people are certainly far from perfect in the application of correct policies/strategies in normative situations. The simplifying techniques, or heuristics, that people use in order to cope with their everyday lives have been shown to be often fallible in normative situations. The three main heuristics of representativeness, availability and adjustment/anchoring have been repeatedly demonstrated to produce systematic biases in Kahneman and Tversky's discrete incident research. Consideration of environmental aspects, however, introduces the role and importance of feedback in allowing the decision-maker the opportunity to continuously revise and refine his methods. From this it is clear that both judgement and choice ('what') depend crucially upon the context in which they occur ('when') and the cognitive representation of that context.

The question of 'who' makes decisions has been addressed in terms of group and corporate decisions. The main issue in group decision-making is the resolution of conflicts that form within the group. Corporate decisions, on the other hand, are a means of formally distributing the components of the decision-making process within the hierarchy of an organisation. In both cases, the systematic acquisition and communication of information is seen as a major factor influencing decision-making performance. The next chapter examines the characteristics and potential of such systemised decision-making in contracting organisations.

2

Systematic decision-making by contracting companies

Types of decisions

Ansoff (1965) divides business decisions into three categories –
strategic decisions, administrative decisions and operating decisions.
Strategic decisions are primarily concerned with external rather
than internal problems of the firm, involving the consideration of
such issues as the nature of the firm's objectives and goals, and
diversification strategies. Administrative decisions are concerned
with structuring the firm's resources in a way which creates a
maximum performance potential. One part of the administrative
problem is concerned with organisation: structuring of authority
and responsibility relationships, work flows, information flows,
distribution channels and location of facilities. The other part is
concerned with the acquisition and development of resources:
development of raw material sources, personnel training and
development, financing and acquisition of facilities and equipment.
Operating decisions usually absorb the bulk of the firm's energy
and attention, the object being to maximise profitability of current
operations, involving such major decisions as resource allocation,
scheduling of operations, supervision of performance and applying
control actions.

These categories typify the 'management' approach to decision-
making, in relating decisions to the functional divisions of the
organisation. Strategic decisions are seen as being made by
senior managers, whose decisions influence policy and affect
the organisation's relationships with its external environment.
Administrative and operating decisions are carried out by middle
management, whose decisions affect the internal functions of

production, accounting and finance, marketing, personnel research and development, and operational management at the foreman or supervisory levels.

Recent studies of leading companies, by Peters and Waterman (1982) for instance, suggest that the most successful organisations have little regard for such a strict managerial hierarchy. Many of the companies investigated were found to have a very loose decision-making structure, apart from a firm centralisation of 'core' values.

An alternative is to classify decisions as being either 'strategic' or 'tactical' decisions. These are defined as 'what shall we do?' and 'how shall we do it?' decisions respectively. The former includes attempts to answer such questions as, 'what are we trying to achieve?'; 'what are our objectives?'; 'what opportunities are open to us?'; 'what are our strengths and weaknesses?'; 'what are our current strategies?'; 'what strategic choices do we have?'; and 'what should we do?' Tactical decisions are the operational decisions involved in estimating, buying and accounting. In this sense, strategic decisions are those which are very important to the company.

For contracting companies, the opportunities for strategic decisions are limited.

One such opportunity occurs in relationships with other organisations. These relationships may involve the permanent unification with another organisation in the form of an acquisition or merger, a project-specific temporary unification such as a joint venture, and a project/process-specific temporary indirect unification by licence or agency.

Another major decision concerns the internal organisation of companies and the arrangement of the physical, human and financial resources, often termed the organisational structure.

A further, and vital, recurring decision for contracting organisations is the selection of suitable projects. The majority of construction contracting companies rely almost exclusively on project work obtained by competitive tender. The type and location of projects obtained has been said to be by far the most important factor in determining the direction of the construction organisation (Lansley et al. 1979).

The formalisation of major decisions may be expected to be expressed in terms of a corporate decision system of some kind. The next section examines the existence of such systems in contracting organisations.

Corporate decision systems

Generally

Contracting companies have, for some time now, been urgently recommended to exercise some forethought before taking decisions and subsequent action. Argenti (1974) and Ansoff (1965) in the general business field, for instance, and Grinyer (1972), Diepeveen and Benes (1978), Lansley (1981b), Fellows et al. (1983) and many others in the construction literature have all advocated the application of long-term planning as the basis for short-term effective action, on the grounds that inadequate planning inevitably leads to failure.

At the corporate level, planning may been defined as simply basing decisions on purpose, facts and considered estimates; or, organisationally, as the systematic process of determining a firm's goals and objectives for at least three years ahead and developing strategies to achieve these objectives (Rajab 1981: 1); or, managerially, as a continuous process of making entrepreneurial decisions systematically and with the best possible knowledge of their futurity, organising systematically the effort needed to carry out these decisions (Drucker 1955).

The notion of objectives is often stated to be inextricably bound up in the corporate planning systems. Cheetham (1980), for instance, has been a strong advocate of management by objectives (MBO) for construction companies.

Murray (1978) has identified six basic evolutionary corporate planning models: Allison's (1971) 'Rational Actor' model, in which the decision-maker is a kind of 'super-person' who always behaves in a perfectly rational manner; the 'Organisation Process' model, which emphasises the impact of processes and procedures of organisations on the strategic planning process in the tradition of organisational theory; the 'Bureaucratic Politics' model, in which decision-making is assumed to be a political process wherein agreement is reached through bargaining games; Steinbrunner's 'Cybernetic' model, in which the central focus of the decision process is the business of eliminating the variety inherent in any significant decision problem; Steinbrunner's 'Cognitive' model, containing cognitive models and belief structures modified by inputs from the real world; and Mintzberg's (1975) 'Contingency' model, in which alternative explanations are provided for phenomena under different conditions.

Many benefits have been claimed for corporate planning

49

systems. Rajab (1981), for instance, in investigating the nature and extent of corporate planning in construction companies, found that corporate planning makes managers think about the future and the effects of decisions on the future; encourages an understanding of the company aims leading to a better understanding of operations; focuses managers' attention on developing the business; quicker decision-making; better co-operation between departments; and increased competency of managers by making them face up to key decisions.

Use by construction companies

There appears to be little use of any formal decision systems in industry. Operations research techniques, for instance, are generally not well regarded or used by decision-makers (Bonder 1979: 209), and particular problems have been found in introducing operations research into such activities as marketing and devising competitive strategies (such as product pricing and bidding) (Wagner 1971: 1269).

Wong (1978), Stark (1976) and Lansley (1983), among others, have found that contractors do not favour the use of bidding models. Barnard's research (1981) found that, in the construction industry, in common with most industries, there is little use made of corporate planning.

Humphreys's study (1977) of eighteen Merseyside construction companies found little evidence of the operation of formal policies, although annual turnover forecasting was widely practised together with cash flow forecasts at monthly and quarterly intervals, mainly to ensure the availability of capital to finance projects.

Cusack's investigation (1981) of decision-making in construction companies, six in some depth, concluded that decisions were made intuitively, based mainly on experience. The study did find, however, that plenty of information was available but not in the right form.

Rajab (1981) did locate five companies using corporate planning systems, but was unable to determine whether the use of these systems benefited the companies. Some differences were observed between the systems operated by the companies themselves and those recommended in the literature. A substantial number of companies, for instance, did not carry out very systematic internal appraisals.

Yet another study (South 1979), of twenty-three construction companies between 1970 and 1976, found a considerable variability between companies' performance and policies.

Studies of organisations outside the construction industry suggest that the most important contributions of corporate planning systems are actually in the 'process' rather than in the 'decision' realm in that they create a network of information that would not otherwise be available.

Apart from isolated cases, management by objectives, or other long-range plan-based methods, seem not to have been adopted by construction companies. Recent studies suggest that most construction companies use a form of contingency rather than long-range planning (Edwards and Harris 1977; Lansley *et al.* 1980).

Reasons for lack of use

Rajab (1981) has identified five major problems associated with corporate planning systems in construction organisations: co-ordination of aims and objectives of various units in the organisation; communication problems; forecasting results and accuracy; restrictions due to capital policies; and political or economic uncertainty overseas.

Fryer (1977) has suggested that lack of managerial skills could be responsible. In a survey of twenty-nine managers in construction companies, he found that, although decision-making was the second highest rated skill (after 'social' skills), such decisions were normally concerned with short-term, day-to-day issues rather than strategic aspects of management.

Many of the problems may well be due to special characteristics of the industry itself. Economists, for instance, seem to have frequently failed to understand the industry due to its extremely complex technological and institutional constraints; imperfection of knowledge about future markets; lack of an adequate theory of human capital; concentration on the demand side because of historical excess capacity; lack of importance of time in neo-classical production theory; the local nature of the industry; and the small effect on the economy (Burton 1972: 1). The effects of this can be far-reaching for, in Burton's view, many current national problems can be traced to the fact that economists and operations research specialists have not provided the level of understanding of the construction industry necessary for the solution to these problems.

Many of the difficulties in objective decision-making appear to stem from the complexity of the construction process. The immense number of variables involved, and the uncertain environment result in the absence of necessary data for managerial decisions (Burton 1972: 86). Difficulties in accurately assessing long-term demand and the non-continuous volume of work from clients, particularly the government, makes long-term forecasting and planning so much guesswork (Goodlad 1974).

Another aspect is the limited amount of time the decision-maker has available to make each decision. Prosper (1984: 24) has noted the difficulties in finding the time to apply 'correct' management techniques.

The combination of lack of relevant information and lack of time seems to be a big factor in restricting the use of formal decision systems.

Problems have also been encountered in the relevancy of the techniques available, a particular problem being the involvement of specialists. Some criticisms of operations research, for instance, are of the relevance of current mathematical developments and that techniques and methods are being developed by individuals who have more of a disciplinary allegiance to mathematics and economics (Bonder 1979: 210), resulting in there being 'too much optimisation, the results of which are usually irrelevant to decision-making' (Jensen 1976).

Aspects of a decision system
Scope

The characteristics of an effective decision system are essentially those attributed to effective management but, as Ball observes, these are not easy to define in any unique sense:

> clearly part of the process of defining effectiveness is by results . . . [but] success also has a time dimension. Short term success can mean long term disaster. The tasks and decisions of management have themselves different time horizons which have in some way to be brought together to show some index of effectiveness. But even when we believe that this can be done, it is not enough to stop there since, in the social system, both of the organisation and of the wider social system of which the organisation is part, it is not a matter of indifference as to how results are achieved. To some degree, this is because managerial

> behaviour will be governed by acceptable social values and
> modes of behaviour and these values may change over time.
> (Ball 1977: 4).

In making decisions, therefore, it is necessary to consider the
interaction between decisions and the environment (social system)
over time. One view is that the organisation simply responds to
direct environmental 'stimulus', providing a service to satisfy the
demands of the environment, the 'outside-in' approach. A more
recent recommendation in the construction literature is to adopt a
more aggressive policy of attempting to influence the environment
by promotional activities, for instance the 'inside-out' approach
(Ewing 1968: ch. 6). Rajab's study (1981) of construction companies
indicated that both approaches are necessary.

The construction company's environment is often conveniently
divided into two separate groups, the internal and the external.
Different companies need to consider different environments. In
Dressel's view (1965), the essential differences between companies
are in their capacity, size and structure. Commonality, however,
does exist in such basic resources as people, property and finance.

The shift in emphasis in environmental perception in recent years
has been marked, perhaps even on the scale of a Kuhn paradigm
(Cotgrove 1980). Table 2.1 indicates some of the changes noted
by Cotgrove.

Ansoff's renaming of the firm as an 'environmental serving
organisation' further evidences the alternative approach. It follows, therefore, that a decision system will ultimately need to
recognise cultural, political and social inputs in an open system,
renegotiated environment (Murray 1980). These considerations lead
to the increasing necessity to analyse both internal and external
environments to identify power groups' and individuals' values
(Johnson and Scholes 1984) and pursue social objectives (Andrew
1973: 18). It is important, as Toffler (1971) suggests, to recognise
in organisations an array of goals other than economic ones and
growing increasingly sensitive to changes in the non-economic
environment.

Bahrami's studies (1981) of fourteen corporate planning systems
found these consistent features in all the systems: they facilitated
the adaption of the company's strategic posture to the emerging
opportunities and threats to its environment; an integrative function
by facilitating communication and flows of information; and a
control function to implement strategic priorities by evaluating

Table 2.1 Competing environmental perceptions

	Dominant social paradigm	Alternative paradigm
Core values	Material (economic growth)	Non-material (self-actualisation)
	Natural environment values as resource	Natural environment intrinsically valued
	Domination over nature	Harmony with nature
Economy	Market forces	Public interest
	Risk and reward	Safety
	Rewards for achievement	Incomes related to need
	Differentials	Egalitarian
	Individual self-help	Collective/social provision
Polity	Authoritative structures: (experts influential)	Participative structures: (citizen/worker involvement)
	Hierarchical	Non-hierarchical
	Law and order	Liberation
Society	Centralised	Decentralised
	Large-scale	Small-scale
	Associational	Communal
	Ordered	Flexible
Nature	Ample reserves	Earth's resources limited
	Natural hostile/neutral	Nature benign
	Environment controllable	Nature delicately balanced
Knowledge	Confidence in science and technology	Limits to science
	Rationality of means	Rationality of ends
	Separation of fact/value, thought/feeling	Integration of fact/value, thought/feeling

Source: Cotgrove (1980: 129, Table 2).

proposals and monitoring performance. The construction industry, it has been observed, has not been noted for its speed of reaction to environmental events, such as changes in demand. A sudden and substantial increase or decrease in demand in a major sector or geographical area has not normally been matched as quickly by an appropriate increase or decrease in capacity (Campbell *et al.* 1974: 21). However, as Sidwell (1984) has commented, moving into new and unfamiliar markets places greater strain on the efficiency and skills of the company. What appears to be needed is some preparedness for a future state. Uncertainty of the exact nature of future environmental states is a big problem in this respect but, ironically, as Ansoff points out, the greater the uncertainty the greater the need to be prepared.

Lansley (1981a) suggests that construction companies who followed the 'traditional doctrines' in the 1970s either went out of business or diminished in size. The only firms who survived were those who were flexible and responsive to the needs of the changing market. Diepeveen *et al.* (1985: 113) suggest that contractors should evaluate future technological developments which may affect the business structure, implying that 'scenario writing' may be an effective approach. It is suggested that management should work out two or more possible future alternatives which are intrinsically consistent (Benes and Diepeveen 1985: 29). This recommendation closely resembles contingency planning, previously found to be successfully employed by some construction companies, but *ahead* of, instead of *after,* environmental changes. One approach to this is through the concept of 'weak signals' (Ansoff 1984: 5.4) where the effects of possible changes in the environment are examined. Another, interdependent, approach is by simulation studies.

One final aspect of the scope of a decision system is the criticism by Murray (1980) of Ansoff's approach to strategic management in that a 'rational-actor' model is assumed, that is the decision-maker is seen as a remote 'super-person' dedicated to some optimising or maximising strategy. The increasing amount of decentralisation of decision-making currently being reported, together with the sometimes rather irrational and decentralised method of the 'excellent' companies (Peters and Waterman 1982), does indeed suggest that Ansoff's assumption may be misplaced. In terms of a decision system, this implies the existence of several option selection procedures. What really seems to be needed is a system that can inform the executive as to the likely effects of decision strategies that he has himself formulated and therefore permit a manager to evaluate decisions that satisfy his personalised rationality (Wagner 1971).

Practical needs

Analysis of attempts to introduce decision systems into construction organisations reveals that certain practical aspects need to be considered.

The major problem is in the cost of implementing and monitoring the system, which will depend on the depth to which the decision-maker is prepared to go. Limiting the set of options, limiting the number of evaluation criteria, approximating option evaluations, simplifying selection procedures illustrate possible approaches. Neale (1985) recommends the adoption of simple systems with a minimum data demand. Cusack (1981) found no shortage of data, but what was missing was a quick and accurate method of analysis that enables alternative solutions to be compared. Levinson (1953), for instance, has suggested using a combination of formal and informal methods by allowing the operations research department to solve those fragments of a total problem that are amenable to quantitative formulation. The sub-optimised solutions can then be considered by the decision-maker, together with intangibles, the unquantifiable elements of the problem. The executive decision will, in some cases, be based partly on the operations research solutions, partly on other data produced by the company, and partly on the judgement and intuition of the management (Levinson 1953). What is proposed is an economic trade-off between more elaborate models that require greater data processing and more approximate models that need less data to apply (Wagner 1971). The issue is, of course, centred on the tensions between risk and cost, the reconciliation of which is a decision problem in itself.

The number of decision options is a measure of the versatility of the system as decision-makers need alternatives that can provide them with more flexibility over time (Bonder 1979). Retaining the flexibility of decision options has been dealt with to some extent by Rosenhead et al. (1972), Merkhofer (1977) and Pye (1978) by focusing on the size of the alternative action space available to the decision-maker, the flexibility being reduced to zero when a specific alternative is chosen for, as Merkhofer (1977) notes, all flexibility is lost when an irrevocable commitment is made to a specific alternative. Clearly, some compromise between versatility and cost is necessary and, although the versatility ideas are still imprecise, and methods are not available to assist in their implementation, we can and should pursue the spirit of the concept in our planning and analysis support to decision-making (Bonder 1979).

Risk is also a problem associated with the option evaluation process. Estimating the outcome of decisions is bound to be a rough and ready business, especially when the outcomes are often only fully realised at some quite distant time in the future. Unfortunately, the construction industry is particularly vulnerable in this respect. The methods of obtaining work and the length of contracts, for instance, together with the fragmented nature of the industry, the customised product and the unstable nature of the environment in which the construction process takes place make risk assessment particularly unattractive. In fact, one of the main reasons for the high failure rate of construction companies may be the under-estimation of risks (Langford and Wong 1979). It is possible that risk assessment can be improved by formal feedback systems but, in many cases, the decision-maker has to rely on more subjective information.

System design

In designing a decision system a sensitive system of indicators geared to measuring the achievement of social and cultural goals, and integrated with economic indicators is an absolute precondition (Toffler 1971). Informational support, it is suggested, would come from a Strategic Data Base (SDB) representing the major conclusions regarding the environment and the organisation's clientele (King and Cleland 1978: 95). A Management Information System (MIS) is a form of SDB, being specifically designed to formally present information required to support managerial decision-making.

The properties of a MIS include: provision of information from both internal and external sources necessary to support a range of specific management activities and decisions; provision of information in a manner and at a time relevant to managerial decision-making; and flexibility to adapt to and accommodate organisational and environmental change (Booth 1981). A MIS in support of the strategic planning process would, it is suggested, provide information on the general environment, economic, technical and political (including legislation); factors of productions; and competition, future demand for products/services, policies of competitors etc.

One approach to MIS design is through analysis of the current decision-making process. There are, however, some limitations in this approach as it results in an essentially static, rational view of decision-making; users' descriptions are biased towards expectations; it tends to rationalise decision-making, oversimplify goals and underplay uncertainty; modelling of uncertain/complex phenomena involves simplification; and it is difficult to foresee information needs to support future decisions. Booth suggests that a contingency framework focusing on the 'if – then' relationships of the problem situation would provide a more appropriate starting point.

An outgrowth of the notion of management information systems has been the currently in-vogue notion of decision support systems. A decision support system is a management information system that also has some processing capacity designed to help the decision-maker use the information. A common form of such processing capability is the ability to ask 'What if . . .?' questions about possible courses of action and quickly receive answers from the computer. How helpful such a capability is depends on the problem at hand. It seems to be quite helpful in some business decision contexts because it informs the decision-maker of the long-range consequences of the available options (Von Winterfeldt and Edwards 1986). The nature of the contract bidding problem suggests that decision support systems may well provide a viable approach.

Information systems are normally associated with some type of environmental scanning activity. Aguilar (1967) has identified four types: undirected viewing, involving considerable orientation by the scanner in selection of particular sources; conditional viewing, where the scanner is sensitive to particular types of data; informal search, where information wanted is actively sought; and formal search, a programmed or quasi-programmed search to a pre-established plan, procedure or methodology. Etzioni (1967) advocates a method of mixed scanning involving broad surveys of the problem area and detailed investigation of areas adjudged to merit such attention.

An implicit prerequisite in any information system is to provide adequate forecasts of future events. This is a particular difficulty in the construction industry where operations are often short-run and on a project basis because of the need to continuously re-allocate with shifts in market demand. Gill (1968) has even opined that it is not possible to forecast plans from one project through a succession of projects. There are, however, techniques available to enable some predictions to be made. Raiffa (1968), for instance, has shown how probability theory can be employed in general decision situations involving risk. Benjamin (1969), Langford and Wong (1979), Wolf and Kalley (1983) and others have attempted to introduce aspects of the decision-maker's preferences into a probabilistic approach by means of utility theory. Still others have conducted simulation studies (e.g. Bennett and Fine 1980; Morrison and Stevens 1980).

Before designing a MIS or decision support system, an understanding of the major underlying characteristics of the system is needed. Booth (1981: 232) refers to this as the 'conceptual design stage' and is of fundamental importance in MIS design and which requires that a clear understanding of the decision environment and process is developed. In such complex and dynamic conditions as those prevailing in the construction industry, one approach is to model the complexities involved.

Decision models

Several models have been proposed for the construction industry decision-maker but it is common for research papers to develop a thesis, usually in the form of a mathematical model, without adequate mention or consideration of underlying assumptions and characteristics of the environment. In many instances, particularly in contract bidding, these assumptions are demonstrably untenable (Stark 1976). It has been observed that despite the enormous literature concerned with pricing, economists have devoted relatively little space to the consideration of pricing in the construction industry. The literature that does deal with construction pricing concentrates on the formulation of optimal bidding strategies for contracts, while largely neglecting the fundamental issue of presenting a detailed analysis of the interaction of the chief factors, both quantifiable and unquantifiable, that influence the contractor's bidding decision (Lange 1973: 91).

What is needed is a model that reflects the truly pivotal factors in the environment being modelled, especially with regard to the types and amounts of available data and the ability to process this information rapidly enough to be useful to the decision-maker (Wagner 1971). The construction literature reveals no existence of any such substantive approach to decision model building.

In the previous chapter the basic elements of the decision-making process were examined. These appear to be concerned with the choice among options involving such considerations as the size of the choice set and the means by which choices are made. This can be regarded as a three-stage process of option identification, evaluation and selection (Johnson and Scholes 1984).

The identification of interesting options is often a function of the evaluation and selection process. In practice, possible options which are difficult to evaluate may be omitted while options more easily evaluated may be consistently included. Another factor influencing the inclusion of a potential option is the quality and quantity of information needed and available, and the associated time and costs.

Time is also a factor in constraining the number of options that can be identified, depending on the speed of identification. A further factor is the ability and the preconceptions of the optioner himself which will be related to some extent to his education, experience and motivation.

Fortunately, the number of types of realistic options are relatively limited for the construction organisation. The major difficulty lies in the evaluation stage. However, some recent findings by Lansley *et al.* (1980) suggest that flexibility is an increasingly important attribute for the success or survival of the construction organisation. One aspect of flexibility would seem to be the willingness to bring an increasing variety of options into consideration.

A popular approach to the option identification problem is to apply a feasibility technique which allows a cost-effective procedure to reduce the option set. This involves quickly sifting out the least likely options before employing a more sophisticated evaluation. An often recommended procedure is to bring the companies' objectives and policies to bear on the problem. A policy to concentrate entirely on house building, for instance, would certainly be a very cheap option identification aid, but its effectiveness in identifying all the best options will depend on the policy formulation procedure.

Evaluation of each option implies that some knowledge is available of the future outcome of the decision option. As in the option identification problem, the extent of this knowledge will depend on the quality and quantity of information available, and the associated cost and time.

Accuracy of evaluation will also depend on the evaluator. A further aspect of option evaluation is that the outcome of a decision is not necessarily independent of the decision-maker, who may well participate in the implementation process.

In order to best help the selection procedure, each option will need to be evaluated in a similar manner, which implies the presence of some criteria.

Having identified and evaluated the various options available, the selection process ought to be relatively straightforward. Difficulties occur in accommodating conflicting criteria, particularly those evaluated non-quantitatively. The problem can also be exacerbated by the need to make several decisions, either simultaneously or sequentially. This latter aspect is a decision choice process in itself, involving the identification and evaluation of sets of decisions.

Once again, information, cost, time and the ability of the selector are important aspects.

It is clear then that each of the stages of option identification, evaluation and selection contains its own problems and involves some knowledge of the future. The contingency approach suggests that the identification of options should be widened to consider not only those presently available, but also those that may become available. The evaluation of options is essentially a report on the likely changes in the future environment as a result of the choice of each option. The selection process will involve consideration of several, probably conflicting, criteria representing interesting aspects of the environment.

One operational characteristic of the decision model is concerned with the sequencing of the three stages – is it necessary to identify all options prior to evaluation and is it necessary to evaluate all options prior to selection? It is suggested that the evaluation of options is normally done *as they are identified* as search activity is often conducted within the constraints of time and cost (Booth 1981: 133). This approach logically leads to an iterative model of decision-making where each option is in turn identified, evaluated and compared with the previously best selection. This comparison will determine whether the previously 'best' selection should be replaced by the current option or not. Such a procedure has the great practical advantage of allowing the decision-maker to search among a feasible set of options of his own, choosing for as long as he wishes. The basic model then, illustrated in Fig. 2.1, is envisaged as an iterative process occurring within, and interacting with, the environment.

Lindblom's (1959) 'The science of muddling through' involves a similar incremental procedure. Some of the problems associated with this approach include the possibility that an important variable is missed; policies may be overlooked; it may reinforce indifference to new technologies; and that it relies on satisfactory present policies, continuity in the nature of the problem and continuity in the means for dealing with the problem (Dror 1964). It is necessary, therefore, to identify all of the variables involved and the variety of policies available in an open system contingent on environmental change.

Criticisms levelled at the 'muddling through' approach, such as the use of subjective evaluations, stopping at the first 'good looking' selection and late responses to problems unresolved by earlier decisions, are idiosyncratic of the decision-maker rather than the incrementation procedure. The advantages claimed of the incremental approach are, however, relevant to the proposed

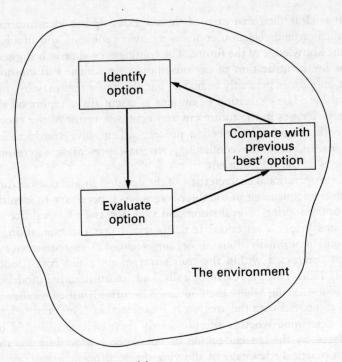

Fig. 2.1 Basic decision model

model in that it is intended to be relatively quick and efficient, more flexible, does not demand explicit objectives and makes use of the decision-maker's experience (Grinyer 1972).

Conclusions

There are many decisions faced by a construction company in the ordinary course of its business, ranging from the major strategic decisions taken by top management to operational decisions taken at lower levels. Recent research suggests that the more successful companies place more emphasis on the decision than on the level of management concerned with the decision. Formal management-oriented decision aids, such as corporate planning systems, have received little attention from construction companies. Major difficulties appear to stem from organisational issues and, perhaps more importantly, knowledge acquisition. These two interrelated aspects involve difficulties in co-ordination of aims and objectives and communication in the former and time-constrained informational needs in the latter.

Particularly difficult problems in the construction industry are due to its complex and uncertain nature. Another major informational difficulty encountered by a construction company is the necessity to forecast events over the life span of a project and beyond.

The basic model proposed in Fig. 2.1 represents a possible basis of a practical decision system. In developing the model for contract bidding, it is first necessary to concentrate on one particular type of decision, referred to by Bischoff (1976) as 'one of the central problems of corporate planning' – the project selection decision. In so doing, an approach often found in the operations research literature has been adopted, in which the uncertain and dynamical aspects of the model are treated separately. The following chapter, therefore, deals with the complexities of a static/deterministic project selection model.

3

Deterministic project selection models

Introduction

This chapter aims to specify the construction company's project selection decision problem within the framework proposed in Ch. 2. In order to do this it has been found expedient to restrict considerations to 'wisdom' aspects of the problem, that is 'perfect knowledge' is assumed to exist. The effect of this is that only the *kinds* of knowledge that are directly relevant to the problem are examined here (indirect aspects and knowledge acquisition are dealt with in Ch. 5). A further expedient has been to largely ignore time-dependent aspects such as cash flow and the impact of current decisions on future decisions (these are dealt with in Ch. 4). The chapter concludes with the consideration of some possible approaches to developing a solution technique.

The decision environment

A decision model has been proposed in Ch. 2 in which decisions and actions are viewed as a process within, and interacting with, an 'environment'. This view necessarily implies a contextual definition of the environment as anything which affects or which is affected by the decisions or actions. The decision environment would, therefore, include such bodies as clients, competitors and even governments, in addition to personnel, property and finance thought to exist generally within the organisation.

'Resources' are defined here as those parts of the decision environment which are at the decision-maker's disposal in accommodating the decision. Resources would, therefore, usually include personnel, property and finance but not clients or competitors (Ansoff 1965: 17).

A further point is in the distinction between decisions, actions and outcomes. For the purposes of model building, decisions may be regarded as processes involving the three components of option identification, evaluation and selection. Actions here are presumed to take place once a decision has been made and is therefore a separate issue. Similarly, implementation is taken to be synonymous with action and is also a separate issue. This is not to say that actions and implementation are not considered in the decision process, but that the operational aspects of decisions do not need to be modelled except insofar as they affect the decision itself. Outcomes then are a set of environmental states or changes in states associated with a particular decision–action sequence. With the perfect knowledge assumption, the interest is in the (predictable) relationship between the decision and the outcome, and 'action' is simply subsumed within 'outcome'.

The environment is continually changing. The effect of a decision, then, is to produce an outcome which is different to that of other decisions, or no decision. The project selection decision problem is essentially targeted at identifying the decision which will result in the most favourable outcome.

The decision-maker is interested in two facets of the environment, those aspects of the environment which generate work opportunities (projects), and those which are affected by the decision (outcomes).

The outcome environment

The outcome environment consists essentially of people (aspirational environment) and property (non-aspirational environment). The aspirational environment includes workmen, managers, administrators, executives and directors within the organisation (internal aspirational) and shareholders, clients, sub-contractors and competitors outside the organisation (external aspirational). The aspirational environment can be further sub-divided into individuals and groups.

The non-aspirational environment is often classified into monetary aspects (e.g. liquid assets and cash) and non-monetary aspects (e.g. buildings, land, plant and equipment).

A further convenient distinction between outcome environments concerns those aspects directly affected by the decision (resources) and those indirectly affected by the decision. The latter environments include competitors and the project-generating environment.

People

The extent to which people are affected by the decision process depends on their aspirations, expectations, attitudes and personal philosophies. These attributes are termed by Johnson and Scholes (1984: 116) as 'values'. Rockeach (1973) makes a finer definition wherein 'attitudes' are considered to reflect a level of affect towards a specific object or situation while 'values' are thought to transcend objects and situations and be connected with the satisfaction of higher-order personal needs, thus occupying a more central position in an individual's personality, make-up and cognitive system. This distinction has been found useful by Hackett and Guion (1985), for example, where absenteeism was found to be a result of a decision process involving the individual's personal values rather than attitudes to job satisfaction.

Recent studies indicate that the performance of tasks within an organisation fulfils some essential psycho-sociological needs of the individual. Kahn (1981), for instance, found that about three-quarters of employed men and the majority of employed women would carry on working even if they did not need a wage. The major reasons for this were considered to be due to the presence of friends at work and the fact that the occupation helped to reduce boredom.

Many interrelated factors have been associated with individual and group needs: activity, meaning, reward and social status (Kahn 1981), for instance. In the construction organisation context, non-monetary objectives such as 'leisure' or 'partaking in civic duties' (Fellows et al. 1983: 40), 'maintaining a way of life' (Hillebrandt 1974), 'personal security' (Fellows et al. 1983: 18) and 'serving the general community' (Barnard 1981) are valued. Attitudes to such objectives, however, would seem to be tempered by the current state of need fulfilment of the individual.

One study of operative motivation (MacKenzie and Harris 1984) has used Maslow's hierarchical need state structure as a framework for comparing operatives' and managers' views on operative motivation. Maslow's theory implies the existence of five states of need: psychological; safety; belonging; esteem; and self-actualisation. An individual is said to progress through each state, from psychological to self-actualisation, as the needs associated with each state are satisfied. MacKenzie and Harris's results, together with the ranking of operatives' views of the importance of incentives from an earlier study by Wilson (1979), is shown in

Table 3.1. These results, although indicative of the type of factors affecting operatives, strongly suggest the inapplicability of Maslow's system in providing collectively mutually exclusive need states for the operatives. It is possible, however, that *individual* operatives may provide a better fit.

Despite extensive research into human behaviour, a brief summary of which is included in Fryer (1985), there is little consensus on any basic explanatory theory. The fundamental problem may be in the inconsistency of the human decision process.

Table 3.1 Comparison of operative incentive rankings

Theoretical ranking (after Maslow)	Operative ranking (A. J. Wilson)	Management ranking
Physiological needs		
Earnings	3	1
Short travel to and from work	7	—
Safety needs		
Physical/safety/working conditions	1	7
Welfare conditions	2	6
Job security	18	4
Belonging needs		
Friendliness of site	4=	10
Work with people as a team	12	9
Work on a well-organised site	4=	2
Good relations with management	14	3
Fringe benefits	15	8
Needs for esteem		
Recognition from management/ workmates	10	—
Working for a successful company	18	—
Working for a modern company	15=	—
Need for self-actualisation		
Challenge in the job	17	—
Job freedom	9	1
Plenty of time for personal/ family life	6	5
Prospects for promotion	21	12=
Opportunities for training	20	12=
Ability to make use of, and develop, skills	8	—

Source: MacKenzie and Harris (1984: Table 3).

Group behaviour presents no less of a problem. In many respects, the needs and aspirations of groups are identical to those of individuals. The interactions of individuals within groups are of particular concern, however, power and social context being important factors. Recent studies by Tjosvold (1985) suggest that social contexts involving co-operative, individual or competitive-related activities were more important than vested power.

Inter-individual and inter-group relationships are usually referred to in terms of such manifestations as 'politics' or 'power'. Here the tendency is to rely entirely on overtly expressed values of power groups such as unions (Johnson and Scholes 1984).

'Corporate harmony' has been implied to be a characteristic of a successfully progressing company (Fellows *et al.* 1983: 48). Recent studies by Peters and Waterman (1982), however, have found instances of some very successful companies thriving on internal competition.

One power group that has attracted particular interest in the construction literature is that of senior management. Managers have an additional role in the organisation, which is to be formally responsible for resources. Insofar as human resources are concerned, this responsibility requires a concern for welfare (Lansley *et al.* 1980: 43), satisfying employees (Moore 1984: 20) and their aspirations (Barnard 1981) and encouraging and supporting individual growth and development (Fryer 1985). The basis of this responsibility is, according to Fryer (1985), in the provision of secure employment (though not highly rated in MacKenzie and Harris: Table 3.1), a friendly and co-operative atmosphere and fair compensation for the efforts of employees. Much of this managerial task is covered by such functional terms as personnel management, health and safety, and labour relations.

Conflicts that exist within and between resources are particularly notable where managerial responsibilities are concerned. The conflict between personal and company interests has been discussed by Cyert and Marsh (1963), although Hillebrandt (1974: 90) considers such conflicts to be minimal in construction companies where there is a substantial overlap of ownership and control. The major area of conflict appears to be in the management and control of monetary and non-monetary resources.

Control of resources

The construction industry, according to Sidwell (1984), relies heavily on the flexibility and initiative of its people and as a result firms which rely on standardised systems and procedures are particularly restrained in this respect. Controls based on performance standards and direct supervision have been found to be less constraining. What appears to be needed is a means by which people can obtain clear and consistent views of their own roles, the roles of colleagues and the firm's objectives, and co-ordinate their activities (Lansley *et al.* 1980: 43). There are times, though, when rather more than communicative and co-ordinating support are needed. One such occasion is in the preparation and management of change, particularly when resistance to it is anticipated. In this case, the system can be used to *manipulate* resources. Similar manipulation activities occur in *balancing* resources. A company may, for instance, increase monetary resources at the expense of human resource development, and vice versa. The provision of such manipulatory facilities are obtained through control systems, usually embedded in the *organisational structure* of the company.

A wide variety of organisational structures exists in the construction environment. Lansley *et al.* (1979: 3, 74) have identified four basic structure types: ideal bureaucratic, with high control and integration; mechanistic, with high control and low integration; organic, with low control and high integration; and anarchic, with low control and low integration. Their study of twenty-six national and regional construction companies involved in general contracting, housing and services found national firms tending to display relatively high levels of control but with no one structure being favoured by any of the different types of firm. Performance, however, was found to be 'strongly related' to higher levels of integration, while control was of 'little importance'.

The apparent lack of influence of control may be due to the existence of an 'adhocracy' form (Mintzberg 1979), typically found in construction organisations because of the temporary and diverse nature of project activities (Ireland 1985: 60). As a result, construction organisations have been urged to concentrate on developing structures and systems which enable effective location of technical and specialist support and systems on site, integration between staff and their activities, and communication of information (Lansley *et al.* 1980: 43).

The relationship between corporate decisions and organisation structure has been extensively studied by Chandler (1962) and others, resulting in the now accepted thesis (Smith 1985: 176) that the organisation of the enterprise develops to match its decisions. Studies by Newcombe (1976), however, of a number of construction companies of various sizes and types found that delays in developing an appropriate organisation structure can be fatal. Ansoff (1965: 179) has proposed the adoption of an administrative strategy to manage the organisational evolution of the firm. Such an administrative strategy could, according to Ansoff, be elaborated further into specific organisational relationships and provisions for growth of organisational resources. Several researchers, however, have noted a distinct lack of application of administrative strategy in construction companies, evidenced by the lack of suitable teaching and training material which could be used to develop the abilities of the managers (Lansley *et al.* 1979: 1, 65), for instance. The reason for this may be that the very factors responsible for the existence of adhocracies mitigate against controlled organisational development.

Peters and Waterman's study (1982) of 'excellent' companies suggests a simple organisational form of the adhocratic type to be most appropriate. This study found senior managers to be relatively few in number and demands; the focus of the attention to be on people, particularly the customer and the workers, and the product; a bias for action, to cause and react quickly to changing circumstances.

Property

Property, termed 'physical resources' by Johnson and Scholes (1984), consists of such physical assets as land, buildings, machines and materials. The extent to which such property is directly affected by the project selection decision is often minimal, except perhaps in the case of very large or unusual projects, as many effects are of a temporary nature. Some of the more permanent effects can be the need to increase the size of the head office to accommodate an expanding permanent staff, which may involve the acquisition of further land and buildings. Plant and materials are normally acquired for the duration of the project, although the residue of some large items of plant, such as a tower crane or batching plant, will have an impact. The acquisition of plant or manufacturing facilities for larger projects can have longer-term implications in generating possible decision options involving permanent and separate business operations.

Money

Monetary resources are usually classified into long-term/medium-term finance. Long-term finance is used to purchase buildings, plant and equipment and to carry stocks of materials (Harris and McCaffer 1983: 312). Short term finance is used to overcome immediate cash-flow problems, such as the purchase of materials, plant hire and payment of sub-contractors (Harris and McCaffer 1983: 312). The project selection decision will, therefore, predominantly affect short-term finance and generally only indirectly affect long-term finance. Typical sources of long- and short-term finance are given in Figs 3.1 and 3.2.

The acquisition of finance generates benefits (assets) and costs (liabilities). The liabilities incurred in the acquisition of finance consist of internal liabilities, for example debts owed to ordinary and preference shareholders, and external liabilities, such as sums owed to debenture holders, the Inland Revenue (for taxes), banks (for loans and overdrafts), and trade creditors (Adam 1965: 226). Liabilities can also be short-term (current liabilities), such as those payable to trade creditors, or long-term (deferred liabilities), usually more than one year (Adam 1965: 226).

Assets can similarly be divided into current and fixed depending on the time period involved. A further relevant distinction is between liquid and illiquid assets. Working capital comprises the liquid or near-liquid assets needed to lubricate the daily transactions of business. It is represented by the difference between current assets and current liabilities, and is locked up in a continuous cycle, shown in Fig. 3.3.

Interrelationships in the outcome environment

Many aspects of the outcome environment are interrelated and often conflicting. A common feature is the clash of interests between power groups, such as senior management and unions, where changes in the environment which are beneficial to one group are detrimental to the other. Similarly, improvements in levels of financial resources of one group of people usually implies a reduction in financial resources in another. The successful progress of the organisation depends exclusively on the balance of benefits received by these sections of the outcome environment.

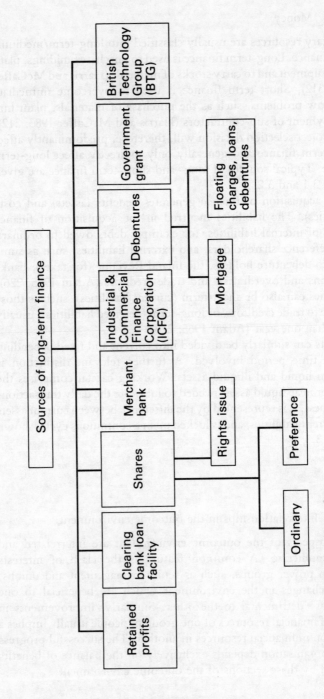

Fig. 3.1 Sources of long-term finance
Source: Harris and McCaffer (1983)

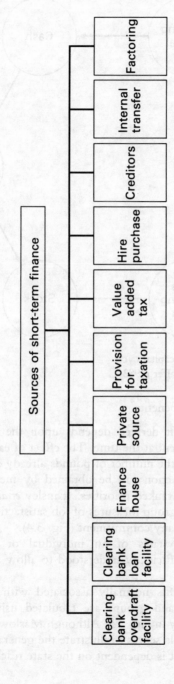

Fig. 3.2 Sources of short-term finance
Source: Harris and McCaffer (1983)

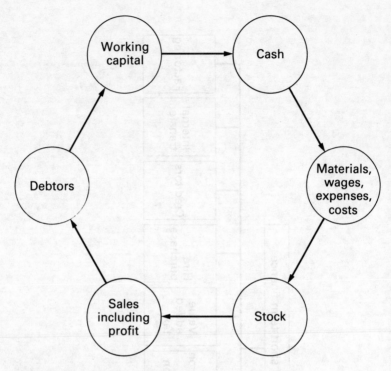

Fig. 3.3 The working capital cycle
Source: Harris and McCaffer (1983)

Measures of benefits

The degree of benefit derived depends upon the development state of the environment at the time. The effect of earning £1, for instance, depends on the number of pounds already earned.

Measures of satisfaction can be obtained by means of questionnaires to provide ranked priorities. (Lansley *et al*. 1979: App. F, 23) have obtained group measures of job satisfaction, company satisfaction and company commitment (Fig. 3.4).

The development states of an individual or a group of people are not yet sufficiently understood to allow any universal classification.

Some of the benefits normally associated with internal and external individuals and groups are tabulated using Maslow's needs/drives hierarchy in Fig. 3.5. Although Maslow's system has many defects, the table serves to illustrate the general proposition that the size of benefit is dependent on the state reached.

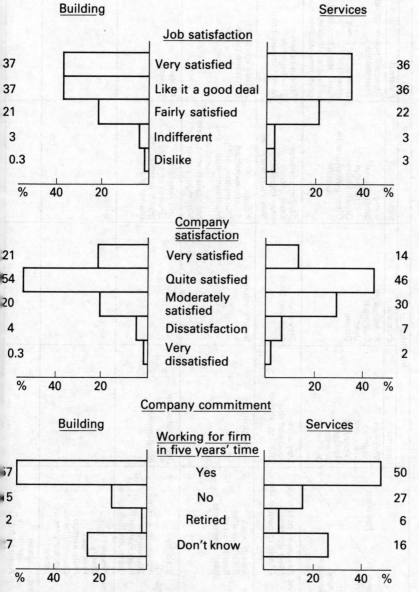

Fig. 3.4 Measures of satisfaction with job and company
Source: Lansley et al. (1979: App. F, 23)

Recipient / Maslow's needs/drives (Owner, Hierarchy, Development status)	Individual		Group	
	Internal	External	Internal	External
	Workmen, Foreman, Site agent, Executives, Manager, Director, Owner	Shareholder, Customer, User, Others	Gang, Site/regional, national, Organisation, Other power groups – unions	Attached power groups – Shareholders. Unattached power groups – Sub-contractors, suppliers, unions, ecological, government, client bodies
Survival Pay/cover overheads, Meet debts, Obtain minimum work	Stay alive, Food and drink, Clothing, shelter	Stay alive, Food and drink	Stay in business, Keep licence, Stay together, Minimum workload	Stay in business, Stay together, Minimum workload
Safety Steady work, Steady income, Resolution of basic grievances	Job security	Secure income	Assets, Steady workload, Minimum growth, Minimum profits and turnover, Maintain market share, Minimum power	Steady workload, Minimum power
Love (belonging) Stability, Increasing income, Stimulation, Participation in decisions (influence)	Job satisfaction, Personal development		Job satisfaction, Growth of assets, profit, turnover and market share	Power, Growth
Esteem Respect, Status, Prestige, Philanthropy, Community service, Advisory (non-power)			Growth	
Self-actualisation Philanthropy, Assured future				

Measures of monetary benefits are well accepted. 'Profit' and 'turnover' are of major interest, but several other descriptive statistics are used. Calvert (1981) has identified the ratios commonly used:

1 Current assets to current liabilities (working capital ratio)
2 Liquid assets to current liabilities
3 Outstanding debts to sales
4 Illiquid assets to sales moving annual total
5 Cash to current liabilities
6 Current profit to invested capital
7 Current profit to sales
8 Direct labour to turnover
9 Average credit period
10 Overhead percentage

Taxation and cash flow are two further considerations. Real property is normally evaluated in monetary terms. Depreciation is an important factor in such evaluations and also affects taxation liabilities.

Project characteristics

Relationship between project characteristics and the outcome environment

The types and kinds of projects undertaken by a construction organisation have a considerable impact on its outcome environment. Deliberate moves into a new area of work have been found to be an important means of developing mobile management, for instance (Lansley *et al*. 1979: 1, 59). Project value also has an important bearing on financial resources.

The characteristics of projects are necessarily a function of the construction industry itself, which encompasses a whole range of diverse activities such as civil engineering works, building works, public and private sector work, large capital utilities, development work and refurbishment involving contracts obtained under competition, negotiation or a variety of cost reimbursement forms (Sidwell 1984: 22).

In examining the nature of industries generally, Smith (1985) has suggested key factors as being the type of products produced and the market served, the technology of production and the nature of the materials required. The diverse nature of the construction industry, however, makes these factors rather difficult to define.

77

Hillebrandt (1974) defines the construction product as basically the service of moving earth and material, of assembling and managing the whole process. However, as this service and management varies according to the technical processes involved, the industry is viewed as consisting of many sub-industries coming under the umbrella of the industry concept. A more appropriate analysis is proposed by Hillebrandt to be the *market* . . . in which a group of firms, whose products are more or less substitutes for each other, operates. Lange (1973) has termed these determinants, with the addition of industry branch, 'sub-markets'. Size, complexity and industry branch are often referred to as 'type' (Lansley *et al.* 1980) or 'size and type of work' (Harrison 1982), Lansley *et al.* (1980) proposing 'client' as a further sub-market.

These sub-markets, i.e. type of work, client, location and competitors, define the 'nature of the work' (Mannerings 1970) coming from the construction company's 'immediate environment' (Foster 1974). A recent study by the Building Economics Research Unit (Cusack 1981) has found that the sub-markets collectively account for over 97 per cent of reasons underlying the decision to tender for projects.

Type of work

The type of work available in the construction industry is reflected in the activities of large construction companies ranging from general building and civil engineering to materials manufacturing, property development, trade specification and even open-cast mining, together with peripheral services such as materials supply, plant hire and project management (Fellows *et al.* 1983: 1). A building company's services can include a building on its site; a building for assembly on a site provided by the client; an assembly service, for a building designed on commission to the client; or one of a series of contributory services brought together and co-ordinated on behalf of the client to erect a building to a design commissioned by him (Jepson and Nicholson 1972: 5).

Types of buildings are usually denoted by function: residential, commercial, industrial, educational and recreational being typical groupings. The building's function will largely be associated with benefits to the consumer.

The physical and monetary size of a project affects the company's resources and, particularly, management and finance. Productivity has been associated with project size (Clark and Lorenzoni 1985).

Large contracts can develop managerial skills, for instance, provided the personnel have reached a suitable stage of development (Harrison 1982). Monetary resources similarly need to be sufficiently high to withstand cash-flow pressures.

Lansley *et al.* (1979: 3, 5) have found that the technology of the project, expressed in terms of size, complexity and method of construction required, significantly affects organisational and managerial aspects of the company when an unfamiliar technology is involved. In such situations, the organisational structure tended to become more flexible. Different organisation structures occurred on large contracts involving many complex tasks (e.g. hospitals and hotels) than on smaller and less complex contracts. Distinctions between organisation structures for civil engineering and building projects were not found to be significant, however, although many building companies considered the acquisition of technical expertise and understanding of the commercial aspects of civil engineering to be an insurmountable difficulty.

'Technology', although of potentially great value in expressing relationships between project characteristics and the outcome environment, has been found difficult to completely define. Theoretical developments are still needed in this respect (Lansley *et al.* 1979: 1, 64).

Types of client

Jepson and Nicholson (1972: 4) have identified four types of client: a speculator, investing in building for profit; a public body, investing in building on behalf of, or for the benefit of, the community; an occupier with a family or commercial activity or an industrial process to house; and a person or body seeking a monument. Public construction demand is about 30–40 per cent of overall demand (Diepeveen 1985: 111).

Two main client influences on outcomes have been found to be 'ability to pay' and 'relations' (South 1979). The latter also includes the client's advisers, the architect, engineers and quantity surveyor. Relations have been found to affect the contractor's efficiency and cause delays in settling variations and the final account (Cusack 1981).

The factors related to the client organisation and the construction project are procurement methods and contractual arrangements. Ireland (1985) has identified six procurement methods in common use: a single lump-sum contract on a fully documented project;

provisional or partial quantities contracts; cost reimbursement (cost–plus); package deal (design and construct or turnkey); construction management; and project management. There appear to be no satisfactory criteria which uniquely separate each procurement method. However, four important aspects have been suggested to be the arrangements for determining the cost of the project and identifying the contractor to be used; the roles and relationships of the specialists used, including the possibility of having the contractor available to contribute to the design; the process structure adopted, including such aspects as the overlap of design and construction, the use of multiple prime contracts and the staging of these; and details included in the conditions of contract such as provision for extensions of time for industrial disputation of inclement weather etc. (Ireland 1985: 77).

The value (cost to the client) of the project is considered to be related to the cost determination and contractor selection method used. Negotiated contracts are generally agreed to increase value, while open tenders generally decrease value (Smith 1981). However, as Adrian (1973: 370) observes, the price offered by the contractor needs to be comparable with potential competitors, even in the absence of direct competition.

The contractor's contribution to the design necessarily affects his resources. The overlap of design and construction generally reflects the desire for speedy completion. The speed at which the project is needed has important repercussions on estimating resources (Mannerings 1970; South 1979) as well as production resources.

The conditions of contract mainly affect risk (see Ch. 4). Specific instructions regarding the type (e.g. sub-contractors, materials) and use (access, storage, permissible working times) of resources have direct implications.

Some specific clients may have a special interest in the company through a previous relationship, for instance. In these cases, the client may have a particular influence in selecting the second lowest tender, for example, and thereby modifying the market value principle.

Geographical location

Dressel (c.1980: 14) distinguishes between 'home' markets (consisting of town, area, region, county, province and country) and 'abroad' (consisting of neighbouring country, developing countries and overseas).

Lansley *et al.*'s (1979) studies of several construction companies in the South East, South West and East Midlands of Britain revealed that most firms worked over a small area, mainly within a maximum radius of forty miles from their base. Even national contracting firms were found to have interests centred upon their local or regionally based units, which generally adhered to similar boundaries.

The distance of the project from the company's local base affects operatives, who appreciate short travel and welcome the extra free time it produces (see Table 3.1, rankings 7 and 6 respectively). Local craft can, of course, be employed, but this often adversely affects productivity (Clark and Lorenzoni 1985) and hence monetary resources.

Transportation costs are another important factor, together with the costs incurred by non-productive travelling time and subsistence allowances. The organisational structure can also be affected by the need to make special communication arrangements between the site and local, regional or head offices. Remote sites and overseas projects can have special influences due to weather conditions and cultural differences.

Competitors

From the market viewpoint it is the company's competitors that determine the value of the project and, as the deterministic model presupposes that competitors' bids are known, then the value must also be known. The factors influencing bid levels of competitors will be the same as the company's factors. Ease of entry to the industry or market, for instance, simply reflects the position where the option to enter the industry or market is associated with beneficial and preferential outcomes.

Summary

Four project characteristics, type, client, location and competitors, have been considered in relation to influences on the outcome environment. These characteristics are themselves interrelated as, for instance, certain types of client always want certain types of buildings, or always build in the same locality. A simple causal model is shown in Fig 3.6. A more complex model would accommodate possible relationships between type and location (e.g. nuclear power stations should be on remote sites), competitors and

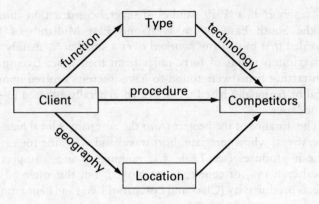

Fig. 3.6 Relationships between project characteristics

client (e.g. the existence of a well-established package dealer may influence the procurement type decision), competition and type (e.g. a company's known ability to produce certain pre-fabricated components may influence the design) etc. Other environmental factors such as governmental and social legislation also affect the project characteristics. These are dealt with in Ch. 5 as 'indirect' influences.

Figure 3.7 summarises the relationships between the project characteristics and the outcome environment briefly introduced in this chapter.

Figure 3.8 shows the essentials of the project selection model, consisting of the available projects, decisions and outcomes, their influences on each other, together with indirect environmental influences. The dotted influence line between outcomes and projects is the dynamical link required for the dynamic models examined later. The requirements of the contingent approach to decision-making demand that *potential* options which may not currently be actual project opportunities are considered, and these have been accommodated in the decision 'box' for this reason.

Selection criteria

The project selection decision is a result of considerations of the beneficial effects of the decision on the outcome environment. The decision-maker, however, places differing levels of emphasis upon different aspects of the outcome environment. The internal outcome environment, for instance, is usually of more concern

Project characteristics	Outcome environment		
	People	Money	Real property
Type (function) (size) (technology)	Consumer Management Organisation & management Sub-contractors Suppliers (technology)	Finance (size) Profit (technology)	Materials (technology) Plant (technology) Head Office (size)
Client	Estimators (procedure) Designers (procedure) Sub-contractors (contract)	Finance (ability to pay) Profit (procedure) Finance (procedure)	Materials (contract)
Location	Operations (travel, free time) Organisation & management (communications) Local labour, sub-contractors, suppliers	Finance, profit (cost of transport) (weather) (accommodation and subsistence) (production) (communications)	Transportation Vehicles Communication devices – telephone
Competitors		Value (finance, profit)	

Fig. 3.7 Relationships between project characteristics and the outcome environment

83

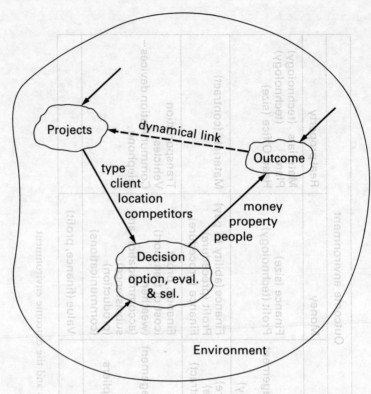

Fig. 3.8   Project selection model

than the external outcome environment. These aspects of the environment are, effectively, project selection criteria, and the degree of emphasis placed upon each criterion is indicative of its relevance to the problem. Relevant criteria are closely associated with the decision-maker's objectives and goals.

The primary objective of the company has been said to be in its continued existence and further development (Dressel c.1980: 2). Special objectives involve market, supply, production, financial, personnel and organisational aims. These are dealt with here as monetary, non-monetary and market-related objectives.

Monetary objectives

The desired changes in levels of monetary resources are usually expressed in terms of profits or profitability. The conventional

84

economist interpretation of company objectives is in the maximisation of profits, although Simon (1957) has found profit 'satisficing' to be a more appropriate description of the general business aspiration.

Profit maximisation has been considered by many writers in the construction industry to be a rather naive view of the project objective (see Fellows *et al.* 1983: 40; Hillebrandt 1974: 89; Woodward 1975: 170, for instance). It has been suggested that the company's primary objective is to make 'adequate' profits (Hillebrandt 1974: 92), 'normal' profits (Hillebrandt 1974: 93), 'modest' profits (Fellows *et al.* 1983: 40), 'target' profits (Niss 1965; Hillebrandt 1974: 89) or minimise losses. Profits have been measured in absolute terms, or as the level of return on investments (Barnard 1981; Mannerings 1970). A further distinction is between before- and after-tax profits.

An alternative approach concentrates on the growth of earnings (Barnard 1981), commonly referred to as 'turnover', where similar objectives such as 'target' turnover (Hillebrandt 1974: 91; Niss 1965) or 'limited expansion' (Hillebrandt 1974: 89) have been identified, often involving annual turnover forecasts (Humphreys 1977).

Other objectives

A frequently reported objective concerns the utilisation of resources. This includes the efficient use of resources (Fryer 1985) such as labour and materials (Barnard 1981; Niss 1965) and filling plant capacity (Benson 1970). Maintaining the size of the workforce (Cusack 1981) or keeping key workers (Niss 1965) have also been found to be important objectives.

Objectives involving people in the environment have already been discussed to some extent in this chapter in identifying human developmental characteristics. Other objectives include serving the client well (Fryer 1985; Barnard 1981), also the general community (Barnard 1981) by maintaining and improving quality and service (Niss 1965) and avoiding such activities which endanger the environment and public health (Fryer 1985). Retaining the confidence of suppliers and sub-contractors has also been found to be important (Moore 1984: 19).

Market-related objectives

Objectives are sometimes more conveniently expressed indirectly in terms of the market, instead of as specific desired states in the outcome environment. These aspirations, termed product-market scope (Ansoff 1965: 98), include such objectives as increases in market share (Fellows *et al.* 1983: 118; Barnard 1981), staying in existing markets (Adrian 1973: 371) such as construction type (Cooke 1981) or location (Foster 1974), entering new markets (Woodward 1975: 170; Foster 1974) and growth in a number of markets (Barnard 1981; Fellows *et al.* 1983: 27). Product-market scope is, however, a 'means' rather than an 'end' and, as such, constitutes more of a 'strategy' than an 'objective' (Ansoff 1965: 100). The decision model adopted in this book relies purely on the consideration of outcomes arising from the decision. A strategy is, therefore, regarded as a means of pre-empting the workings of such a model by some global mechanism such as, in this case, attributing market-related factors to outcomes. Such a global process, it is maintained, would be only enabled *through* the model. A useful purpose can be served, however, in comparing known successful strategies with those revealed by the model as part of the validation process. These are described in Ch. 6.

Multiple objectives

Studies by Bengtsson (1985) have failed to reveal the existence of any single unambiguous company goal. Multiple objectives are required if the relations of an organisation to the environment are to be understood (Bengtsson 1985: 33). Conflicting objectives were found, particularly between monetary objectives (e.g. 'profit within own area of responsibility', 'company profit') and human needs and aspirations (e.g. 'stimulating tasks and internal training programme', 'job security', 'work environment', 'safety' etc.). The emphasis placed on each objective, the 'goal profile', was found to differ between individuals. An analysis of eighty-six individuals in construction companies suggested differences in goal profiles to be associated with different managerial hierarchical levels in the organisation and different quantities of expertise. There is, as Bengtsson observes, no simple method for evaluating goal profiles.

Selection strategies

Selection strategies can be classed as either 'rational' or 'irrational'. In both cases the objective must be to make the best possible choice from a set of alternatives. The identification of rational strategies is referred to as the 'optimisation problem', which is usually expressed in mathematical terms, involving the minimisation of some function (the objective function or criterion function). In problems where several criteria exist, this function is variously referred to as the 'vector criterion', 'multivariate criterion' or a 'multidimensional criterion'. When several criteria are combined into a single criterion the result is termed the 'scalar criterion'.

Methods of handling optimisation problems containing several criteria are called 'multiple criteria' or 'multi-attribute' methods.

Multiple criteria decision evaluation

There is a practical need, in the face of multiple decision criteria, to develop a strategy for presenting all those potential courses of action which might reasonably be regarded as attractive without obscuring what is at best likely to be a complex decision by the presence of many less desirable possibilities (Kmietowicz and Pearman 1981: 106).

In recent years, an increasing number of papers have appeared concerned with both the theory and practice of multiple criteria decision-making. French and Dutch authors, in particular, have made significant contributions to the field. While the majority of early formal work appears to have emanated from psychologists and management scientists in the USA, many potential areas of application exist. Public policy decisions, for example, frequently involve the consideration of a wide range of consequences which affect many different groups of people in different places and in different ways.

It is apparent, however, that no single multiple criteria technique exists which is unambiguously superior to all others, the most appropriate method or combination of methods varying from problem to problem (Kmietowicz and Pearman 1981: 106).

One possible approach is to construct a multi-attribute function covering the whole range of monetary and non-monetary outcomes which could potentially arise from the decision to be taken. The best-known methods for reducing multiple consequences to a single dimension are in financial appraisal and cost-benefit analysis. In the former case, market prices are used to evaluate the different consequences of a course of action. In the latter, account is taken of consequences which may not have a market and for which shadow prices have to be substituted.

The multi-attribute function, termed the 'global preference function' by Ibbs and Crandall (1982: 191), can be formulated in several ways. Keeney and Raiffa (1976) have considered four of these formulations: additive; multilinear; multiplicative; and general.

MacCrimmon (1973) has identified four major categories of solution technique: weighting methods; sequential elimination methods; mathematical programming methods; and spatial proximity methods. At one point or another, a weighting method is central to the evaluation procedure of most practical multiple criteria decision-making models, the main difference between methods being the techniques used for establishing the weights (Kmietowicz and Pearman 1981: 107).

Evaluation of the preference function

Examination of the construction industry literature reveals two approaches to the formation of the global preference function evaluation process in the project selection problem. Although both of these approaches are presented in a non-deterministic context, they, nevertheless, serve to illustrate the potential use of the multi-attribute technique.

Study 1 (Fellows and Langford 1980 and Fellows et al. 1983: ch. 3)

Fellows and Langford give an example of a weighted additive multi-attribute utility function approach to the construction project selection problem. They consider five courses of action (options): returning the tender documents; submitting a cover price; providing detailed estimates and a tender conversion; preparing a tender based upon approximate estimates; or reworking the tender. Each of these possible outcomes is evaluated on five criteria: speed of obtaining solution; accuracy of solution; cost of solution; client/consultant consideration (risk, attitudes etc.); and benefits, success potential to firm (profitability potential, employment of resources, continuity of work etc.). Adjustment for the relative importance of each criterion is made by a utility weighting device before values are summed into an aggregated outcome evaluation. Under the reasonable assumption that the decision-maker is interested in maximising the utility of the various consequences resulting from his decision, the 'best' decision will be that associated with the highest aggregated outcome evaluation. 'Sensitivity tests' are recommended by the authors in assessing the effect of changes in the utility weightings and 'the criteria themselves'.

Study 2 (Ibbs and Crandall 1982)

Ibbs and Crandall have considered the use of weighted additive and multiplicative multi-attribute functions. In their example there are three (unspecified) decision options, the outcomes of which are evaluated as three criteria: profit return; contract size; and 'regulatory aspects'.

The multiplicative formulation relies on the existence of Utility Independence (UI) and Multi Utility Independence (MUI). Tests for the existence of these states involves the construction of a standard lottery to check the decision-maker's indifference to relative changes in permutations of criteria values. In the additive formulation, MUI only is a necessary condition.

Weighting factors in the multiplicative formulation are required for all attributes, together with an attribute independent scaling factor. As Ibbs and Crandall show, the value of this attribute independent scaling factor can be computed from the attribute values and weightings and, in particular, that when the attribute independent scaling factor obtains a zero value the multiplicative formulation reduces to the additive form. Indeed, it would seem that the attribute independent scaling factor can be used as a decision variable in determining the method of aggregation to adopt.

The resulting global preference function value is computed for each decision and, as in the previous study, the 'best' decision is considered to be that associated with the highest-valued global preference function.

In addition to the recommendations for sensitivity tests on the weighting factors and the criteria used, several further observations are made. Precise definition of the decision variables is considered to be important in order to avoid confusion of the variables measured. 'Profit return', for instance, may have a variety of valid sub-measures, such as absolute monetary profit or return on investment, which reflect different value levels. The independence checks, involving all permutations of the criterion variables, can become 'unwieldy' in the presence of more than 'five or six' criteria. If none of the independence conditions can be found among the decision criteria, other steps may be necessary. Special formulations are available, but difficult, or some method of criteria parsimony applied by isolating offending variables or combining variables by an orthogonalising technique such as factor analysis.

Three final operational comments are made. Firstly, some decision-makers have difficulty in expressing a preference function for the criteria. Secondly, there are situations in which decision alternatives are assigned scalar values outside the original limits of the analysis. It could be, for instance, that the decision-maker considers a criterion variable to be more important than an alternative which has already been assigned a maximum value on the weighting index. Finally, a related feature, and one which appears to be a recurring problem in the utility approach, is the instability of utility values in the weighting scheme. These values, it seems, must be continually monitored as the firm's preferences change.

Conclusions

The project selection problem, in its deterministic and static form, centres on the consideration of three fundamental and interrelated aspects of the outcome environment: people, money and physical property. Four interrelated project characteristics, type, client, location and competitors, have a significant influence on these environmental aspects.

It is considered that, in order to pursue the successful progress of the company, the 'best' decision should be the one which will most benefit all these often competing aspects of the outcome environment. This will normally entail the evaluation of criteria including profits, profitability, earnings and turnover for monetary outcomes, the type, value and usage of physical resources, the usefulness and aspirations of individuals and groups within the organisation, the level of the client and community satisfaction of the company's quality and service and the confidence of the suppliers and sub-contractors. The value of these criteria, it is argued, will be relative to previous levels, referred to as the developmental state.

The final stage of the decision model outlined in Chapter 2 involves the comparison of the evaluated criteria with those of an alternative decision. Where only one criterion exists, profit for instance, the comparison is trivial. The presence of multiple criteria is, however, clearly an essential feature of the problem. Before any attempt can be made at a solution, it is apparent that some method of weighting must be applied. This is regarded as an aspect of the selection phase of the problem in order to preserve the generality of the evaluation phase.

The proposal to combine the weighted criteria into a single scale is, perhaps, the most controversial issue. The major criticism with this approach is that, in reducing the multiple-dimensional consequences of an act to a single dimensional evaluation, information is inevitably lost. If there is no doubt about the rates at which decision-makers are prepared to trade off different consequences against each other at all different levels of attainment of those consequences, then reduction to a single dimension should cause no great problems (Kmietowicz and Pearman 1981: 106). Ibbs and Crandall's study indicates that this is not likely to be the case, some difficulty being encountered in acquiring consistent trade-off values.

Kmietowicz and Pearman (1981: 106) suggest two possible approaches to this problem. One is the comparison and ranking of selection strategies on the basis of more than one decision. The other is in the reduction of the dimensionality of the problem by fixing acceptable weights to the different consequences of strategies and the exploration of the implications of some tolerance in the precise values of those weights.

Both of the studies reported have adopted the latter approach in attempting to attach weights to the various criterion variables and in recommending some sensitivity analyses. The need to perform extensive independence checks and the difficulty in assigning weights suggest that the approach may not be without its problems, even in the deterministic model.

It is noted, however, that whatever solution technique is employed, some formalisation of the decision process does have value in helping to clarify both what is being aimed at and the relative importance of conflicting goals. Furthermore, communication with other decision-makers and affected parties is facilitated if some framework for presenting and comparing the consequences of different courses of action exists.

4

Time-dependent aspects

Introduction

The previous chapter was concerned with the relationship between the project selection decision and the immediate environment of the decision-maker, assuming perfect knowledge and, generally, without regard to time-dependent aspects of the problem. The purpose of this chapter is to explore such time-dependent aspects while still maintaining focus on the immediate environment and assuming perfect knowledge.

Time-dependent aspects of the decision-making process have two major implications in terms of the project selection model. One is the causal relationship between the outcome environment and projects, shown in Fig. 3.8 as the dynamical link. The other implication is that time introduces a new dimension to the problem.

The relationship between the outcome environment and projects

The previous chapter examined the problem of selecting a project or set of simultaneous projects which would best benefit the outcome environment without regard to any further selections that may be required in the future. However, it is clear that future decisions will be significantly affected by current ones. The problem can, therefore, be restated as that of selecting the set of *sequential* projects which will best benefit the outcome environment. Problems involving sequential decisions are said to be dynamical problems. The dynamical version of the project decision problem demands knowledge of the effect of the outcome environment associated with each project on the quantity and characteristics of future projects.

The generation of project opportunities is normally regarded to be a result of some marketing activity. Until relatively recently, marketing has not generally been considered appropriate for construction companies, as they belong to a service industry largely waiting to be asked for their services (Sidwell 1984). Lansley *et al.* (1979), however, found some rather more aggressive contractors who actively sought opportunities through market research and by cultivating contacts with prospective clients. It was also found that contractors who normally adopted a passive attitude became more aggressive when work was short.

The marketing aspects of the project selection decision are only a small part of the total possible marketing effort, and very little literature is available on the subject at the time of writing.

An obvious point of interest is the client, who is part of the outcome environment *and* project characteristics. Enhanced benefits for a particular client may well generate further project opportunities. Jepson and Nicholson (1972) term this general strategy 'image building' or the development of 'goodwill'. Such enhancement necessarily implies reduced benefits in other aspects of the outcome environment. It may require, for instance, the unquestioning assumption of liability for the errors and failings of employees and associates and that profit may thus be lower (Jepson and Nicholson 1972: 78). The opposite approach, termed 'milking' the project, is aimed at enhancing non-client aspects of the outcome environment and with the possible consequence of reduced future project opportunities or modified project characteristics.

This means of influencing potential clients extends to other aspects of the outcome environment. Knowledge of benefits received by one client may influence other potential clients. Benefits received by a section of the community may also influence potential clients in a similar way. Even benefits obtained internally, such as the well-being of the workforce, may engender a special attitude in potential clients towards the benefits they may receive should they wish to employ the company.

Unless clients possess perfect knowledge, then communication of events that take place in the outcome environment to potential clients is an important issue. Such communication usually implies some advertising or promotional activity by the company. The project selection decision can provide some assistance in this through the selection of certain prestigious projects, for instance, or projects associated with well-publicised designers or causes. In these cases, enhanced promotional benefits may be preferred to short-term monetary gain.

The time dimension

The effect of time considerations is to introduce an additional dimension to the problem, as changes in the decision environment occur at different points in time.

Major implications occur in the outcome environment. The extent of benefits received by people is, as discussed in the last chapter, influenced by the stage of development reached at the time. These benefits are received continuously, in the case of human resources, resulting in continually changing developmental and aspirational states. Also, as people join and leave the organisation, fluctuations in quantity as well as quality occur.

Performance levels are affected by time, instanced by such phenomena as the learning curve. The time of the year can affect output by up to 50 per cent (Cusack 1981: 54). Overtime working and bonus schemes also provide other time related aspects. Construction sites suffer particular difficulties in the co-ordination of sequential activities as operatives frequently change work places (Bennett and Fine 1980).

The acquisition of a new project involves some degree of disruption to personnel, depending on the project characteristics, although craft-based organisations, such as construction companies, have been said to respond quickly and effectively to major changes in demand (Burton 1972: 72). Lansley *et al.* (1979), however, have found evidence of resistance and reluctance to change due to incompatible individual development strategies (rigidity of views and attitudes); the frequency of changes, especially those not providing benefits to the individuals; lack of involvement in the decision, causing the change or its implementation; and poor communication of decisions and their anticipated effects on the individuals concerned.

The extent and frequency of change has an effect on the organisational structure of the company, a tendency to a more flexible structure occurring with increasing change (Lansley *et al.* 1980) depending on the present size of the company (Lansley *et al.* 1979). Movements in monetary resources are primarily linked with the project duration, resulting in the consideration of cash-flow implications. Cash flow has been found to be affected mostly by such project characteristics as the size, the type (e.g. speculative housing), the client (e.g. private work) and bias in the progress valuations (caused by 'front end loading') (South 1979). The client's conditions of contract further impact on cash flow by restricting

94

income (retention) and reimbursement of changes in the value of money (fluctuations). The cost of creating liquid assets (interest rates) and the timing of payments to suppliers, sub-contractors, shareholders etc. are further important aspects.

Time effects on physical property include the provision of temporary buildings and the acquisition, maintenance and disposal of materials and plant. These aspects are normally treated in monetary terms, such as depreciation or sinking fund provisions.

Changes also occur in the project characteristics. Design modifications take place during the course of construction. These affect the management and organisation of the work, productivity, cash flow and even the contract period. Changes in client or consultant personnel can affect working relationships, sometimes quite dramatically. Such changes (e.g. change in quantity surveying personnel) can also affect monetary resources.

Implications for evaluation and selection

Consideration of time-related aspects of project selection introduces the notion that outcomes take place over time. These outcomes can be regarded as being discrete events or as continuously developing, as represented by discrete or continuous time systems. An outcome, in these terms, is effectively the state of the outcome environment *at some point in time* after the decision has been made. Points of time that are of interest occur in the short-, medium- and long-term (Adrian 1973: 370). For construction companies, short-term is associated with the duration of a particular project, medium-term has been said to be about three years (Bahrami 1981), although in recent changing times twelve to eighteen months has been considered more appropriate (Benes and Diepeveen 1985), and long-term some distant future of a minimum of ten years ahead. Such distinctions are quite arbitrary however. Cash-flow analysis, for instance, attempts to predict monetary outcomes at quite frequent, usually monthly, intervals and is particularly useful in identifying times when financial problems will occur. Ideally, a system would indicate the state of the outcome environment *at any moment in time*.

The influence of the outcome environment on project opportunities raises special strategic issues. Sacrificing profits to enhance opportunities, for instance, is one such strategy (Fellows *et al.* 1983: 40, 188). Strategies aimed at stabilising profits, return on investments and turnover are all evident (Barnard 1981). Development strategies

95

also exist to enable exploitation of opportunities (Fellows *et al*. 1983), particularly organisational development (Lansley *et al*. 1979). Marketing strategies of this nature are termed forward integration strategies (Moss 1981).

These considerations suggest that the project selection decision will require evaluation of the state of the *project generating environment* in addition to the outcome environment. Strategic decisions also require evaluations of the *nature of changes* in the relevant environment. This would require knowledge of the rate of change or the existence of trends, for instance. It is contended, however, that, as noted in the previous chapter, such strategy-oriented aspects are necessarily concerned with behaviours manifested by, rather than incorporated into, the model, except as a simplifying expedient.

In the 'systems' context, changes in the environment can be regarded as an iterative process and any decisions affecting these changes are adjustment processes. The competitive economy, which is a particular organisational form in which all members are regarded as acting in competition with each other, has received some attention in this respect. The competitive economy has been described as consisting of agents, involved in a competitive process, who act in response to their changing 'environments' and to actions by other agents resulting in 'messages' (prices). An adjustment process in this organisation is a kind of scheme or process which this organisation reveals at each iteration and which would satisfy certain properties to the best of all its members. In this context, an adjustment process can be viewed as a sequence of aggregated actions (behaviour patterns) taken by each agent (Gottinger 1983: 178).

For a different class of environment, Hurwicz (1959) has studied adjustment processes in terms of differential equations in which agents respond to messages from other agents including themselves (memorising). The behavioural pattern of such an economic system can be studied in terms of a particular social welfare function satisfying an optimality criterion given an environment of a particular kind. On the basis of the adjustment process new states will be generated up to a point where the final state is compatible with the welfare criterion. Some important results in this area have been obtained, notably by Hurwicz (1959) and Gottinger (1983: 179), although always depending on some simplifying assumption such as the existence of a 'classical' environment or a Pareto-like stabilising tendency. Major criticisms of these results turn on informational efficiency, giving rise to controversies about the choice of economic systems, and the goal-compatible behaviour patterns of economic agents in which a competitive system is satisfied, given the classical environment, by assuming profit and utility maximisation.

A further difficulty with this approach is that the agents in the project selection environment do not simply respond to environmental stimuli, but attempt to influence stimulatory parts of the environment (evidenced by the 'marketing' effort), neither do the agents act in a purely competitive manner.

The complexities of the various interactive elements in the decision environment over time have been modelled by Gottinger (1983) by a device termed a 'sequential machine'. The sequential machine is a finite-state dynamic system possessing five general characteristics:

1. *A set of inputs,* e.g. those changing parameters of the environment which will affect the system behaviour in a predictable way.
2. *A set of outputs,* i.e. those parameters which act upon the environment leaving observable changes in the relationship between the system and the environment.
3. *A set of states,* i.e. those internal parameters which determine the relationship between inputs and outputs and which may reveal all necessary information embodied in the part.
4. *A state transition function,* which determines the dynamics of how the state will change when the system is fed by various inputs.
5. *The output function,* which determines what output the system will yield with a given input when in a given state.

(Gottinger 1983: 17)

A sequential machine is then defined as a function $f:\Sigma A \rightarrow B$ where A is the basic input set, B is the basic output set and $f(a_1, \ldots, a_n) = b_n$ is the next input at time j $(1 \leqslant j \leqslant n)$. A is a non-empty set of ΣA, i.e. $\Sigma A = \{(a_1, \ldots, a_n):n \geqslant 1$ and $a_j \in A\}$. Looking inside the machine, a circuit C is defined as a quintuple $(A, B, Z, \lambda, \delta)$, where Z is the (non-empty) set of internal states, $\lambda:A \times Z \rightarrow Z$ is the next-state function, and $\delta:A \times Z \rightarrow B$ is the next output function

$$C_z(a_1) = \delta(a_1, z);$$
$$C_z(a_1, \ldots, a_n) = C_x(a, z)(a_2, \ldots, a_n) \text{ for } n \geqslant 2$$

The basic idea of a sequential circuit C is then

$$C:z = z_0 \xrightarrow{a_1} z_1 \xrightarrow{a_2} z_2 \xrightarrow{a_3} \ldots \xrightarrow{a_n} z_n$$
$$\downarrow \qquad \downarrow \qquad\qquad \downarrow$$
$$b_1 \qquad b_2 \ldots \qquad b_n$$

Gottinger's perspective is to consider sequential machines as basic analogues for modelling complex 'humanistic' systems (organisations), and to treat adjustment processes in terms of transformations on the set of states of a machine. One consequence of the sequential machine concept is that any biological, ecological or economic system evolving in time can be viewed as a transformational semi-group (tsg) in which time is an irreversible resource.

The first task in building such a machine is to decompose the system into component parts or sub-systems. This is done by first identifying the external state vector $x_t = [x_{1,t}, x_{2,t}, \ldots, x_{n,t}]$ representing exogenous factors driving the system from 'outside'. In terms of the project selection process, these exogenous factors include such indirect influences as government policy and social attitudes. Exogenous factors are not incorporated into the decomposition.

The next step is to choose a kind of partition of the overall system into parts that comprise the main activities of the system. Gottinger suggests that this can be achieved by a decomposition into three types of machine, a message machine, a decision machine and a payoff machine. In terms of project selection, this implies project opportunities and characteristics (message machine), project selection/rejection (decision machine) and the outcome environment (payoff machine). The payoff machine, for instance, would resemble the configuration shown in Fig. 4.1.

Each part enclosed in dotted lines is itself an automaton called a component. The interaction of all components with feedback constitutes the realisation of the entire system. The transformations relating to each component are each described by a set of structural equations taking into account input or feedback stimuli from other components. Each stimulus for a component is composed of an external stimulus, together with all state-output configurations of all previous components plus the feedback responses to subsequent components. The overall design complexity is determined by the structural complexity of the components and the computational complexity of the interaction between components, the length

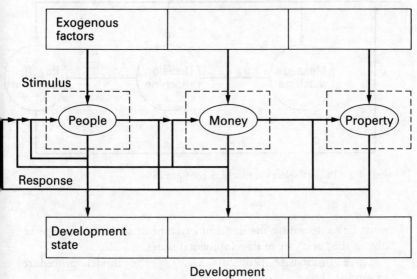

Fig. 4.1 The payoff machine
Adapted from Gottinger (1983)

of computational strings to arrive at solutions. The control complexity is a kind of complexity that satisfies some bounds in the performance boxes in order to keep the system in harmony and stability. A refinement of the payoff machine shown in Fig. 4.1 would further decompose the outcome environment into individual people, separate types of monetary assets and individual items of property.

Figure 4.1 illustrates a cascade decomposition. Other types are available, such as serial and parallel decomposition. Machines can also be decomposed in similar ways or combination of ways. Figure 4.2 indicates a possible machine configuration for project selection. General environmental factors (external stimuli) affect all the machines involved. The projects and their characteristics affect the decision machine. The outcome environment (payoff machine) loops back to influence (future) environmental influences.

The project selection process is then, in terms of this model, controlled by the decision machine, the key developmental results being formed in the payoff machine. The solution to the problem

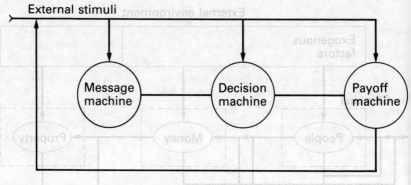

Fig. 4.2 Project selection machine configuration

must be in operating the decision machine in such a manner as to obtain the 'best' set of developmental states.

Three immediate problems arise in the model procedure examined above:

1. As the number of components (particularly in the payoff machine) and sufficiently strong connections among components increase, the behaviour of the system becomes increasingly obscured by complex interactions which resemble very much non-linearities in the total system's behaviour in correspondence with size.
2. The structure and size of components themselves present a potential source of complexity depending on whether and to which extent a component system is sensitive to disturbances, errors, threshold phenomena etc.
3. As the number of components and interdependencies in the system enhances, increasingly longer sequences of calculations are required to deduce the behaviour of the system which results in computational complexity.

The solution to these three problems would enable us to determine the complexity of the system on-line, as it is running from some initial time to some target time in the future. But knowing the complexity would permit us to design control strategies which are effective in guiding the system towards relative stability or harmony. In order to understand the complexity of the systems, it is important that we should be able to understand the strongly connected, coupled nature of its sub-systems. For this purpose we need a measure of complexity that reflects the structural performance of each of the connected sub-systems in terms of state space configurations, plus the number of computational links that are established among the various sub-systems and that reflect the richness of state representations in the global trajectory space of the entire system (Gottinger 1983: 119).

A recent approach to dealing with the computational complexities involved has been to reconfigure the computer hardware in such a way as to arrange the processing elements to match the structure of the problem. This has resulted in an entirely new kind of computer, the 'connection machine' (Hills 1985) which, in terms of the project selection problem, implies a separate processor for each aspect of the problem environment, e.g. each individual member of the organisation.

It is clear from the literature, however, that insufficient knowledge is yet available to determine the complexity of the system to the degree recommended by Gottinger. Even the assumption that the objective is to guide the system towards relative stability and harmony is as yet untested.

Conclusions

This chapter has outlined the dynamical and dimensional effects of time on the project selection problem. An approach to conceptualising the problem along the lines of Gottinger's sequential machine has been proposed as a means of handling the complexities involved. It is anticipated that this, together with some type of multi-attribute analysis discussed in the previous chapter, may form the basis of a useful and realistic approach to developing appropriate solution techniques. Before attempting such a task, however, it is necessary to consider a further (and most critical) aspect of the problem – the effects of imperfect knowledge.

5

Non-deterministic project selection models

Introduction

The aim of this chapter is to consider the implications of relaxing the 'perfect knowledge' assumption. The effect of this is to reduce our decision-maker to a mere mortal faced, as will be seen, with a task of rather unearthly proportions.

Imperfect knowledge introduces uncertainties, in the most general sense, into the problem. One such uncertainty, the value of the project, is of particular relevance in the competitive situation in that the decision-maker can no longer be certain of obtaining the project he has selected. Problems involving this characteristic are normally termed auction, bidding or tendering problems upon which a body of literature already exists. The following extract is, perhaps, a suitable introduction to the subject.

> To many people, the whole subject of bidding and tendering appears to defy analysis and is cloaked in a certain amount of mystery. One reason for this is that there are so many variables that are not well understood when they interact, that it becomes very difficult to make specific predictions. Some of the more important of these variables are related to the cost of the completion of the work, for example the price of materials, labour rates, labour productivity, plant usage, ground conditions, weather, variations instructed as to the detailed work to be completed and additional costs associated with delays caused by shortage of materials or lack of information. A second reason for the mystery surrounding bidding is that it is a very sensitive area to many contractors and they are unwilling to discuss it. This is largely due to the desire to keep methods of estimating work and the prices used confidential to the company, but a more subtle and seldom quoted reason for secrecy is that many contractors do not themselves fully appreciate how their prices are arrived

at, and may indeed have very little or no systematic approach to bidding whatever.

(Woodward 1975: 168)

Imperfect knowledge

The model of the project selection decision process thus far developed relies on the decision-maker 'knowing' the exact effect of potential decisions on the outcome environment, placing some value on each of these effects and selecting the 'best' decision by comparing these values. The reality of the situation, however, is that 'exact' effects can seldom, if ever, be predicted. The difference between predicted and actual outcomes, here termed 'errors', are, therefore, a direct result of the imperfect knowledge of the decision-maker. The nature and magnitude of these errors have a significant impact on the problem.

If the 'real world' is defined as the 'prototype' (after Aris 1978) and the individual's perception of the real world is defined as the 'model' (after Kelly 1955) then the fundamental cause of all errors is in the discrepancy between the prototype and the model. This does not, of course, imply that a model generating no predictive errors must necessarily be a perfect compositional mapping of the prototype (although such a model may often be considered to be a 'perfect' model). The formula for predicting the expansion of a piece of metal, for instance, is not, although virtually error-free, in any way composed of the actual physical process involved. Although, in essence, simple or 'top-down' predictive models ('simple' in this context is equated with 'elegant') are highly desirable computationally, the instability associated with non-physical prototypes (people!) invariably inhibits their development. The logical action, therefore, is to adopt the 'bottom-up' approach of concentrating on the compositional aspects of the prototype, at least until 'top-down' modelling is sufficiently well-advanced.

Compositional discrepancies between the prototype and the individual's model are due to the prototype information received or not received by the individual together with the individual's ability or inability to model the prototype once the information is received. Interdependencies have been found to exist between the prototype, the individual and information. Skitmore (1985), for instance, in a brief review of the psychology of expertise has noted the profound differences in the way experts and novices handle contextual information.

In the context of the project selection decision, discrepancies between the prototype and the decision-maker's model are frequently termed uncertainties (in the general sense). One type of uncertainty has been identified as 'inherent uncertainty' (Bennett and Barnes 1979), due to 'chance variations' (Gates 1971), 'chance events' (Woodward 1975: 12) or 'lack of predictability' (Ireland 1985: 62) in the prototype and resulting in an inherent inability to forecast positively the efficiency and, therefore, the production rate for any given crew for any given operation (Gates 1971: 277), for example. Inherent uncertainty is, therefore, intended to represent the cause of those errors which cannot be avoided in any way, in other words, the limit to which the model can approximate the prototype.

Some knowledge of the nature of the prototype/model misfit, however, can be useful. A measure of this misfit is called 'risk'. Risk is essentially a measure of the strength of belief that an undesired event will occur or a desired event will not occur, and is usually expressed as the chance or probability of occurrence or non-occurrence. The definition of risk is usually extended to all events to which the chance of their occurrence can be quantified in some way. The definition of uncertainty is then confined to inherent uncertainties for which no measure of their chance occurrence is available.

A general structure of risk assessment is given by Otway and Pahner (1980), reproduced in Fig. 5.1. This structure separates the tasks of risk estimation, based on intuitive or formal estimates, from risk evaluation, based on experimental or statistical data, the object in this case being to gauge the environmental consequence of risk acceptance. Risk evaluation is a complex process of determining the meaning, or value, of the estimated risks to those affected, referred to by Hafele (1974) as the 'embedding' of risks into the 'sociosphere'. Evaluation has been considered by Otway and Pahner (1980) to be a process of ranking risks so that their total effects, both objective and subjective, may be compared for acceptability.

Attitudes to risk vary between individuals from cautious to adventurous. Studies by Dickenson (1979) suggest that risk-experienced people tend to be more cautious in their attitude to risk. Building contractors, although no evidence is yet available, are also thought to be generally risk-averse and this, too, may be a result of risk exposure. While not wishing to make risky decisions, however, it would appear that people in the construction industry are able to adequately cope with risky situations. Indeed, the Tavistock

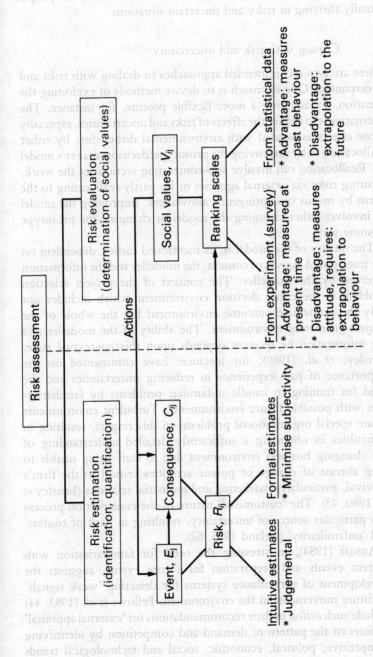

Fig. 5.1 The general structure of risk assessment   *Source:* Otway and Pahner (1980)

Institute's study (1966) paradoxically found evidence of people actually thriving in risky and uncertain situations.

Coping with risk and uncertainty

There are two recommended approaches to dealing with risks and uncertainties. One approach is to devise methods of exploiting the situation, by adapting a more flexible posture, for instance. The alternative is to reduce the effects of risks and uncertainties, especially those effects associated with environmental disbenefits, by either reallocation or by improving the prototype/decision-maker's model fit. Reallocation can involve sub-contracting sections of the work, insuring risks via external agencies or by partly reallocating to the client by means of contingency allowances. Improving the model fit involves either changing the model or changing the prototype in some way.

The quality of the model is, as mentioned earlier, dependent on the interrelated aspects of context, the modeller and the information received by the modeller. The context of the project selection problem is the entire decision environment which includes not only the immediate outcome environment but the whole of the project-generating environment. The ability of the modeller and the information he receives depends upon this contextual state. Lansley, *et al.* (1980), for instance, have commented on the importance of past experience in reducing uncertainties and the need for training to handle unfamiliar problems by familiarisation with possible future environments. Turbulent environments create special organisational problems in this respect, resulting in difficulties in obtaining a sufficiently detailed understanding of the changing business environment due to staff being unable to keep abreast of change or pursue activities critical to the firm's survival, particularly marketing and industrial relations (Lansley *et al.* 1980: 43). The 'customised' nature of the construction process is a particular source of uncertainty, resulting in 'lack of routine' and 'unfamiliarity' (Ireland 1985: 62).

Ansoff (1984), in stressing the need for familiarisation with current events and preparation for future events, suggests the development of surveillance systems for detecting 'weak signals' of future movements in the environment. Fellows *et al.* (1983: 44) include such action in their recommendations for 'external appraisal' to forecast the pattern of demand and competition by identifying competitive, political, economic, social and technological trends in the project-generating environment. Their 'internal appraisal' covers internal aspects of the outcome environment.

Foster (1974) indicates the major sources of information of these environmental states (Fig. 5.2) as inputs to his management services system. As Erikson *et al.* (1976) observe, however, such information is not always readily available, mainly due to the competitive nature of the environment. A further problem, as

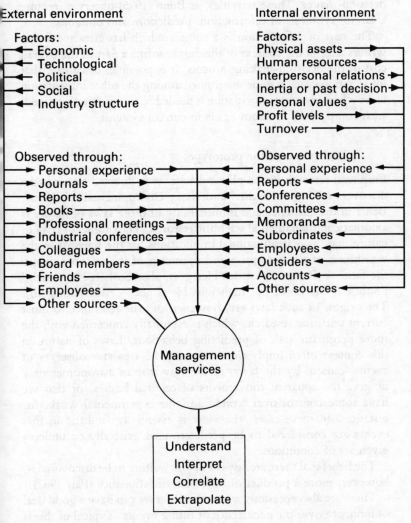

External environment

Factors:
- Economic
- Technological
- Political
- Social
- Industry structure

Observed through:
- Personal experience
- Journals
- Reports
- Books
- Professional meetings
- Industrial conferences
- Colleagues
- Board members
- Friends
- Employees
- Other sources

Internal environment

Factors:
- Physical assets
- Human resources
- Interpersonal relations
- Inertia or past decision
- Personal values
- Profit levels
- Turnover

Observed through:
- Personal experience
- Reports
- Conferences
- Committees
- Memoranda
- Subordinates
- Employees
- Outsiders
- Accounts
- Other sources

Management services

Understand
Interpret
Correlate
Extrapolate

Fig. 5.2 Basic sources of information *Source*: Foster (1974)

noted in Chapter 2, is that the information does not always exist in the most appropriate form. Gilchrist (1984), for instance, discusses the problems of aggregated information which may be simply averages of some highly variable observations. The information may also contain errors which implies the same considerations as errors occurring in the decision problems generally. Further difficulties occur in interpreting and communicating information to the decision-maker and assimilation of the information by the decision-maker. These activities, as Bunn (1975) observes, require a careful synthesis of information, predictions and opinions.

The cost of information is a subject which has attracted many writers and, in the context of this book, forms a part of the overall cost of the decision-making process. It is possible, of course, that information costs may be distributed among the other information users where identical information is needed but, as previously noted, such compatibility seldom exists in current systems.

Behaviour of the prototype

Empirical research in the physical sciences is directed towards the discovery of 'laws of nature' underlying environmental behaviour. Belief in the existence and immutability of those laws of nature is axiomatic in fundamental scientific research. The origins of laws of nature may have motivational implications for the scientist in the worthiness of the enterprise and optimism of its outcome, hence the famous 'Raffiniert ist der Herrgott, aber boshaft ist er nicht' ('Subtle is the Lord, but malicious He is not' – Albert Einstein). The origins of such laws are, however, of little relevance to most current scientific research, which is essentially concerned with the more pragmatic task of predicting behaviour. Laws of nature in this context often imply the scientist to be a passive observer of events 'caused' by the laws, in the way that an astronomer may observe the apparent movements of celestial bodies, or that we have some control over 'conditions' (in experimental work, for instance). In these cases, the view is essentially fatalistic in that events are considered to be predetermined generally or under a given set of conditions.

The belief that there are laws of nature waiting to be discovered is, however, more a product of faith than of rationality (Pais 1982).

There are also occasions where the observer can have a good deal of influence over the occurrence of future events. Typical of this is in the occurrence of observer bias in psychological and sociological work. Another example is in the interaction between predictions and outcomes. While a piece of metal expands under heat in a way that is independent of any predictions about its ultimate state, the same cannot be said in situations where the experimentee is aware of the experimentor's predictions.

Interaction between predictions and outcomes exists in the project selection problem. In many cases, the decision-maker's prediction, say that a certain profit will be achieved, will be treated as a target. Similarly, predictions of low rates of personnel development can generate low expectation of personal progress. Complete interaction between prediction and outcome is termed a 'self-fulfilling prophesy' in which the prediction can be said to be the cause of the outcome. Some further discussion on this aspect is to be found in Skitmore (1981a).

The extent to which the outcome environment can be manipulated into its predicted state depends on the decision-making processes of individuals in the outcome environment. Major inhibitors within this manipulation process include errors, unforeseen and unpredictable events, lack of information and human factors (Cusack 1981) which are precisely the factors associated with the lack of fit between the prototype and the decision-maker's model.

Conclusions

Lack of perfect knowledge opens up whole new areas of the project selection problem. As the decision-maker can no longer be regarded to have direct access to the 'real world', he/she must attempt to create an internalised version from his perception of that world. The closeness to which the internalised model aligns with the 'real world', it is argued, determines the quality of the model and hence the quality of decisions. The degree of alignment is considered to be dependent on the contextually interdependent aspects of the modeller and the information received by the modeller.

Little is known of the abilities demanded of the modeller except that experience, training and, perhaps, some innate characteristics are beneficial. Informational requirements are, on the other hand, rather better known. Information directly relevant to the problem is, however, never complete. Some kinds of information are either too costly to obtain or simply unobtainable. These practicalities dictate the need for relatively inexpensive information concerning the entire decision environment. Further issues centre on the accuracy and usefulness of information and its relationship with the decision-maker.

The decision environment

Bahrami (1981) considers the general 'contextual' environment of an organisation to consist of: economic factors, including inflation, interest and exchange rates; political factors, including the political ideology of the government and political developments on the international scale; social factors, including changes in life styles and values; technological factors, including the impact of new technology on specific industries; and legal and legislative factors, including the impact of government legislation on such matters as 'lead in petrol' on oil and motor vehicle companies. Smith (1985) actually reduces these five factors into four by combining legislative with political factors. These factors have been variously termed the organisation's 'background environment' (Foster 1974) or the environment 'outside the building process' (Tavistock Institute 1966).

Political and economic factors are interdependent. A construction organisation at the local level is affected by the need to obtain planning approvals and also by the state of local public sector building programmes. Besides being an important client to the construction industry, the national government acts indirectly through legislation on safety, tax, noise, employment etc. Construction demand is closely related to the health of the economy at local, national and international levels. Economic trends in regional development, the treatment of urban decay, the regulation of the economy, the manipulation of interest rates, and national economic growth and decline are important factors (Fellows et al. 1983). Foster (1974), however, considers that the effect of government policy and its economic consequences on the industry's output 'would not be sufficient to disrupt a long range planning exercise', a rather surprising statement considering events taking place in 1974!

Social factors, which include demographic movements, changes in education, working hours, housing, leisure, retirement, sports promotion and holiday patterns, are said to have an 'enormous' impact on the decision environment (Fellows et al. 1983: 46). Pressure groups, such as those concerned with conservation, have also become a particularly important social phenomenon.

The combination of economic, political and social factors has been identified by the Tavistock Institute (1966) with sources of uncertainty attributable to government departments, planning authorities, public bodies, client organisations and the general public. The same combination has been studied more recently by Murray (1980) in respect of social values, concluding that the type and stability of values are dependent upon the interrelationships between social structure, policy and culture.

Technological factors mainly affect the construction organisation's site or business systems. There are also technological implications in the demand for certain types of construction due to increased need for computer component manufacturing facilities, for instance. Foster (1974) suggests that there are important informational implications caused by changes in technology, knowledge being needed in particular of the impact of new materials, new methods and processes, and working in new environments. Fryer (1985: 14), however, maintains that the construction industry does not have to cope with rapid technical change, but the market for buildings is changeable and unpredictable.

The implications of these major environmental factors on the market, or in the terminology used here, the project-generating environment, are examined in more detail in the next section.

The project-generating environment

Successive governments of the post-war era have gradually changed in their policies from direct intervention towards demand management (Budd 1978). Direct intervention still exists in the construction industry in the form of public client organisations such as the Property Services Agency and regulatory action through building, fire and safety regulations and planning legislation. Indirect measures occur in the form of grants and fiscal policies which affect the demand for construction, the building land market, capital money markets and industrial and competitive practice.

Changes in government policy as a result of either internal or external matters or events can and do affect the demand for construction services (Moore 1984: 21). The size of the government budget and changes in public expenditure policy, involving cuts, reflation attempts and moratoria on cash limits, are particularly significant for the industry (Lansley et al. 1979: 1, 9). Foreign policies influence events on the international scene, in construction for military projects, for instance. Entry to the European Economic Community and associated changes in taxation, legislation for equal opportunities and protection of employment are further important influences (Lansley *et al.* 1979: 1, 9).

Many important economic features are related to the health of the economy – balance of payments problems, sterling crises, high interest and mortgage rates, high inflation, rising unemployment and low economic growth being particular examples. Economic factors are of prime importance as the decision to build is the result of a favourable analysis of the marketing situation that shows future increased product demands or the need for new and different products or the research department may develop new products with high sales potential, or new government or social requirements may dictate the need for new facilities. The ultimate reason, in virtually every case, is economic (Clark and Lorenzoni 1985: 2).

Two particular instances of economic factors are given by Moore (1984). One is in the effect of the oil crisis, resulting in a concentration of construction activity in offshore projects, in terminal sites such as Aberdeen, energy-saving schemes, energy-creating projects such as nuclear power stations, and projects involving new types of energy generation. The other example concerns the growth of container transport and the consequent need for projects involving port facilities, storage and roads.

Social factors influencing the demand for construction arise from the basic needs and aspirations of individuals and groups of people. In general terms these influences are connected with leisure, education, shelter, mobility and environmental concern (Moore 1984).

Constructional implications associated with leisure include such facilities as sports and recreational centres, swimming pools, squash courts etc. The increasing popularity of dining out involves the construction of clubs, extensions to hotels and public houses, and car parks. Holiday activities create the demand for extensions and alterations to hotels, additional airport buildings and runways, and docks and landing facilities for overseas travel.

Educational and domiciliary building activity is affected by changes in population levels and the state of the existing building stock. A declining birthrate implies less demand for schools and teacher-training colleges, for instance, while deteriorating housing involves the renovation or replacement of dwellings in the form of new housing estates together with associated amenities.

Increased mobility and the greater use of the motor car has created a need for the provision of more suburban facilities

– supermarkets, department stores, and surface and multi-storey car parks.

Environmental pressure groups have had a significant impact on the nature of construction projects, such as motorways, roads, airports, nuclear power stations and waste disposal plants.

Science and technology, and also the products of research and development, have provided a further impact on the nature of demand for construction projects. Technologically based production facilities, such as those involved in the manufacture of computer hardware and other electronic equipment or those utilising such products (such as computer centres or robotic assembly lines), are typical examples.

Predicting project opportunities

Predicting project opportunities clearly involves obtaining knowledge of the frequency and characteristics of future projects. Such knowledge is, invariably, acquired through market intelligence, which can be obtained directly from clients and architects, although this approach has its problems as architects' offices often react unfavourably to the visits of salesmen, and the levels at which interviews are usually negotiated with local authorities may be of more use to suppliers than to contractors (Jepson and Nicholson 1972: 51).

An alternative approach is to seek market intelligence indirectly. One such indirect method involving records of approved planning applications has been found to be significantly associated with the volume of subsequent work (SEBI c.1965). Majid (1967) has studied 'with some success' (Jepson and Nicholson 1972: 50) this use of planning applications in predicting housing trends in the North West of England. Difficulties exist, however, in that local authority procedure is not uniform and once data are required for a locality extending across local authority boundaries, then standardisation of the format of applications and centralised processing of a periodic summarised return from authorities becomes necessary. A further problem is that not all relevant information on project characteristics is available. There are, however, some commercial organisations who exist to provide this type of information to contractors.

The more long-term changes in the project-generating environment can be predicted by assessing trends in the demand for construction. Such assessments depend on knowledge of future changes in the economic, political, sociological and technological factors affecting demand. Political trends may be observed from statements made by influential politicians (see, for instance, Freeson 1977), Acts of Parliament, white and green papers etc. Economic trends may be revealed by economic indicators including population statistics, indicators of regional prosperity, industrial structure, investment etc. (see, for instance, Lansley *et al*. 1979: 2, 22). Demographic analysis of census statistics have been used to predict changes in housing demand, for example (Parry-Lewis 1968).

Many of the informational sources used for evaluating aspects of the market are detailed by Harris and McCaffer (1983: 182–8), including such periodicals as *The Economist*, *National Institute Economic Review*; government publications such as the *Monthly Bulletin of Construction Statistics*, *Housing Statistics*, *Sample Census Statistics*, *Regional Economic Reports*, *Local Planning Reports* and *Monthly Digest of Statistics*; and other publications such as *BMP Weekly Publication* and *Construction Trends*.

The extent to which the organisation attempts to predict the action of the project-generating environment is largely dependent on its marketing policies. Rajab's survey (1981) suggests that the most attention is paid to externally compiled statistics (100 per cent), external market researchers (33 per cent), trend projections (14 per cent), consumer surveys (11 per cent) and economic modelling (11 per cent), commercial intelligence being preferred to government reports. Most forecasts and information on the external environment were found to be obtained on a regional basis by lower management.

The general level of accuracy of predictions does not seem to be very good, particularly in changing economic conditions. The hard facts of a collapsing market, growing unemployment, high interest rates, and the dismantling of impressive building concerns have taught us that our forecasts of the early 1970s were far from accurate. Changes in social, political and economic factors have been so rapid in recent years that forecasting on the basis of extrapolation of existing trends is now far from reliable (Benes and Diepeveen 1985: 27). Causes of demand fluctuations have often been attributed to government measures to alter the level of activity in construction (e.g. public work moratoria) or the whole economy through construction (by public expenditure cuts) (Campbell *et al*. 1974). More recently, however, there has been some evidence to suggest that the government has tried to stabilise demands on the industry by planning its expenditure and operating a more effective system of monitoring and controlling local authority expenditure (Cannon

1978: 13). The extent to which the government is successful in this is not clear for, although it is suggested that there are very few examples of turbulent environments in construction (Harding 1985: 220) and the construction environment only moderately uncertain (Brown 1974), Diepeveen (1985) is still adamant that public sector demand is very unstable despite efforts to create stability. One possibility is that the environmental changes occurring are of a more fundamental nature outside governmental control, the 1970s, for instance, having witnessed a series of probably fundamental changes both in the determinants and in the structure of demand more sporadic and unpredictable than have hitherto been experienced since the war (Lansley *et al*. 1979).

Predictions in the outcome environment

The bulk of the literature dealing with predictions in the outcome environment is concerned with monetary aspects and particularly predictions of expenditure by the contractor, usually termed the cost estimate. Moyles (1973), for instance, has considered in some detail the factors affecting the accuracy of this cost estimate under the groupings labour, materials, plant, sub-contractors, overheads and profit. Fellows *et al*. (1983) use similar groupings as a means of identifying fixed, variable and semi-variable costs (in the economic sense) together with direct (project-related) and indirect costs.

Figure 5.3 indicates the basic relationship of the factors in the outcome environment proposed in this book, which is essentially concerned with project characteristics and their influence on people, money and property. The central issue in this model in determining costs is that of productivity or performance which, together with the nature of the tasks generated by the project, largely determine expenditure.

The influence of project characteristics

The project characteristics are seen as influencing the tasks to be done and the income to be received by the participants in the construction process.

The information available for predicting the extent and nature of the tasks is contained formally in tender documents in the competitive situation. These, in the UK, may comprise the drawings and specification and/or bills of quantities. The accuracy of task predictions has been found to be affected by errors and omissions in

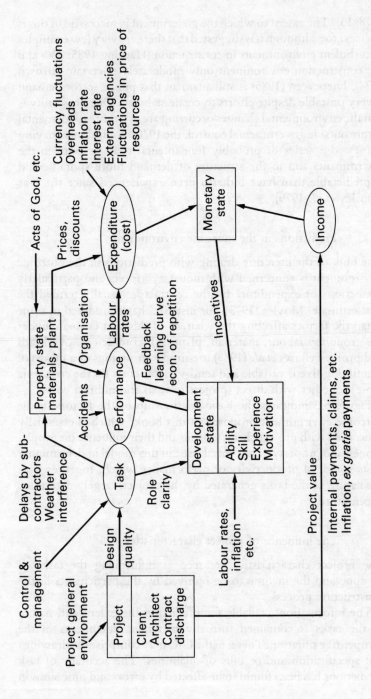

Fig. 5.3 Relationship of factors in the outcome environment

the drawings (Bennett and Ormerod 1984) or by misinterpretation of contract requirements (Gates 1971) over, for instance, the suitability of 'equal substitutes' (Gates 1971) or 'quality of work' (Moyles 1973: 51; Bennett and Ormerod 1984). Mistakes occur through computational errors (Langford and Wong 1979) and omission and commission (Gates 1971). Quantity errors are of particular concern (Langford and Wong 1979) resulting in undermeasurement or omission of items (Park 1966). The generality of quantity descriptions also provides a source of error, the extent of which has been said to be dependent on the level of measurement (Bennett and Barnes 1979). It is possible, however, that misestimates in quantities can sometimes be anticipated (Stark 1976). Many criticisms have been made of the lack of association between quantity items and the nature of the construction task. Task–oriented quantities have been proposed to improve predictability (Flanagan 1980 and Thompson 1981, for instance).

Further project-associated information regarding tasks can be obtained by site visits and enquiries to the client or his advisers. The kind of relationship with the client and his delegates has a bearing on this and future events (Cauwelaert and Heynig 1978).

Difficulties occur due to 'unknown work' (Bennett and Ormerod 1984), which in the post-contract period can be a result of design changes, which are mostly attributable to client requests (Diekmann and Nelson 1981), involving 'major scope changes' (Clark and Lorenzoni 1985). Delays caused by the client and architect are a further factor which can, in some cases, develop into delays of a more permanent nature, such as financial failure of the client (Langford and Wong 1979), resulting in the early discharge of the contract.

Many of the project factors which influence tasks also have implications in predicting income. The main determinant of income is the price offered by the contractor at the tender stage, this price being determined by the project selection decision, one consideration of which is the predicted monetary state caused by the amount of expenditure incurred. The heavy emphasis usually placed on monetary aspects, together with the difficulties involved in predicting the market value of the 'customised' construction project, often results in a situation where predicted price and cost are closely related. The construction contractual arrangements are, in many respects, aimed at monitoring this relationship by providing some expenditure-related income adjustments. These are mainly project-based in covering such events as errors and omissions in drawings, specifications and quantities, and client interference in the form of design changes. Environmental changes can also be accommodated in reimbursements for inflation and other unforeseen events. Income fluctuations are, however, seldom exactly the same as fluctuations in expenditure as some form of surrogate measure is often employed. Design changes, for instance, are usually valued by quantity-related measures rather than by an exact record of expense incurred. Time-related aspects are also important as, in construction contracts, income is received some time after the expenditure has taken place. These cash-flow aspects can be exacerbated by delays in client payments, particularly where outstanding claims are involved.

Tasks and performance

The ways in which tasks are defined and executed are attributable to a combination of project characteristics and other events of differing degrees of predictability. The weather, especially in the early stages of the construction process, is clearly an important factor, as is the extent and quality of management and control (Gates 1971; Duff 1976). Delays in obtaining management approvals is a source of variability (Bennett and Ormerod 1984). Adequate advance planning by means of network analysis, for instance, can improve predictability but there is no evidence of its widespread use in the construction process (Cusack 1981). The complex and dynamic arrangement of tasks on a construction site is, as demonstrated by Bennett and Fine's (1980) simulation studies, an important cause of variability.

Performance is influenced by the task and its associated working conditions, the state of materials and plant resources and the development and aspirational state of operatives. The degree of difficulty presented by the task is difficult to predict due to the variability in tasks and condition between projects. A complete workforce is seldom transferred from job to job so, while a competent site agent may obtain favourable results in one situation, there is no guarantee that this programme will be repeated in another (Moyles 1973: 46). Predicting learning curves or the economies of repetition for similar reasons is also problematic (Foster 1974). Performance is linked to incentives although the cost of the work often remains the same (Moyles 1973: 49); the saving in time and the reduction of people utilised, however, can affect expenditure by reducing on-costs and overheads. Labour outputs can also vary

118

from area to area as some parts of the country have traditionally poor output and strong union militancy although these are fairly well recognised by local and national contractors with experience of working in those areas (Moyles 1973: 50). Labour unrest (Gates 1971), disputes (Barnes 1974) and strikes (Clark and Lorenzoni 1985) are particularly sensitive factors in performance predictions.

Fryer (1985) intimates several personal factors – personality, experience, motivation, ability and skill, and stress – to be important determinants of human performance. Other factors include role clarity and feedback, in addition to task demands. Feedback, in general, has not been thought to be adequate in construction (Flanagan 1980), although measurement techniques of work study and activity sampling do exist.

Efficient working is also dependent on the requisite materials being delivered at the right time and in the desired place (Moyles 1973: 50). The use of power tools and other items of plant has a major impact on productivity (Niss 1965; Cusack 1981). The occurrence of illness and accidents are further factors (Clark and Lorenzoni 1985).

Many other factors are involved in determining performance levels, a complete review of which is beyond the scope of this book. It is clear, however, from this brief review, that performance rates are 'highly variable' (Bennett and Ormerod 1984) and their prediction is probably the most uncertain aspect of the entire project selection problem.

Outcome states

There is very little reference in the construction literature to the prediction of human development. Such literature as does exist is concerned primarily with human development as a means to further improve the company's monetary state, via improved efficiency and productivity for instance. Human development in such cases may be measured in terms of responsibility, position in the organisational hierarchy, remuneration, courses attended and qualifications acquired. A more indirect measure of human development (but more directly relevant to the monetary state), particularly at the operative level, is productivity, which is, to some extent, a reflection of the individual's abilities and skills, experience and motivation. Predicting human development *per se*, however, may involve the assessment of other factors more directly associated with well-being. The only such measures that appear to

119

be available at the moment seem to be evaluated intuitively, in that '. . . the workforce is reasonably content', or by the frequency of disputes which, as has been noted earlier, may be regarded by some individuals and groups to be aspirational events in themselves. The only other alternative that seems to be available lies in the use of questionnaires, although this approach has currently been restricted to research activities.

Predictions of property states are, in the project context, normally confined to changes in the materials and plant levels. Various control techniques are available to influence the level of stocks and which are applied with varying degrees of success. Plant and particularly materials supply has been shown to be virtually perfectly elastic (Burton 1972), although delays do occur resulting in variabilities caused by late deliveries (Bennett and Ormerod 1984; South 1979); mechanical breakdown and malfunction of equipment are a further source of variability (Bennett and Ormerod 1984).

The price of labour and materials and plant combine to impact on monetary states. Material substitutes can affect the accuracy of predictions, for a careful search of the market alternatives may yield better goods at competitive prices (Harris and McCaffer 1983: 181). The acceptability of such substitutes to the client, however, is not necessarily assured though, and is in itself a further cause of prediction error. The fluctuating prices of materials is a cause for concern although trends can be predicted to some extent (Cauwelaert and Heynig 1978). Fluctuations in discount levels are a further difficulty.

The effect of labour costs on monetary levels is dependent on productivity and rates of pay. Rates of pay can fluctuate for many reasons, including changes in government legislation, union agreements, responsibility and incentive schemes. Labour-related expenses also exist in the form of overtime payments, supervision costs, national insurance contributions etc.

Further fluctuating expenses stem from changing interest rates, inflation and currency rates. Prediction errors can also occur in the failure to allow a sufficient amount for overheads (Park 1966).

The effect of sub-contracting

The incidence of sub-contracting has greatly increased in the post-war era, probably due to the complexity of modern buildings, labour shortage, structuring of large firms and taxation policy (Moyles 1973: 59). There are exceptions, however, as some companies are actively pursuing closer links with sub-contractors through acquisition. These changes are seen as an indication of the companies' preference to increase control over their operational environment through 'internalising' the activities upon which they are dependent or by attempting to reduce uncertainty by externalising parts of their business (Lansley *et al.* 1979: 1, 59).

The extent to which control is lessened is largely dependent on the relationship between the company and the sub-contractor. The continued use of a sub-contractor should be beneficial in this respect, although this is not always possible due to contract requirements (nominated sub-contracts, for instance) or financial considerations. The degree of uncertainty is similarly dependent on familiarity with the sub-contractor. An important source of uncertainty occurs when the contractor has to estimate sub-contract prices instead of obtaining quotations.

Delays by sub-contractors have been found to be a particular cause of prediction error (Langford and Wong 1979).

The prediction process

The very need to predict future environmental states generates processes which themselves affect the decision environment. The degree of accuracy of predictions, dependent on the contextual relationship between the predictor and his information, largely determines the level of effect.

Predicting movements in the project-generating environment is usually regarded as a marketing function. Little is known of the personnel and monetary consequences of this relatively recent activity in construction companies.

The functional process of predicting changes in the outcome environment, especially the monetary aspects, is better documented. Predicting future project-related costs is normally performed by the estimator or estimating department. The size of the estimating department is often related to the company's turnover (Humphreys 1977), the amount of resources needed being determined by project characteristics such as the type and size of project, its location and the time available for tendering, together with the estimator's expertise and information. The time available for tendering has been found to be particularly important (Cusack 1981). The frequency of estimates appears to be season-related, Humphreys' (1977) study noting a peak period between February and March during which time a total of fourteen to sixteen estimates were being compiled simultaneously.

The direct effect of the estimating process on monetary states has been investigated by several researchers. Broemser's (1968) analysis of one construction company found the cost of estimating to represent 9.1 per cent of total assets and 1.8 per cent of total receipts, this figure being equivalent to 0.18 per cent of the value of each project estimated, as only 10 per cent of the estimated projects were actually obtained. Park (1966) places this figure higher at between 0.5 per cent and 2.0 per cent of project value, offering a rule of thumb used by some contractors on large projects to be

total estimating cost = 0.005 × estimated direct materials costs + 0.015 × estimated direct labour costs

equivalent to 1 per cent on a $1m contract. Rubey and Milner (1966) suggest that, for a 'good bid', estimating costs would be perhaps 1 per cent of the total bid. Harrison (1981) is of the view that estimating costs vary quite widely between 0.1 per cent and 10 per cent of project value, depending on the degree of repetition involved and the experience of the estimator.

Larew (1976) has used a multiple regression analysis technique to identify possible causal associations in the time spent by one contractor in estimating twenty-two project costs in the early 1960s. The results of this analysis suggest that high activity may be caused by the presence of many speciality items: excessively detailed specifications, and reference to exotic standards; high-quality finish; the insistence that contractors satisfy owners' every desire; and where the contractor seems to be held responsible for the errors and omissions of the designers. Medium levels of activity are associated with some specialities, but not to an excess; reasonable and understandable contract documents; the requirements for a good and workmanlike finish; the contractor being responsible only for work shown on plans and in the specifications; where the designer accepts responsibility for the contract documents; and where the contract assures a fair, prompt and impartial mediation of disputes. Low activity is associated with very few specialities: abbreviated specification; open structures with low quality of finish; simplicity in every respect; and relatively straightforward production work is needed. Estimating time was also shown to be less for 'in town' projects and more for 'out of town' projects, due to the necessity for the estimator to visit the site. Larew (1976) has also obtained evidence that estimating costs are a logarithmic function of project value.

All of the research indicated above, however, was conducted prior to the introduction of computer aids. Since that time, several inexpensive estimating systems have become available on the construction market and have attracted some considerable interest. One such system is known to be installed in over 1000 locations at present (Hunt 1986). The effect of this on project estimating costs is likely to be quite dramatic.

Accuracy of predictions

As has been previously discussed, the accuracy of predictions relating to the project-generating environment is not thought to be generally very good. There are no specific figures available in the literature concerning accuracy levels achieved and some research in this direction, particularly in relation to project characteristics, the abilities of the predictor and information used, would be advantageous.

Accuracy in predicting the outcome environment is, however, known to be rather poor. Estimating construction costs is probably the most researched area and the process has been found in practice very approximate and crude (Benjamin 1969), relying on haphazard methods often grossly in error (Neil 1978). Ashworth and Skitmore (1983) have examined estimating accuracy in some detail, considering the various measures available and noting the extensive use of subjective judgement involved. Their findings suggest that the extent of complexities and uncertainties in the process results in accuracy being determined more by the ability of the predictor than the project information available. In view of the facility to 'control' work to some extent in the post-prediction period, it is reasonable to assume that the cost estimate can often be considered to be self-fulfilling to some extent, in which case only a reasonable figure is needed. There is, however, a bias in the process due to the need to avoid excessively low estimates of expenditure. Such low estimates are avoided by including contingency allowances (Harrison 1981) or risk premiums (Portsmouth Polytechnic 1974; Barnes 1974) to cover possible errors, particularly those caused by uncertainty or risk. This can result in uncertain cost being 'padded two or more fold' (Case 1972). Clearly there are limits to this procedure as increasing estimates of expenditure in this way will result in a totally false impression of the predicted monetary state.

A further difficulty is that the predicted price of the project, if based on expenditure predictions formulated in this way, may well be in excess of the price the client wishes to pay. One way of avoiding this is to exclude any allowance for such unpredictable events as strikes, bad weather, major scope changes, acts of God, currency fluctuations etc. from the estimate and any other item with less than a 50/50 chance of occurrence, and making full allowance for other events (Clark and Lorenzoni 1985: 117).

An alternative approach is to consider the probability of occurrence of an event and the cost associated with its occurrence, the product of which is the 'expected value' to be incorporated into that estimate (Gates 1971: 277). The suitability of this approach depends on the risk attitude of the decision-maker who may or may not be happy with this averaging technique. Case (1972) and Stacey (1979) have both proposed a method of deriving a probability distribution of cost estimates from an indication of the most likely lower and upper bounds of the predicted cost of individual items. Such a technique is anticipated to accommodate the preferences of decision-makers to varying risk attitudes.

Selection strategies and the non-deterministic model

Kmietowicz and Pearman (1981: 105) have considered three models for decision-making with multiple criteria. These models cover situations of uncertainty, risk and 'incomplete knowledge' (where criteria can be ranked only).

Although they acknowledge that it may ultimately be possible to develop a strategy for handling simultaneously the twin problems of uncertainty and multiple criteria, current practice is nowhere near this point.

Four approaches encountered in the construction literature are concerned exclusively with the second model where a cardinal scale is used to assess the relative importance of different criteria. The first two of these approaches, by Hillebrandt (1974: ch. 13) and Benjamin (1969), attempt to evaluate preferences directly from the decision-maker, based on Shackle's (1952) degree of potential surprise in the former and utility theory in the latter. The two other approaches, by Fellows and Langford (1980) and Ibbs and Crandall (1982) use a multi-attribute utility function.

Study 1 (Hillebrandt 1974: ch. 13)

Hillebrandt's approach is to first construct an index of potential surprise of a specified profit/loss outcome for a specified bid value. The next step is to identify the profit and loss outcome on the potential surprise index which will generate the greatest stimulus to the decision-maker. These outcomes, called standardised focus gain and standardised focus loss, are then evaluated on a gambler indifference map to ascertain the ultimate focus gain. Ultimate focus gains are found for all possible bid values and the bid value associated with the maximum ultimate focus gain is adjudged to be the best decision.

A further development proposed by Hillebrandt is to allow for competitive aspects of the problem by plotting the ultimate focus gains and the degree of potential surprise of obtaining the contract associated with each bid value on a bidding indifference map.

Although seemingly complicated, Hillebrandt's approach is simply a formalised intuitive procedure. In accommodating a whole range of subjective judgements, the approach represents an admirable attempt to avoid many of the criticisms normally levelled at bidding decision aids. The benefits of this form of analysis are suggested by Hillebrandt as being helpful for understanding the reasons for decisions on tender prices; in locating the reasons for difference of opinion between persons sharing the entrepreneurial function within contracting firms; in assessing how the bidding theory based on the probability approach can help in tendering decisions; and hence, altogether, in making the process of tender decisions more logical and efficient.

Study 2 (Benjamin 1969)

Benjamin identifies three aspects of the selection strategy problem: (a) a probability distribution to express the relationship between the cost estimate and the actual monetary cost of performing the work, (b) a non-linear utility function which scales the decision-maker's preference for different amounts of money and (c) a means of assessing the probability of obtaining the project with different bid amounts.

In deriving the probability distribution of the cost estimate, it is proposed that such factors as sub-contractors' bids, materials availability and costs, labour availability and productivity, methods of performing the work, season in which the work is done, location of job, type of building or type of construction and supervisory capacity are taken into account.

The utility function transforms the monetary value of the outcome to a different scale which satisfies the decision-maker's ordering of preferences for different amounts of profit or loss with a given bid. Further work by Willenbrock (1972) has developed the work into a sophisticated technique.

In estimating the probability of obtaining the project, the characteristics of the project and the 'bidding environment' are considered.

Study 3 (Fellows and Langford 1980)

The value on the five criteria (speed, accuracy, cost, client and benefits) are assessed by the decision-maker. The aggregated outcome evaluations, together with the probability of each outcome, are then analysed by means of a decision tree. Sensitivity analysis is recommended to assist in identifying the best decision route.

Study 4 (Ibbs and Crandall 1982)

The values of the three criteria profit return, project size and 'regulatory aspects' are assumed to be derived by 'conventional procedures'.

Estimating scalar values for the preference function is suggested to be an often imprecise task. For a decision problem such as the search for new business markets, the American authors recommend sources such as 'Dun and Bradstreet' statistics as providing some relative indication of possible expected profit margins. Various government agencies and owner's representatives may supply future bidding volume and project size information. In the final analysis, though, the authors maintain that it is the decision-maker who, with the assistance of the decision-analyst, must make these estimates.

In their example, the mean estimated scalar value and the estimated standard deviation about that mean is assumed. A sensitivity analysis of the decision alternative is then conducted by a Monte Carlo simulation procedure for 100 iterations.

Conclusions

Of the four selected published accounts of non-deterministic approaches to the construction project selection problem with several criteria, the first, by Hillebrandt, relies entirely on the decision-maker's judgement.

Benjamin's approach estimates the monetary effect of a decision based on some knowledge of the probability distributions of

126

estimated/actual costs and 'our' bid/competitors' bids. These probability distributions are suggested to be obtained as far as possible by objective analysis. The estimated value of the preference function is derived from some non-linear function of the estimated monetary value of the project.

Fellows and Langford and Ibbs and Crandall both estimate values of individual criteria by relying mainly on the decision-maker's judgement. Sensitivity tests are recommended to test the reliability of outcome evaluations.

The additional difficulties associated with the multiple criteria project selection problem in the non-deterministic model are in the reliable assessment of criteria values. While an assessment by empirical means would seem desirable, the frequent recourse to the decision-maker's judgement in these assessments prompts the view expressed by Hillebrandt (1974: 184) that most of the factors are so varied and qualitative that it seems better to use judgement for quite wide groups of variables together.

Dynamical aspects

The effects of imperfect knowledge are essentially two-fold. One factor is that uncertainties in the immediate decision environment introduce the necessity to consider more indirect influences, particularly in the project-generating environment. These indirect influences also result in considerations of other aspects, including organisation and control, together with marketing decisions. In terms of the sequential machine approach discussed in Chapter 4, this would suggest a revised model along the lines of Fig. 5.4.

Here the project decision machine is envisaged as being one of several such decision machines, including an organisation and marketing decision machine, all causally related to the project-generating machine and the outcome machine. The project-generating machine consists of a set of four internal 'states', economic, governmental, societal and technological, which are determined by exogenous variables such as government ministerial policy decisions, changing international economic conditions, shifts in societal attitudes and general technological developments, generally influencing the demand for construction work. Other determinants of the project-generating machine states emanate endogenously from the outcome machine in what may loosely be termed as marketing inputs. The outputs of the project-generating machine determine the frequency and characteristics of project opportunities for input

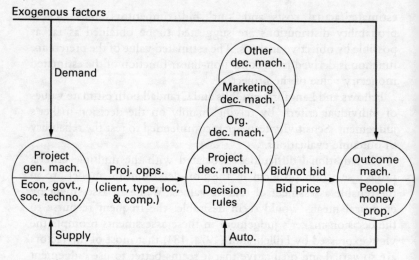

Fig. 5.4   The project decision system environment

into the project decision machine. The project decision machine output in the non–deterministic situation consists not only of the dichotomous project selection variable, but also of other features which may determine project acquisition, such as the price and contract duration offered. The result of the project decision, together with such exogenous factors as societal aspirations, interest and inflation rates, forms an input into the outcome machine affecting its three states of people, money and property. The connection between the outcome machine and the project-generating machine forms the dynamical link in the system, and the control link (shown dotted) suggests a means by which the decision machine can be automated to respond in a rational manner to changes in outcome states.

The second factor turns on the predictive difficulties associated with the system components. The five general characteristics of each machine, inputs, outputs, internal states, state transition and output functions, have some degree of unpredictability, usually extremely high. The way in which environmental changes affect project opportunities is largely unpredictable and little appears to be known of the effect of project characteristics on the state of personal well-being. Perhaps the most knowledge that is available concerns the effect of project characteristics on monetary outcomes although, as discussed in this chapter, there is still a considerable degree of uncertainty involved. These predictive difficulties are further exacerbated by the need to forecast future events, preferably over a period of several years.

The situation is, however, not entirely hopeless. One of the great contributions of J. von Neumann (1969) is to have proved the fact that a predictable system can be built from unpredictable parts. An outstanding example of this is Bennett and Fine's (1980) construction project simulator (CPS) which, by repeated simulation of a stochastic construction process model containing many highly varying elements, generates fairly stable probability distributions of project cost and duration. The CPS typifies what Gottinger (1983) has termed dynamic systems of 'intermediate complexity'. Gottinger outlines four points on which he would like to see computer models developed in order to cope successfully with systems of intermediate complexity. Firstly, the model should be aimed at achieving improvements rather than optimality. Secondly, sensitivity analysis should be preferred to formal statistical hypotheses testing. Thirdly, the computer model should consist of an interaction between human beings and machines. And, finally, the system should be integrated as far as possible with other similar such systems.

These points coincide well with the work described in the last section in prescribing a judgement-related system with a facility to observe the effect of errors by means of sensitivity analyses. The improvement-related approach has already been proposed in Chapter 2, Fig. 2.1, where options are evaluated consecutively for improvements.

Relationships with other systems have already been considered, and these other systems have been introduced in Fig. 5.4 as other decision machines, the organisational and marketing machines being seen as particularly relevant. Computer simulation, an essential ingredient in systems of intermediate complexity, also aligns with the need to anticipate changes in the environment in contingency planning or other 'scenario' type approaches to flexible management.

129

6

The project decision system

Introduction

This chapter completes the specification of the project decision system by defining the various options available to the decision-maker. Some means are discussed whereby the system can be utilised in the search for decisions which will best enhance the outcome environment. Further references are made to the construction literature to determine possible appropriate search methodologies by means of decision rules and strategies. The chapter concludes with a final proposal for a project decision system with an indication of some devices necessary for its practical operation.

Decision options

The decision options considered in this section are restricted to the set of outputs associated with the project decision machine shown in Fig. 5.4. Options that are associated directly with organisational and control decisions, marketing decisions etc. are outside the scope of this book. These other decisions, however, interact with the project decision and references will be made where the interaction occurs.

Ansoff (1965) recommends five possible alternative courses of action in project screening: reject the project; provisionally accept the project; add it to the reserve list of approved projects; remove a project from the reserve list and replace it with the same project; and remove an active project, discontinue it and provisionally accept the present project. As contractual issues prevent the practical implementation of any of these alternatives once the contracting organisation is formally employed by the client, the relevance of these options will be restricted to the pre-contract period and, in particular, the tendering (bidding) period.

The limited amount of time available for bidding limits the use of reserve lists to a minimum, the usual options being restricted to acceptance or rejection of the project. Harris and McCaffer (1983) suggest that this decision to bid must be made at three possible points in the bidding process: during the pre-selection stage, if a pre-selection process is being used; after receiving all the contract documents; and after the cost estimate has been prepared.

The decision that the project is not required generates two options, not to bid or to bid with a 'cover' price. The decision that the project is required generates several options, including alternative price levels and what Simmonds (1968a) terms 'non-price features' such as quality, contract duration and design facilities. The breakdown of price also creates options for front loading (South 1979; Diekmann *et al.* 1982) to enhance cash flow. Further options are theoretically available in the combinations of price, non-price features and loadings.

Selection of 'best' options

The basic decision model proposed in Fig. 2.1 involves the sequential identification, evaluation and comparison of decision options as a means of locating the 'best' option. In terms of the project decision system, this would entail the evaluation of various bid levels, non-price features and loading arrangements, and all combinations of these, for a sequence of project opportunities over a suitable period (about 1½ years). The uncertainties in the system environment imply that the frequency and nature of project opportunities, changes in the outcome environment and exogenous variables together with their interrelationships are not known very well.

One approach to finding the best set of options in these circumstances would be to evaluate every conceivable combination of options and events. There are, however, clearly extremely severe computational difficulties in this approach. An alternative procedure is to confine the process in some way to a reduced set of alternatives. This approach effectively introduces a further decision into the system, i.e. which option or set of options to evaluate next. This decision is termed here the option identification decision (OID) and a procedure for determining this is termed an option identification decision rule (OIDR).

The literature reveals many (non-random) OIDRs, often of a qualitative nature, that are applied by construction project decision-makers. In almost every case the options considered are whether the project is wanted and, if so, the level at which to bid. The next section examines the nature of the OIDRs commonly employed.

Option identification decision rules

The magnitude of a decision, it has been said, will normally be judged in terms of resource commitment its implementation will require and the risk factors associated with this commitment in relation to the expected outcome (Cusack 1981: 24). The substantial effect of project decisions on resources, together with the associated high levels of risk and uncertainty known to exist, indicate that the project decision is of paramount importance. The guidelines for making such decisions are determined by the organisation's business policy. Business policy statements are of the type 'When faced with a situation of the type X, always choose course of action A, rather than B or C . . .', and as such would seem to be eminently suitable potential OIDRs. The rather subjective manner in which policies are formulated, as a result of moral, political, aesthetic or personal considerations rather than as a result of logical and scientific analysis (Kempner 1976: 63) and their influence in the project evaluation and selection process in determining the choice among multiple criteria, strengthens this view.

Policies are normally devised to coincide with the managing director's objectives (Lansley et al. 1979: App. E, 11–13), the board of directors and senior management (Cusack 1981: 39) or in consultation within a group of companies (South 1979).

Business strategies appear to perform a similar role to policies. Strategies have been defined as 'broad policies' (Bahrami 1981: 2, 5) describing 'patterns of decisions' (Andrews 1980) resulting from or enabling the continuous process of making entrepreneurial decisions (Drucker 1959). The distinction between strategies and policies, on this basis, is not very clear and, indeed, some 'considerable confusion' is known to exist (Kempner 1976: 63). It has been said that policy decisions refer more often to the character and nature that the company wishes to adopt, while strategy refers to the means to be employed in bringing about these desired characteristics (Kempner 1976: 63). This suggests that, in terms of the project decision system, the view on what constitutes the most desirable states in the outcome machine is determined by policy while the internal mechanics of the decision machine which generate these states is determined by strategy. In other words, the OIDRs are determined by strategy and the 'best' set of OIDRs are determined by an 'optimal' strategy.

The high level of uncertainty surrounding the project decision problem has an important effect on strategies and policies (Frazer 1981), mainly due to prediction difficulties (Benes and Diepeveen 1985). Uncertainties can occur exogenously by changes in the levels of demand, for instance, and endogenously by the results of the decision mechanism. The combination of these situations is considered here in terms of high-/low-risk exogenous factors and strategies.

Low-risk exogenous factors and strategies

Harding (1985) has identified two types of low-risk exogenous sets of factors, the placid, randomised environment and the placid clustered environment. Low-risk strategies in the placid randomised environment are essentially 'stick with the knitting' (Peters and Waterman 1982) in terms of project characteristics with attention mainly focused on the outcome environment especially in terms of production (Lansley *et al.* 1980) and backward integration (Moss 1981). Typical objectives in these situations are to achieve target profits and monetary return (Niss 1965) and limited or selected growth (Fellows *et al.* 1983; Barnard 1981; Porter 1980: xvii) with some preference for growth (Fellows *et al.* 1983). The emphasis is on the correspondence between projects and resources, which Moss (1981) terms the focusing effect resulting in responses to project opportunities limited and influenced by the size of the company (Jarman 1978; Lansley, *et al.* 1979: 3, 2). This simple response mechanism, termed 'operational' (Lansley *et al.* 1979: 3, 2) or 'tactical' (Harding 1985: 216) can influence the type of work chosen (South 1979), although smaller builders appear to be less affected (Jarman 1978).

The focusing effect has been observed in most construction organisation strategies. South's (1979) examination of twenty-three construction companies, between 1970 and 1976, found little effort to change markets except from public to private housebuilding. Most companies had limits on work types, geographical range from head office and value ranges of work. In comparing differing sized construction companies, Jarman (1978) concluded that large companies do not tackle business ventures with little knowledge or expertise. Medium-sized companies usually concentrated in one area, both spatially and by product. Small companies specialised in maintenance and repairs which the large companies generally avoided unless as a rolling programme. Housebuilders, on the other hand, could do any type of job within reason, local-authority housing and small industrial units being specified alternatives.

Outcome-oriented strategies are essentially concerned with the need for work reflected in the level of utilisation of resources. Low-risk strategies recognise limitations in capability and capacity, concentrating on the availability of resources by means of capability profiles (Fellows *et al*. 1983: 18) for instance. Project workload has been found to be the single most important factor in determining the bidding decision (Mannerings 1970) affecting the organisation's ability to tender and resulting in the decision to return a tender, reduce margins or be more selective in projects (South 1979).

The availability of personnel has been found to be a major factor affecting the bidding decision, one reason being due to the policy of keeping the work-force together (Niss 1965). Plant and skilled operative constraints exist, craft shortages occurring because of redeployment difficulties caused by barriers to entry between crafts (Burton 1972). Utilisation of equipment is one objective of construction companies (Niss 1965) and materials availability has been found to affect the bidding decision as it can influence the contract duration and thus the level of project overheads (South 1979). Low-risk monetary-oriented strategies include minimising capital usage (Rajab 1981) or utilising available capital sufficiently to avoid financial over-extension (Park 1972: 24, 4), an essential constraint being that the project must generate sufficient profit to cover overheads (Humphreys 1977).

Harding's second type of low-risk exogenous factors, the placid clustered environment, implies the existence of some predictable movements in the project-generating environment which can be exploited by the organisation. Such identifiable trends can lead to low-risk demand-related pricing strategies based on forecasts of future project opportunities and levels of competition (South 1979). Medium-sized organisations, for instance, being more susceptible to down-turns in demand, may respond by increasing specialisation (Jarman 1978) or competitive advantage. A more coherent market-oriented strategy can be adopted to enhance company image and reputation and, to some extent, influence demand by adopting a passive attitude on claims (Harris and McCaffer 1983: 181), co-operating with clients in improving the design and contract (Harris and McCaffer 1983: 182) and generally increasing client satisfaction (Rajab 1981; Peters and Waterman 1982).

Low-risk responses to change in demand imply that output trends will be a delayed and smoothed version of demand trends. Evidence of this lagged and damped effect (South 1979) suggest that low-risk exogenous factors and strategies typify the construction industry.

High-risk exogenous factors and strategies

High-risk exogenous factors are associated with Harding's (1985) disturbed reactive environment and Ansoff's (1979) turbulent fields. Turbulent fields imply a gross increase in relevant uncertainty where effects are amplified and become unpredictable; where there is little relationship between a decision, its resulting effects and the next decision to be made; and where the future appears to be disjointed and discontinuous. There are, fortunately, few examples of turbulent environments in the practice of construction (Harding 1985: 220), the construction environment being found to be 'moderately uncertain' (Brown 1974) and not significantly disruptive other than through the inflationary mechanism (Foster 1974). Turbulence, however, can be induced if the organisational structure is inappropriate to the demands placed on it, or if the quality of management declines (Harding 1985: 220). Low-risk strategies of the kind outlined in the previous section can have similar effects.

Swift changes in demand can cause 'overheating' in the industry. With low-risk strategies the various parts of the construction industry cannot increase or decrease output as quickly as orders. But when orders increase too rapidly, the industry becomes overheated and contractors spread work forward, and vice versa when demand is inadequate. The results of such overheating or inadequate demand can be observed by such indicators as the ratio of vacancies to unemployed, level of brick stocks, the rate of increase of earnings and bid prices in construction compared with other industries, architects' new commissions, and bankruptcies in the industry (Campbell *et al.* 1974).

Perseverance with low-risk strategies in high-risk environments can have undesirable consequences in the form of defensive take-overs or liquidation. There are difficulties, however, despite this knowledge, in changing strategies to accommodate fluctuations in demand because of commitment to the focusing effect and general resistance to change. The project decision model implies that commitment to the focusing effect is inappropriate except as one means of identifying plausible options. The organisation and management of change is considered to be a function of the organisation machine (Fig. 5.4).

The high-risk environment has a two-fold effect on the organisation. The fluctuating and unpredictable changes in demand represent increased and varied opportunities and threats. Successful low-risk strategies are associated with avoiding threats and concentrating on survival (see, for instance, Fellows *et al.* 1983: 188; Hillebrandt 1974: 89, 92; Woodward 1975: 170; Harrison 1982), while high-risk strategies attempt to exploit opportunities as a means of further growth (see, for instance, Lansley *et al.* 1979: 3, 86; Niss 1965; Fellows *et al.* 1983: 188; Rajab 1981). The former strategies can lead to controlled regression (Benes and Diepeveen 1985), decline (Fellows *et al.* 1983: 32), the desire for stability (Niss 1965; Rajab 1981) or a constant volume of work (Niss 1965). Growth strategies lead to the desire to progress and expand (Niss 1965: 92) by increasing the level of operations (Woodward 1975: 170), size and turnover (Fellows *et al.* 1983: 188).

In high-risk environments, both low- and high-risk strategies require a certain 'fleetness of foot' regarding market orientation. Low-risk strategies are essentially passive in that attempts to influence project generation are kept to a minimum except in times of need. The accent is on market specialism until circumstances dictate otherwise. Stability strategies (Lansley *et al.* 1979: 3, 87), emphasis on quality of product (Rajab 1981; Niss 1965), strategies to keep out competitors (Woodward 1975) and maintain or increase market share (Foster 1974; Cusack 1981; Fellows *et al.* 1983: 188) are typical. Entry into new markets, when necessary, can present difficulties, however, depending on the costs of starting up and the chances of obtaining more work in that market. One approach to this difficulty is the 'foot in the door' strategy (Foster 1974) involving a gradual transition between markets. Information on new markets is clearly a vital factor.

The main emphasis with low-risk strategies in high-risk environments, however, is in the outcome environment. The chances of survival can be improved by increased productivity by better and more flexible use of resources through sub-contracting or redeployment of workmen, for instance, to increase efficiency and minimise costs. Increased flexibility has been found in at least two cases, plant and staff workload, to minimise the impact of resource levels on the bidding decision.

High-risk strategies, under the definition implied here, are

136

associated with aggressive market–oriented behaviour. It has been suggested that priority to market-related objectives is essential for the modern company (Lansley *et al.* 1980). Such forward integration strategies include expansion and diversification, developing merger potential and growth through acquisition. Grinyer (1972) has postulated the incremental nature of strategic development in diagrammatic form, from existing expansion and diversification to conglomerate diversification (Fig. 6.1). Strategic developments on this scale demand close integration of bidding, organisational and marketing activities in order to be successful. Newcombe (1976), for instance, found that incompatibilities between organisational and marketing strategies can have a terminal effect on the organisation. Organisational flexibility is needed to prevent incompatibility occurring (Lansley *et al.* 1979: 1, 15).

High-risk strategies continually seek new fields of endeavour and attempt to create their own demand. Such objectives necessarily

	Existing services, type of construction, or product	New but related services, type of construction or product	New and largely unrelated products
Existing clients in same geographic area	Existing strategy	Expansion	Expansion
Existing clients in new geographic area	Expansion	Expansion	Diversification
New clients in same geographic area	Expansion	Diversification	Conglomerate diversification
New clients in new geographic area	Expansion	Diversification	Conglomerate diversification

'Construction firms are normally well advised to explore strategic alternatives in the sequence indicated by the arrows.'

Fig. 6.1 Alternative strategies
Source: Grinyer (1972)

imply the existence of good environmental information and active marketing together with appropriate management and co-operation of those involved in the decision environment to overcome long-run limitations of size, organisation and markets (Moss 1981).

Conclusions

The previous examination of the total project decision problem reveals the need to assess multiple conflicting criteria under dynamic and uncertain conditions. The appropriate decision is selected by evaluation and comparisons of options over time. The options to be evaluated include the decision of whether or not the project is wanted and, if it is, the level of price to offer. Options occur due to the presence of project opportunities generated by the general demand for construction together with the marketing efforts associated with previous decisions. The result of the project decision is to influence changes in the outcome environment. The uncertain nature of all aspects of the decision problem, and particularly those important factors which lie in the future, indicates that values and strengths of relationships will need to be estimated. The combined complexities and uncertainties of the problem suggest that some simulation model may be most appropriate, allowing the implication of inaccurate estimates to be examined. Figure 5.4 proposes a schematic system of the project decision incorporating major aspects of the problem in terms of project generating, project decision and outcome machines. A schemata for the project decision machine is shown in Fig. 6.2 incorporating a means of determining future events by simulation.

The project decision machine contains an option generator and evaluator/comparator. The option generator is activated by incoming project opportunities and construction demands together with details of the outcome states. Human input is available through the 'people' outcome state. The option generator contains option identification rules (strategies) while the evaluator/comparator contains rules for comparing multiple criteria (policies). The simulator is a small-scale model of the project decision model, designed to simulate future environments and decisions. The project decision machine contained in the simulator has exactly the same configuration as the project decision machine illustrated in Fig. 5.4. The project decision machine operates, therefore, in a recursive manner, each decision machine containing a nested version of itself. The satisfaction of some termination criterion results in

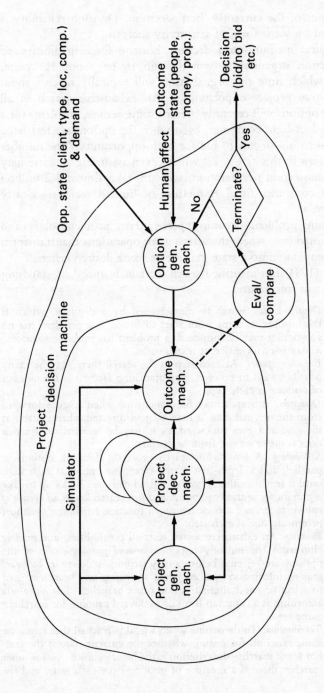

Fig. 6.2 The project decision machine

the output of the currently 'best' decision. Decision reliability is estimated by some form of sensitivity analysis.

A typical medium-term decision horizon for a medium sized construction organisation would seem to be about 1½ years, during which time the organisation will typically receive about seventy-five project opportunities. An exhaustive search of all possible options will certainly present some serious problems for a sub-speed-of-light computer, even when the options are restricted to two – to bid or not to bid for each opportunity. The number of iterations in this case is 2^{75} which, even assuming an extremely fast 1 nanosecond per iteration, will still take almost 1.2 million years of computer time! A method of limited search is clearly necessary.

Searching problems occur in expert systems, problem solvers and robot controllers, where the search is for operations that transform the current state into a state that meets some desired criteria.

Sowa (1984) has identified seven 'certain features' of searching problems of this nature:

> *Depth.* Every search is characterised by a depth *n*, which is the number of steps from start to finish. If a problem has no solution, *n* may be infinite. If a problem has multiple solutions, *n* may vary for different search paths.
> *Branching factor.* At each step in the search there may be many possible ways to proceed. The branching factor *k* is the number of options at each step.
> *Direction.* A search may be *data-directed* when it goes forward from the original data, it may be goal-directed when it starts at the goal and goes backward, or it may be *bi-directional* when it does some searching from both ends.
> *Scheduling.* A *breadth-first* search proceeds along all options in parallel, and a depth-first search takes one option at each step, until it reaches either a goal or a dead end then backs up to take a previously untried option. A *best-first* search keeps an *agenda of options to try, and uses an evaluation* function to choose the most promising one at each step.
> *Pruning.* An exhaustive search tests all possibilities, and *pruning* eliminates the unlikely ones. In *forward pruning* some of the options are rejected before any searching is done. In *backward pruning* information gained while searching one branch is used to select or reject alternatives on other branches. The *alpha-beta* algorithm is a common form of backward pruning for searching game trees.
> *Termination.* To determine when a goal is reached there must be some criterion for testing whether the current state is the end. For some searches the criterion is the binary choice . . . for other searches there is a measure of goodness for each state, and the

criterion is either to find the best state or find one that exceeds a certain threshold.

Heuristics. A systematic guessing strategy can guide or speed up a search. Heuristics may select the best option to try, reducing the branching factor by pruning options or test the current state against the termination criteria. (Sowa 1984: 198)

Strategies for controlling complexity include the introduction of constraints to eliminate redundant or dead-end files; shallow searches; special cases; generate and test plausible solutions; large knowledge bases; and special hardware (Sowa 1984). Various systems combine these strategies. The chess computer, Belle, which has reached master level in competition with human players, uses the alpha-beta algorithm to prune options, an arbitrary cut-off to limit the search, special cases for forcing sequences, heuristics for ordering the search and evaluating positions, a knowledge base of opening moves derived from grand master practice and parallel hardware for generating legal moves and computing the value of a position (Condon and Thompson 1982).

Many of these devices are also applicable to the project selection problem:

1. The problem is likely to have multiple solutions, especially after sensitivity testing, so n may vary depending on the search path.
2. The branching factor k is potentially very large, even infinite, if all real numbers are considered for the set of potential bids. Sensitivity testing, however, is likely to indicate that prices within the range $\pm\frac{1}{2}$ per cent or greater will be sufficient.
3. The project decision model represented in Figs 5.4 and 6.2 implies the use of a data-directed search, no specific goal other than an 'improvement' in outcome state being defined. It is possible, however, that some arbitrary goal such as target profit or turnover may be found desirable in which case a goal-directed or bid-directed search could be used.
4. A breadth-first search could be used to secure short-term solutions, say the best bid to make for the current opportunity irrespective of future opportunities. Sensitivity tests may well reveal that increasing uncertainties of future events reduce their impact on current decisions. The various strategies outlined in this chapter indicate possible heuristic evaluation functions for the best first search. The indications

are that a consistent 'stick with the knitting' market strategy combined with a resource utilisation strategy would suffice unless faced with undue changes in demand in which case a broader search may be more appropriate.

5. Forward pruning could be utilised to remove obvious opportunities that are well outside the organisation's area of expertise. Backward pruning is a possibility where the selection of several contiguous projects is patently linked to create workload or cash-flow overload. The alpha-beta algorithm has a potential application in bidding by enabling some pruning to be made based on the likely actions of competitors leading to a rapid decision not to bid against a leading competitor, for instance.

6. The incremental approach proposed by the model implies that lines of option search are improving the results. A termination procedure might be adopted, for instance, based on a non-improvement heuristic resulting perhaps in an entirely different search strategy.

7. One constraint is immediately apparent – there will be a limit below which certain resources cannot fall. Monetary resources, for example, will have a minimum level. A minimum resource constraint may also be necessary on a continuous basis. A certain sequence of projects could easily generate this state. Sensitivity tests may well reveal the possibility of constraint violation for most combinations of projects.

Part Two

Statistical models

Part Two

Statistical models

7

Statistical models

Introduction

The previous chapter introduced some ideas to ease the computational burden of the project decision problem, mainly centring on possible search heuristics for 'best' decisions. This chapter examines another possibility, the use of statistical models, as a means of reducing some aspects of the problem at least to manageable proportions.

Uncertainty, risk and probability

It is clear from the preceding chapters that uncertainties and risks are likely to be major aspects of the project decision problem. One approach to dealing with these aspects, sensitivity analysis, has already been discussed. Sensitivity analyses, however, exist in many forms although all such techniques are essentially concerned with investigating the effects of uncertainty by inducing perturbations in the data. It is important, therefore, to develop techniques that will permit representation of the uncertainties as accurately as possible. A popular technique for representing uncertainty is by a statistical model in which some variable aspects of the problem are modelled as random events. The advantage of this approach is that the assumption of purely random events implies a special kind of stability, indeed, as Peirce (1980) asserts, '. . . nothing could be imagined to be more systematic'. A further advantage is that the statistical approach enables a potentially substantial amount of theoretical knowledge to be applied to the problem.

There are, unfortunately, few events (if any) which occur in the prototype which will be truly random in the statistical sense, as there are equally few events that are truly deterministic. The best that can be expected, therefore, is a statistical model which will 'reasonably' map some aspect of the prototype. The 'reasonableness' of the mapping is to be judged by the consequent performance of the decision system, and not necessarily the degree with which the model 'fits' the prototype. This will, of course, depend on the 'robustness' of the system in the same sense that statistical tests for means (robust) are less reliant on the assumption of the 'Normal' distribution than tests for variance (non-robust).

The first task, however, is to identify those aspects of the system likely to be amenable to statistical modelling and the type of model which may be most appropriate. The remainder of this chapter, therefore, contains an examination of the literature relating to the statistical nature of variables contained in the project decision model outlined in the previous chapters.

Construction demand and project characteristics

Most modellers consider total demand to be infinite (Atkins 1975) and that project opportunities occur in an infinite (Oren and Rothkopf 1975) or unending sequence (Agnew 1972). Benson (1970) assumes the number of opportunities occurring in a given time interval is known or estimated from previous experience without reference to any frequency distribution. Hossein's (1977) empirical analysis of 106 projects, however, found the frequency distribution of the size of project opportunities to be exponential as adjudged by the chi-square test at the 99 per cent confidence level. A similar analysis by Skitmore (1986) of three sets of data containing 642 building contracts found only the Log–Log–Normal distribution to be appropriate for all the sets.

Ortega-Reichert (1968) suggested the work content of the project to be a random variable. This approach has been developed by Morrison and Stevens (1980) in a simulation study involving the random generation of such constructional features as gross floor area, number of storeys, column centres, building plan, the occurrence and size of basements and types of roofs. Project opportunities were, in this case, generated randomly from a distribution based on the total industry turnover target, average project size and duration.

Models representing the number of competitors bidding for a given project start with Friedman (1956) who suggested a Poisson distribution to be appropriate, an assumption subsequently adopted, but not tested, by Hossein (1977), for instance. Friedman also suggested several methods of estimating the 'average' number of bidders on the grounds that in many cases there is information available to a company about the intentions of its competitors and that this information combined with the experience of its executives may give a good estimate of the number of bidders, an approach reiterated by Rubey and Milner (1966) with particular reference to the type and size of the project involved.

A further approach considered by Friedman, based on an assumed relationship between project size and the number of bidders, was to regress the number of bidders against the company's cost estimates on previous bids. Such a regression has been applied by Wade and Harris's (1976) analysis of 136 bid tabulations from three small to medium-sized general construction contractors located and working in Ann Arbor, Michigan, indicating the existence of a logarithmic relationship between the number of bidders and project value.

A similar analysis has been conducted by Gates (1967), however, but with very poor predictive results. Sugrue's (1977) analysis confirmed this by finding no significant relationships between project size, number of bidders, number of suppliers and sub-contractors involved. Park (1966) has suggested that a non-linear relationship may exist but no evidence has been found to adequately support this notion. Skitmore's (1986) more recent analysis showed the logarithmic linear model to be the most appropriate means of expressing the relationship between contract value and the number of bidders.

Skitmore's (1981a) analysis of bidding data indicated a relationship between the number of bidders and market conditions, although no model was developed. The general lack of predictive models has led researchers to conduct simulation studies based on a randomised number of bidders (Rickwood 1972).

The identities of competitors vary, according to Benjamin (1969), with the type and size of project, the client and the location. However, Morin and Clough (1969) showed that different competitors were met on different classes of work, although the extent of such differences were not revealed. Wade and Harris (1976) have suggested that the identities of the various individual and combinations of competitors can be treated probabilistically, an approach attempted by Skitmore (1986) by means of a log-linear model involving contract values. Shaffer and Micheau (1971: 116) briefly mention a predictive technique termed the multidistribution model (MD) claimed to represent the local structure of the construction industry, '. . . a structure which allows the contractor to predict with a high level of confidence who his competitors will be on a specific project'. The details of this model are apparently given in Casey and Shaffer (1964), a publication to which this writer has been unable to gain access.

Difficulties in predicting the identity of certain competitors, particularly those of whom the company has little or no knowledge, has led to the separate treatment of 'strangers' and 'key' competitors. These and other competitive aspects, however, are examined later in this chapter.

The outcome environment

While no evidence of probabilistic approaches to modelling human development and aspirations was located, some considerable literature is available concerning the physical and particularly monetary aspects of the outcome environment. Monetary aspects are dependent on two major factors, the probability of acquiring the project and the probability of the occurrence of certain monetary states conditional upon the project being acquired or lost. This latter factor is examined first, on the assumption that the project will be acquired, in terms of expenditure (cost) and income probabilities. The probability of project acquisition will be considered in the final section of this chapter.

Expenditure

Cost and estimated cost variables
Although some models assume future project expenditure to be known with certainty (Agnew 1972; Gates 1960; Park 1966; Broemser 1968; Edelmann 1965; Morin and Clough 1969, for instance) it is clear that this is far from the case in the prototype. Several attempts have been made to formulate the problem in a quantitative manner which allows treatment of the variation between expenditure and estimates. One approach adopts the concept of 'true' cost (Whittaker 1970), sometimes expressed as God's cost (McCaffer 1976a) or the Devil's cost! (Fine 1974). This is essentially that of Friedman's (1956) approach who takes the view that the true cost can only be known after the job has been completed and assumes that the distribution of the ratio s of the true cost to the estimated cost can be determined from the contractor's records, this ratio being clearly a random variable (Benjamin 1972). As the

estimate is often assumed to be correct on average (Capen *et al.* 1971), the population mean of this ratio is, therefore, unity with a dispersion, according to determinists, of zero (Casey and Shaffer 1964). Weverbergh (1978) also refers to the random variable S as the ratio of real and estimated costs, where real costs are implied to equal true costs.

A different perspective is provided by McCaffer (1976b) whose model is derived on the basis that different estimators will obviously assess the effects of factors on costs differently and hence a number of estimators are liable to produce a range of estimated costs. This suggests a probability distribution of estimates around some mean. This mean has been termed 'the likely cost' (Cauwelaert and Heynig 1978) and several simulation studies (Fine and Hackemar 1970; Rickwood 1972; Morrison and Stevens 1980, for instance) have been conducted on this basis. The advantage of the likely cost approach is that each project cost estimate can be considered to be a random value drawn from a distribution of possible cost estimates unique to each project, while Friedman's approach implies one distribution to apply irrespective of non-random differences that may occur between projects. This, according to Benjamin (1969), is an important factor for, in his view, there is no single distribution of the ratio of true cost to estimated cost that applies to all jobs without regard to the characteristics of the job. Curtis and Maines (1973) have similar reservations regarding the Friedman approach.

An alternative line has been adopted by Park (1966) who takes the view that the actual project costs are distributed about the estimated costs, this distribution being regarded by Vergara (1977) as symmetrical around estimated costs with actual costs being equal, on average, to estimated costs. This approach suggests that the estimated cost is somehow the target figure, a possibility discussed earlier.

The difference between the 'true' versus 'likely' cost and the 'actual' cost models is essentially that some authors consider estimated costs as a stochastic variable and the true cost as non-stochastic, while others take the true cost as being stochastic and estimated cost to be non-stochastic (Naert and Weverbergh 1978: 362). In statistical terms, this difference, according to Naert and Weverbergh, basically boils down to taking a classical versus a Bayesian point of view.

An alternative way of dealing with this difference has been to treat both the costs *and* the estimates as random variables (Fuerst 1977;

Rothkopf 1980). There is some justification for this approach for, as Fine and Hackemar (1970) demonstrate, variability in estimates of production and costs exists both before and after the event as estimates are guesses at future costs and accounts are guesses at past costs. In their view, the two variables may not be strongly causally dependent, certainly as far as feedback is concerned, for in theory the estimator's guess should be based on accounting data and should be obtained from these by a process of data manipulation and calculation. In practice, data of this kind are of little concern to anyone involved in the process (Fine and Hackemar 1970: 1).

The suitability of a statistical model

Whittaker noted in 1970 that the stochastic nature of estimated costs has been recognised by almost all previous investigators. There has been no discernible change in circumstances since that time, Fuerst (1976) suggesting the cost estimate to be a random variable; Vergara (1977) using probabilistic estimates to treat the cost of the project as a random variable; Carr (1982) assuming estimates of total cost to be random variables; and Rothkopf (1980) considering both costs and estimates to be random variables. Very little evidence exists, however, to support the assumptions and some criticisms have been recorded. Curtis and Maines (1973), for instance, consider that cost estimates are not random but depend on the company position. Ortega-Reichert (1968) implies the cost to be conditional on the work content of the project. Stark and Mayer (1971: 474) suggest that cost dependencies can exist in which economies are anticipated from executing certain combinations of contracts, e.g. the efficient utilisation of supervisory personnel for nearby construction sites. Firms which contract for large construction projects and hence consider fewer bid opportunities might expect their costs to be independent. However, as the number of opportunities to bid increase, cost interactions between projects are more pronounced.

Several aspects of costs and cost estimates have been proposed that may be amenable to statistical modelling. These have been studied, to some extent, by Green (1978) and Vergara and Boyer (1974). Bacarreza (1973) considers the main random variables to consist of: cost percentage of, for instance, labour, materials, plant and overheads; cost 'variances'; cost curves; bidding curves; and contract duration. At a more detailed level, random variables have been said to include the following:

Labour costs Site activity has been modelled as a series of stochastic independent events by Fine (1970) and subsequently by Bennett and Fine (1980), Bennett and Ormerod (1984) and Wilson (1982), among others. Armstrong (1972) has also modelled trends in wages, outputs and performance standards and the ease or difficulty of performing the work in a similar manner. Benjamin (1969) suggests that labour costs associated with the costs of performing the work are random variables whose behaviour may be described by a probability distribution and Gates (1971) has suggested some typical coefficients of variation (Table 7.1).

Table 7.1 Coefficients of variation (V%) of estimated productivity for various operations in building construction industry

Operation	V%	Operation	V%
Unloading and stacking		Concrete formwork	
Packaged material	10	Fabricate	10
Brick, block	10	Erect	10
Loose lumber, bars	20	Strip, clean, oil	10
		Repair	20
Site improvements			
Clearing	10	Concreting	
Grubbing	20	Placing	15
Remove pavements	15	Finishing	15
Pipe culverts	15	Curing	10
Rip-rap	15		
Fine grading	10	Reinforcing steel	
Paving	15	Fabricate bars	10
Sidewalks	10	Set bars	7.5
Power lines	20	Wire mesh	10
Fence	10		
		Structural steel	
Manual excavation		Fabricate	15
Loosen soil	15	Erect	10
Shovel and cast	15	Deck and siding	15
Backhill	10		
Compact	20	Masonry	
Wheelbarrow	15	Trim stone	20
		Set stone	10
Mechanical excavation		Lay brick, block & tile	7.5
Small equipment	20	Point	20
Medium equipment	20		
Large equipment	15	Rough carpentry	
		Cutting, ripping, drilling	

Table 7.1   contd

Operation	V%	Operation	V%
Truck haul	10	Manual	15
		Power	10
Drill blastholes	15	Framing	
		Install	7.5
Sheet piles; drive		Remove	15
Brace and pull	15	Flooring, sheathing	10
		Plaster board	7.5
Foundation piles	20		
		Finish carpentry	
Precast concrete		Exterior siding	10
Manufacture	10	Exterior trim	20
Erect	15	Interior panelling	10
		Interior trim	15
Insulation	10	Cabinet work	15
		Stairs	20
Plastering		Hang doors	15
Lath to walls	7.5	Install windows	15
Lath to ceilings	10		
Stucco netting	10	Roofing	
Plaster	10	Shingle	15
Stucco and gunite	10	Built-up tar & gravel	10
		Flashing	10
Painting			
Walls, floors, ceilings	7.5	Electrical work	
Doors, windows, trim	10	Conduit, cable & wire	10
Structural steel	10	Install fixtures	15
Wallpapering	20	Buried cable	10
Floor, ceiling and wall tile		Plumbing	
Ceramic, quarry,			
structural	10	Exterior piping	15
Asbestos, asphalt,		Interior piping &	
acoustic	7.5	tubing	10
		Install fixtures	10
Glazing	10	Cut and thread	10
		Heating and air	
		conditioning	
		Pipe and duct runs	10
		Fittings	10
		Insulation	7.5
		Install fixtures	15

Source: Gates (1971: 294, Table 2).

Material costs Trends in material costs have been modelled stochastically by Armstrong (1972), Benjamin (1969) suggesting that the theory of stochastic processes (time series analysis in particular) may be used to predict the probability distribution of the cost of materials at the time they are to be purchased.

Sub-contractors' costs Benjamin (1969) suggests that the receipt of a low bid from a sub-contractor could be treated as a Poisson arrival and the relative amount by which it is a low bid could be described by some other probability distribution.

Quantity-related costs Gates (1971) has proposed that errors caused by mistakes are distributed triangularly and symmetrically. Mistakes, according to Gates, include gross mistakes, foolish mistakes and unpardonable mistakes due to carelessness or ignorance. Quantity take-off results in mistakes from plan reading, measurement and related arithmetic as well as ambiguous or incomplete plans. Carelessness results in missing some quantities and even items of work. Fine and Hackemar (1970) and Grinyer and Whittaker (1973) also advocate the use of probabilistic models for mistakes of this nature.

Effects of weather and seasons Benjamin (1969) suggests that since the occurrence of different weather conditions in different seasons are random variables, the costs associated with changes of weather are also random, a view endorsed by Hillebrandt (1974) and adopted in Armstrong's (1972) simulation studies.

Costs of estimating Leech and Jenkins (1978) have performed a stochastic simulation of the tendering system using a distribution of activity times, based on evidence provided by Leech and Earthrowl (1972).

Additional costs Gates (1971) considers that additional costs required by the engineer can be dealt with by probabilistic modelling. The acceptability of substitutes is also recommended for treatment in a similar manner.

Other costs Benjamin (1969) suggests that other costs, such as insurance costs, bonding costs and fringe benefits, which are functions of the above costs are also random variables.

153

Statistical approaches to modelling cost and estimate variability have not gone unchallenged, however. Hillebrandt (1974), in distinguishing between risk (where probabilities can be determined) and uncertainty (where probabilities cannot be determined) suggests that most of the foregoing aspects are uncertain rather than risky and, therefore, considers it questionable whether probability is the right tool (Hillebrandt 1974: 183).

The criticism, however, is not that probabilistic modelling is inappropriate *per se* but that estimation of the parameters involved is likely to be the difficulty.

Estimation of parameters

The complete specification of any probability distribution involves three parameters which have been referred to as shape, spread and location. Although the distribution of costs and estimated cost is, as Naert and Weverbergh (1978) point out, not observable, several indications are available.

Shape

A wide range of shape parameters have been assumed by modellers of project costs. Vickrey's (1961) early work on the application of game theory to auctions assumes costs to be uniformly distributed, an assumption also adopted by later researchers in this field (Griesmer *et al.* 1967, for instance). Fine (1974) and Hackemar (1970) also adopt the uniform assumption in their simulation studies of construction projects, together with McCaffer (1976b), Cauwelaert and Heynig (1978) and Harris and McCaffer (1983), who all assume the range of estimates produced to be the likely cost $\pm A\%$ (Harris and McCaffer 1983: 226) or in the range B to $1/B$, where $B = (100 + A)/100$ (Fine 1974). Beckmann (1974), Naert and Weverbergh (1978), Rickwood (1972) and Mitchell (1977) assume a Normal (Gaussian) distribution of cost estimates to be a reasonable assumption, particularly in those situations where a cost estimate is the sum of a large number of cost components (Mitchell 1977: 192), as implied by the Central Limit Theorem (Case 1972).

Capen *et al.* (1971) and Zinn *et al.* (1975), on the other hand, prefer the Lognormal distribution on the assumption that the cost estimate is the product of variables, Smith and Case (1975) opting for the Loglogistic model for similar reasons. Rothkopf (1969, 1980), Oren and Rothkopf (1975) and Zinn *et al.* (1975) assume the two-parameter Weibull distribution to be particularly appropriate

154

because it is a limiting distribution in the theory of extreme value statistics (Rothkopf 1969: 363), expressing surprise that the Weibull model is not adopted more frequently.

An alternative approach has been to model components of cost as individual probability distributions. An early example of this is Case (1972) who assumed each cost component to be represented by a Beta distribution. A similar procedure has been advocated by Stacey (1979) and others. Spooner (1974) has suggested using the triangular distribution to model cost components, an approach adopted by Wilson (1982), mainly for its simplicity. Recent simulation studies by Bennett and Fine (1980) and Bennett and Ormerod (1984) use a variety of probability distributions to represent the variability of cost components. The resulting total cost and estimate probability distributions in these cases is clearly determined by the degree of dependence between the component cost variables. No studies of these dependencies have, however, been reported.

Construction companies, it appears, have little knowledge of the frequency distribution of costs and estimates as generally no use is made of statistics and probability to systematically evaluate the uncertainty and risk inherent in construction (Neil 1978), perhaps because methods of estimating costs do not attempt to quantify the variability of actual costs (Larew 1976). Benjamin (1969) has suggested the use of three methods to determine the distribution of the total cost of performing the work by convolution of Normally distributed random variables whose elemental distributions are determined by multiple regression; convolution of Beta distributed random variables whose elemental distributions are determined subjectively by the construction cost estimates; and by examination of historical data without regard to the elements or activities of which the job is completed. The first method requires the assumption of stochastic independence which, in Benjamin's view is not unreasonable. Ashworth's (1977) attempts to apply the method, however, encountered severe difficulties in devising suitable explanatory variables. The second method also relies, as mentioned above, on the independence assumption, but no practical applications have been located. The third method, direct assessment, also presents some difficulties for, as Whittaker (1970) has found, details of actual project cost are often not available to the contractor since bulk buying and general stores complicate the task of determining the cost for the project. Further difficulties in estimate/actual cost comparisons are created by post–estimate design changes, for instance.

Despite the difficulties associated with direct assessment, several attempts have been made to determine the probability distribution of costs and estimates in this way by analysis of the ratios of estimated to actual costs for a sample of completed projects. The earliest example of this is by Friedman (1956) who claimed the Gamma distribution frequently furnishes a fit for projects of an unspecified nature. Gates' (1967) analysis of 110 projects completed by a large highway contractor for the Connecticut State Highway Department between 1963 and 1965 found the actual/estimated construction cost ratios to be approximately Normally distributed. Morin and Clough's (1969) analysis of a 'limited sample' of a contractor's cost and estimating data found the distribution of the ratio of actual to estimated cost to be symmetrical. Whittaker's (1970) analysis of 153 construction projects completed by a contractor between 1968 and 1969 purported to show that the use of the Uniform distribution for cost estimates is consistent with, and provides an adequate description of, the real system. Leech and Earthrowl (1972), from a limited amount of information, and Smith and Case (1975) have found a multiplicative model with Lognormal distributed estimates to furnish a reasonable approximation of an actual auction for oil tracts.

An alternative approach, based on the assumption that the difference between different bids for a project is largely determined by the random nature of the costs and estimates, is to estimate the shape of the distribution of bids. McCaffer (1976b), however, suggests that this may be misleading and Skitmore's (1981) analysis of 269 building contracts, indicating a systematic parameter change more closely related to income (price) than costs, would seem to offer some confirmation.

Spread

It has been said that contractors should estimate with an error of considerably less than 10 per cent of their total final cost (Rubey and Milner 1966) and, generally, of the order of ±5 per cent, given a set of quantities and subcontractors' quotations (Park 1966). Experience in process engineering contracts suggest that ±5 per cent is a reasonable figure (Liddle 1979). An opinion survey taken among construction contractors at a seminar in Loughborough also confirmed the view that ±5 per cent is generally appropriate, notwithstanding the lack of supporting data (Moyles 1973). Simulation studies have indicated higher figures to more closely represent those actually obtained by a leading contractor: ±8 per cent to ±11 per cent

(Fine and Hackemar 1970), usually rounded to ±10 per cent (Fine 1974) has been quoted, together with figures between ±5 per cent and ±15 per cent (Hackemar 1970). Morrison and Stevens' (1980) simulation used ±20 per cent labour rates, ±10 per cent materials and ±30 per cent output, the results indicating a mean accuracy of 5 per cent to 7.5 per cent.

Barnes and Lau (1974) judge the average spread for process plant contractors to have an average coefficient of variation (cv) of 7 per cent, the performance of particular companies varying widely from this average, certainly from 4 to 15 per cent. Beeston (1974) reported a cv of 4 per cent found by one civil engineering contractor after careful analysis of the extent of agreement among his estimators when estimating the same project. Gates' (1967) analysis indicated an approximate cv 7.5 per cent while other researchers suggest a cv 5.5 per cent for engineering services 'from experience' (Case 1972) or a cv 2 per cent from an analysis of a limited sample of contractors' cost and estimate data (Morin and Clough 1969).

Barnes (1971), in attempting to overcome some of the difficulties mentioned earlier, has used the ratio of the actual total cost to the estimated total cost multiplied by the ratio of the tender sum to the final account to measure spread. His analysis of data collected for 160 completed British construction contracts indicates a cv 5.8 per cent.

Location

In common with most statistical models, the mean or expected error is normally taken to be the same as the 'true' value. Where the ratios of actual to estimated costs are used, this implies a value of unity, an assumption made by Rothkopf (1980) for instance. Naert and Weverbergh's (1978) discussions with executives frequently engaged in closed sealed building for construction contracts suggest that the expected value of the ratios is often close to unity. Willenbrock's (1972) analysis of data supplied by a road contractor for twenty completed projects, however, showed a 3 per cent increase in costs over the estimate after deducting change orders and claims.

Theoretical considerations of the competitive aspects of the situation imply that some bias must be present in order to avoid the effects of the 'winner's curse'. Winner's curse is said to apply in situations where acquisition of the project is not independent of the cost estimate. Thus, for instance, an underestimate of costs is associated with, and partially responsible for, the acquisition of a project resulting in the expected value of estimated costs conditional upon acquiring the project being somewhat lower than the unconditional expected value of the estimated costs. Friedman (1956) has proposed a means of debiasing estimating costs but, as Simmonds (1968b) observes, the distribution of actual/estimated cost ratios *is* the conditional distribution and, therefore, already debiased to some extent. The situation is, however, complicated by factors associated with competitive aspects for, as Weverbergh (1981) and others have shown, the degree of bias is likely to be closely related (negatively correlated) to the probability of acquiring the project.

Winner's curse may also be an artifact of the model employed. Dependence among errors of estimation between bidders and differing amounts of information (i.e. bidders with different distribution parameters) can remove the effects of the winner's curse completely (Winkler and Brookes 1980). Dependence between estimated and actual costs can also have a similar effect if the estimated cost, as discussed previously, has some predetermining effect on the actual cost of the project.

Relationships between the probability distribution of expenditure and other factors

It has been suggested that the probability distribution of cost will change with the project characteristics. As the variance of the probability distribution of cost is an indication of the riskiness of the job (Benjamin 1969), then it follows that increases in spread are a function of increases in risk. Risk has been said to depend on the type of project (Case 1972), lower risk levels being associated with a company's specialty work and less complex projects (Benjamin 1969) and higher risk levels with large and complex projects (Neil 1978). Both large and small projects, and projects demanding either low or high work intensity, have been associated with high risk (Broemser 1968), although Benjamin considers low-intensity projects to produce lower risks. High levels of sub-contracting are usually associated with low risk (Broemser 1968), providing quotations have been obtained in advance.

One approach to reducing spread is by increasing the estimating effort. Smart (1976) has discussed the possible effect of increasing tendering effort in reducing the variability between costs and estimates.

Summary of overall expenditure distribution parameters

Project expenditure has been modelled extensively by probability distributions. Table 7.2 summarises, in alphabetical order, the

Table 7.2 Distribution parameters for costs/estimates

Modeller	Shape	Spread	Location
Barnes (1971)[h]		cv 5.8%	
Barnes & Lau (1974)[a]		cv 4–15%	
Beckmann (1974)[a]	Normal		
Beeston (1974)[g]		cv 4%	
Capen et al. (1971)[a]	Lognormal		
Case (1972)[c]		cv 5.5%	
Cauwelaert & Heynig (1978)[a]	Uniform	± A%	
Fine (1974)[b]	Uniform	± 10%	
Fine & Hackemar (1970)[b]	Uniform	± 8–10%	
Friedman (1956)[c]	Gamma		
Gates (1967)[d]	Normal	cv 7.5%	
Griesmer et al. (1967)[a]	Uniform		
Hackemar (1970)[b]		± 5–15%	
Harris & McCaffer (1983)[a]	Uniform	± A%	
Leech & Earthrowl (1972)[c]	Lognormal		
Liddle (1979)[a]		± 5%	
Mitchell (1977)[a]	Normal		
Morin & Clough (1969)[c]	Symmetrical	cv 2%	1.0 (median)
Morrison & Stevens (1980)[a]		± 5–7½% (mean)	
Moyles (1973)[f]		± 5%	
Naert & Weverbergh (1978)[i]			close to 1
Oren & Rothkopf (1975)[a]	Weibull		
Park (1966)[a]		± 5%	
Rickwood (1972)[b]	Normal		
Rothkopf (1969)[a]	Weibull		1.0 (exp. val)
Rothkopf (1980)[a]	Weibull		
Rubey & Milner (1966)[a]		less than 10%	
Smith & Case (1975)[c]	Lognormal		
Smith & Case (1975)[c]	Loglogistic		
Vickrey (1961)[a]	Uniform		
Whittaker (1970)[e]	Uniform		
Willenbrock (1972)[j]			+ 3%

[a] assumed for theoretical purposes
[b] assumed for simulation purposes
[c] source of data unknown
[d] analysis of 110 USA road projects
[e] analysis of 153 UK construction projects
[f] opinion survey of UK contractors
[g] analysis of extent of agreement between UK construction estimators
[h] analysis of 160 British construction projects
[i] discussion with Dutch construction companies
[j] analysis of 20 USA road projects

overall shape, spread and location parameters adopted in the cases reviewed in this section.

Income and cash flow

Income is normally assumed to be some function of the value of the bid, the majority of modellers assuming a one-to-one relationship. It is clear, however, that a one-to-one assumption is far from realistic in the prototype, many factors influencing changes between the bid value and the income ultimately received. Most of the factors involved are dealt with on a contractual basis, remuneration often being provided for unpredicted events such as inflation, additional work caused by design changes, uncovering suspected (incorrectly) faulty work, changes caused by fire and flood, and quantity errors and delays outside the company's control. Further income may accrue outside the contractual position in the form of *ex gratia* payments for perhaps exceptionally inclement weather, interest received on invested capital, receipts from the leasing of advertising space on hoarding etc. Of these variations in income only one factor, the incidence of design changes, has been modelled statistically.

Profit, however, is another matter. Estimates of profit are, invariably, taken as the difference between the bid and the cost estimate, usually in percentage terms, and the probability distribution of profit as the difference between the bid (a constant) and the cost (a variable). It is clear, though, that the probability distribution of profit is the difference between the two variables, income and expenditure. As the mechanism of the bidding process often is recognised as being such that the bid is a multiple of a cost estimate (Curtis and Maines 1973), it would seem appropriate that income, expenditure and profit are regarded as being a function of the estimated cost, conditional on the multiple (mark-up) applied. The degree of mark-up will also have a bearing on the likelihood of acquiring the project, an issue which is dealt with later in this chapter.

Models of income and expenditure over time, cash flow models, have been developed. The DHSS's curve formulae, for instance, provide a deterministic approximation of expenditure flows based on projected work value modelled continuously over the project duration, for differing sizes of projects. Similar models have been used by Atkins (1975) to represent the 'cash flow pattern' for differing project sizes and types. The only probabilistic model that has been identified in the work reviewed in this chapter is that adopted by Kangari and Boyer (1981) in the form of a Beta distribution.

Conclusion

Project opportunities and the outcome environment, particularly expenditure, for an individual company have received some attention from statistical modellers encountered in the literature and the indications are that the assumptions implied by the statistical approaches, i.e. the existence of random variables with estimable parameters, may well be appropriate in some instances.

A particularly significant factor in determining the state of the project decision system is whether the project will be acquired or not. This factor would seem to be dependent to some degree on the estimated cost of completing the project and the mark-up applied. Other companies also have a considerable influence in the ultimate appropriation of the project. The next section examines some approaches to modelling the behaviour of these competitors before finally considering probabilistic aspects of project acquisition.

Modelling competitors' bids

Researchers since Friedman (1956) have assumed that by keeping a record of the competitors' past bids it is possible to evaluate its bidding habits, by tracking competition we can develop its bidding behaviour and that history usually can be used as a basis for predicting competitive bid levels just as statistical sampling is used to predict election results (McCall 1977). The prediction of election results, however, by these means has sometimes achieved spectacular failures. It is not surprising, therefore, to find some criticism of this approach insofar as construction project bidding is concerned. One major criticism is that the events taking place are not truly random in the classical statistical sense as the basis of classical statistical theory is that there is an experiment that can be repeated many times in order to gather data from which the parameters of the probability distribution of some random variable of interest can be estimated. A sequence of bidding situations is not really a sequence of performances of the same experiment and each job is unique (Benjamin 1972). While there is no denying the truth of the statement, the same can equally be said for all observed phenomena, as discussed earlier in this chapter. Neoclassical theory simply utilises statistical techniques on the assumption that the underlying mechanisms in the data 'reasonably' resemble the statistical premises, the degree of 'reasonablness' being determined pragmatically rather than by 'goodness of fit'.

Empirical criticisms are more serious. It has been claimed, for instance, that the assumption of randomness is invalid as we know that many subjective factors influence bidding behaviour (Curtis and Maines 1973: 181). Spooner (1971) has also suggested that a random selection process is not a rational representation of behaviour in these circumstances, a view endorsed by Simon (1957, 1959) who also believes that the uncertainty of bidding can and will not be solved through the adoption of probabilistic techniques. The evidence upon which these views are based, however, appears to be rather more circumstantial than factual, and there is a substantial body of opinion holding the opposite view. The general opinion relies on the existence of stable distributions of cost generating stable distributions of bids (Beckmann 1974) based on the long-recognised fact that there is a stability in mass data, although the mass is comprised of erratic individual cases (Gates 1960: 22). This fundamental precept, according to Gates, underlies the basis of actuarial science and is the foundation of the insurance industry, for instance.

A second, and related, criticism concerns what has been termed one of the most serious limitations of the statistical approach which is the basic assumption that competitors will follow the same general bidding patterns in the future that they have in the past (Park 1962). An individual competitor may, for instance, change his strategy, thus rendering past data about him misleading (Beeston 1983: 114). This criticism is essentially aimed at all inductive approaches, for induction necessarily extrapolates from past events to future events. Induction, however, does not attempt merely to extend into the future repetitions that have occurred in the past, but rather by creating the conception of a mechanism (model) that explains the past from which the future may be deduced (Adler 1963: 236). McCaffer's (1976a) analysis of individual bidders suggests that some contractors behave in a matter not entirely consistent with the random model. His series of time-based tests, however, were generally inconclusive and further research may well indicate possible predictor variables in this respect. Despite their reservations, both Park and Beeston concede that in the absence of other information, probably the best guide to the future is the past and that statistical modelling may provide benefits to the organisation.

Some models do, in fact, incorporate other information such as project characteristics and measures to deal with the degrading effects of time, and some of these will be examined later in this section. Two other aspects, which are related to some extent, dependent and non-serious bids, together with problems caused by data acquisition are also addressed later in this section.

The behaviour of competitors

The project decision model, proposed here, is intended to apply to any construction organisation, including competitors. It is clear, however, that the information and computational burden problems implied by attempting to incorporate complex models of competitors' behaviour will be largely insurmountable. This section, therefore, examines some relatively simple models of competitors' behaviour, both collectively and individually.

Collective behaviour

Probably the most detailed and sophisticated analysis of individual and collective bidding behaviour of construction companies has been made by McCaffer (1976a), who found, from his Belgian data, substantial evidence that existing bidding processes are little more than random. The reasons for this may be attributable to the mechanism of the bidding process by which each competitor calculates his cost estimate, which is a random sample taken from his cost estimate distribution, and multiplies it by his mark-up (Curtis and Maines 1973). The implication, therefore, is that each competitor's cost estimate is taken from the same distribution and that the mark-up may also be treated as being taken from a distribution of mark-ups in a similar manner.

The notion of some commonality between competitors' cost estimates does seem to hold some attraction for, as Park (1972: 24.1) observes, taking a single job, most of the competing contractors can also be expected to encounter roughly the same costs of performing the work; they are all subject to the same costs of operation, have access to the same labour supply, use the same types of equipment, obtain supplies and materials from the same sources, and have somewhat comparable, if not equal, supervisory capabilities. As a result, it is claimed that in general building, where there is not a large element of highly specialised work and where there is a number of contractors of similar efficiencies, especially in areas where staff and labour move from company to company, a simplification assumes that the 'likely cost' of a contract to each company is similar (Harris and McCaffer 1983: 226). Many modellers have consequently adopted the assumption that each bidder has identical estimated costs (Larew 1976), true costs (Rothkopf 1980; Rickwood 1972) or that estimated costs are similar (Broemser 1968) or vary around some common mean (Oren and Rothkopf 1975; Morrison and Stevens 1980).

The application of statistical models to the cost/estimate variable has already been examined in the previous section. The variability of mark-ups has been modelled in a stochastic simulation by Rickwood (1972) by the Normal distribution. Grinyer and Whittaker (1973) found mark-ups to vary very little within firms (6.8 per cent $\pm$ 0.35 per cent) and their discussions with other firms have confirmed the impression that they do not vary greatly between firms. A similar analysis of Shaffer and Micheau's data (1971), however, indicates an average mark-up of 5.40 per cent (1.844 standard deviation), quite different figures. Similarities between bidders were observed in Whittaker's (1970) study of UK construction companies who used almost identical methods of determining costs and then all used almost the same percentage mark-up to arrive at their bid prices, inviting the conclusion that different firms attempt to place the same value on a specified contract. The differences that occur between estimated costs are primarily attributable to uncertainty and that the statistical techniques which average the behaviour of competitors and aggregate the results of past competitions are the most appropriate methods with which to study the situation.

Many models assume competitors' actions to be 'purely random' (Morin and Clough 1969) and, therefore, amenable to treatment as random variables and description by appropriate probability density distributions. The distribution of competitors' bids is sometimes expressed in terms of the distribution of the bid/cost estimate ratios, where the cost estimate value is that known by one of the bidders, or bid/average bid ratios (Whittaker 1970; McCaffer 1976a; Carr 1982). It then follows that each time the decision-maker bids on a contract against n competitors, a sample of the size n is drawn from this distribution of competitor bid to cost ratios (Sugrue 1980: 500).

The assumption that all bidders take their bids from the same distribution enables estimation of the distribution parameters to be made by direct observation of the bids made for each contract.

Shape

Vickrey's (1961) early work assumes that all bids are drawn from the same Uniform distribution. Stochastic simulation studies by Fine and Hackemar (1970) have used the assumption that bids are taken from a Uniform distribution, claiming that bids generated in this way compared very favourably with the distribution of bids found in the Costain Construction Company records. Cauwelaert and Heynig (1978) have also assumed a Uniform distribution for mathematical convenience, although they do claim that the assumption is perhaps not far from the truth. Whittaker's (1970) analysis of bids for 153 construction projects by four companies between 1968 and 1969 purported to show the Uniform distribution to be a reasonable model. Whittaker's method of analysis, dividing each bid on each contract by the mean bid for that contract and pooling the resulting ratios, has been severely criticised as being invalid (McCaffer 1976a) mainly because of the distorting effect of the standardising procedure used and the information loss caused by pooling.

Several models have been proposed based on the assumption that bids are taken from a Normal distribution (Alexander 1970; Emond 1971; Mitchell 1977; and Carr 1983, for instance). Morrison and Stevens (1980) also adopt this assumption in their stochastic simulations. Benjamin and Meador (1979) point out that it is the bid/cost estimate ratios that are often taken to be Normally distributed. McCaffer's (1976a) study of bids for 384 road and 190 building projects in Belgium found the Normal distribution to be the most appropriate model, especially for the building projects. Various trend analyses were performed by McCaffer on these data but with little success, inviting the conclusion that the assumption of randomness was perhaps reasonable. Cauwelaert and Heynig (1978: 18), in reviewing McCaffer's work, suggested that the conclusions regarding the Normal distribution and randomness were consistent with the work of other researchers neglecting, unfortunately, to provide any further information.

Park (1966) has used a statistical model of bid/cost estimate ratios that is positively skewed, a model considered to be appropriate by Beeston (1974) for bids for construction projects required by the Property Services Agency. The degree of skewness, however, according to Beeston, was only slight and for practical purposes a Normal distribution would suffice. Another report on McCaffer's roads data proposed an identical conclusion (McCaffer and Pettitt 1976).

The assumption of a Lognormal distribution to model bids is, according to Weverbergh (1982), not doing too bad at least as a first approximation. Klein (1976), for instance, has assumed the Lognormal distribution to be appropriate for bids and Capen *et al.* (1971) have adopted the distribution in modelling estimate value/bid ratios for oil tracts. There would seem, in fact, to be a degree of consensus regarding the Lognormal assumption for oil and mineral tracts bids (Arps 1965; Brown 1966; and Crawford 1970). The consistency in the standard deviation implied by the Lognormal assumption has also been observed by Hanssmann and Rivett (1959) and Pelto (1971) in their analyses of oil tracts and mineral rights sales. Skitmore (1986) also found a form of Lognormal distribution to be the most appropriate for his three sets of data. In this case, a three-parameter distribution was proposed, with one parameter proportional to the contract value.

Friedman (1956) suggests a Gamma distribution to be generally appropriate, an assumption adopted by Dougherty and Nozaki (1975) for oil tract bids. Analysis of pooled bid/cost estimate ratios for 545 civil engineering and 63 mechanical engineering projects has indicated a Gamma distribution to be the best fit (followed by the Lognormal and Normal distributions) (Hossein 1977).

Finally, Oren and Rothkopf (1975) have proposed a two-parameter Weibull distribution to be a suitable model of bids in auctions generally. A summary of shape parameters is given in Table 7.3.

Spread and location

Several researchers have estimated the average spread of bids for individual contracts. These estimates are given without discussion in Table 7.3.

Table 7.3 Distribution parameters for bids

Modeller	Shape	Spread	Location
AICBOR (1967)[o]		cv 6.8%	
Alexander (1970)[d]	Normal		
Arps (1965)[d]	Lognormal		
Barnes (1971)[m]		cv 6.5%	
Beeston (1971)[i]	Pos. skewed	cv 5.2–6%	
Brown (1966)[d]	Lognormal		

Table 7.3 (contd)

Modeller	Shape	Spread	Location
Capen et al. (1971)[d]	Lognormal		
Cauwelaert & Heynig (1978)[a]	Uniform		
Cauwelaert & Heynig (1978)[g]	Normal		
Crawford (1970)[d]	Lognormal		
Dougherty & Nozaki (1975)[d]	Gamma		
Emond (1971)[d]	Normal		
Fine & Hackemar (1970)[b]	Uniform	cv 5%	
Friedman (1956)[a]	Gamma		
Grinyer & Whittaker (1973)[c]	Uniform	cv 6.04%	
Hossein (1977)[k]	Gamma		
Klein (1976)[a]	Lognormal		
McCaffer (1976a)[f]	Normal	cv 6.5%	
McCaffer (1976a)[n]	Normal	cv 7.5%	
McCaffer (1976a)[j]	Normal	cv 8.4%	
McCaffer & Pettitt (1976)[j]	Pos. skewed	cv 8.4%	
Mitchell (1977)[a]	Normal		
Morrison & Stevens (1980)[a]	Normal	19.1% av. range	
Oren & Rothkopf (1975)[a]	Weibull		
Park (1966)[h]	Pos. skewed		
Pelto (1971)[d]	Lognormal		
Shaffer & Micheau (1971)[p]		cv 7.65%	
Skitmore (1981a)[l]		cv 7.65%	
Skitmore (1986)[q]	Normal	cv 6.8%	
Skitmore (1986)[r]	3 param lognormal	cv 13.5%	
Skitmore (1986)[s]	3 param lognormal	cv 7.8%	
Weverbergh (1982)[a]	Lognormal		
Whittaker (1970)[c]	Uniform		1.068

[a] Assumed for theoretical purposes
[b] Analysis of an 'adequate' sample of UK construction contracts
[c] Analysis of 153 UK government construction contracts
[d] USA oil and mineral tracts – source of data unknown
[e] Assumed for simulation studies
[f] Analysis of 183 Belgian building contracts
[g] 'consistent with work of other researchers'
[h] USA construction projects – source of data unknown
[i] Large sample of PSA building contracts
[j] Analysis of 384 Belgian road contracts
[k] Analysis of 545 US civil engineering and 63 mechanical engineering contracts
[l] Analysis of 269 UK building contracts
[m] Analysis of 159 Uk construction contracts
[n] Analysis of 16 Belgian bridge contracts
[o] Analysis of 213 UK motorway contracts
[p] Analysis of 50 USA construction contracts
[q] Analysis of 51 UK construction contracts
[r] Analysis of 218 UK local authority construction contracts
[s] Analysis of 373 UK construction contracts

The location parameter will, of course, depend upon the size of the project. In the absence of any further information, the location parameter may be estimated for each project from the bids for that project. Location parameters for bid/cost estimate ratios represent, under the assumptions of the collective model, a measure of the relationship between a company's cost estimate and bid – in other words, the mark-up.

Relationships between the probability distributions of bids and other factors

Johnston's (1978) analysis of bids for road projects found a significant positive skewness during the years 1970 to 1972, and a slightly negative skewness during the years 1973 to 1975, a change that Johnston attributed to the changing volume of project opportunities. Skitmore's (1981a) analysis of bidding projects data, however, found an opposite trend to exist. Further analysis by Skitmore of parts of bids suggests some relationship of an indeterminate nature may exist between skewness and market conditions.

The spread of bids has been analysed against project value by McCaffer (1976a) and Skitmore (1981a) and a possible but unconfirmed negative correlation obtained. A similar negative correlation has been observed by Morrison (1984) and Flanagan and Norman (1985). Beeston (1983) has suggested that changes in bid spread may be associated with changes in conditions over a few months, the rate of change being an important factor. Skitmore's (1981a) analysis over time shows a dramatic increase in spread in the year 1974 (Fig. 7.1), which coincides with some rather extreme movements in the market at that time. Further analysis by Skitmore of parts of bids implies some relationship of an indeterminate nature to exist between spread and market conditions.

It would seem perhaps that, in view of the indications revealed above, that some further studies of the influence of market conditions may be beneficial.

Distribution of low bids

An alternative approach is to model the winning bids as a probability density function. In this case, the usual procedure is to model the winning bid/estimated project value ratios (Hanssmann and Rivett 1959) or the winning bid/cost estimate ratios (Ackoff and Sasieni 1968; Sugrue 1977, 1980). These ratios are often assumed to follow a Normal distribution (Ackoff and Sasieni 1968; Sugrue 1980), an assumption tested empirically by Beeston (1983) and Sugrue (1977),

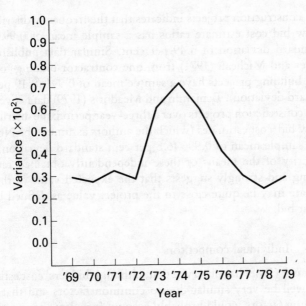

Fig. 7.1 Variance over time

the latter's chi-square test failing to reject the Normal assumption for sixty-eight road low bid/cost estimate ratios. A slightly different version by Sasieni *et al.* (1959) considers the ratios $(B - K)/K$, where B is the winning bid and K the cost estimate, to also follow a Normal distribution.

Weverbergh (1977) has considered, in some detail, two possible procedures, maximum likelihood and an iterative minimum mean square error procedure, for estimating two parameters of the joint distribution of estimated costs and lowest opposing bids. It was concluded that the minimum mean square error method compared favourably with maximum likelihood estimation, although the method of maximum likelihood was particularly appropriate in estimating parameters of multivariate Lognormal distributions, as would be expected. An unfortunate aspect of this study was that both methods resulted in considerable estimation errors, especially for medium-sized samples (Weverbergh 1977: 197), although it was considered that with 'fairly good' a priori knowledge of the parameters of the marginal distribution of estimated costs, estimation of the remaining parameters of the joint distribution would be much easier and more efficient.

Three sets of data have been published which allow some analysis. Broemser's (1968) data from one contractor bidding for seventy-six

169

USA construction projects indicates that the frequency distribution of low bid/cost estimate ratios has a sample mean of 0.993 with a standard deviation of 5.49 per cent. Similar data published by Shaffer and Micheau (1971) from one contractor bidding for fifty USA building projects have a sample mean of 0.991 (8.19 per cent standard deviation). Benjamin and Meador's (1979) data covers 131 USA construction projects over a three-year period: the distribution of low bid/cost estimates (which the authors assume to be Normal) has a sample mean of 0.996 (6.8 per cent standard deviation). The similarity of the means of these independently obtained ratios is striking and strongly suggests that the expected value of the cost estimate may be quite close to the project value as defined by the lowest bid.

Individual competitors

Broemser (1968) has observed that, although bidders' cost estimates may well be very similar due to common factors and that these common factors would probably account for a large proportion of the volume of the job, the things that would be different among contractors would be the management skills in planning and using labour, materials, equipment and sub-contractors. In addition, the bids depend upon the competitors' mark-up which will reflect the bidding policies which are chosen to achieve their own objectives (Mercer and Russell 1969). It follows, therefore, that every competitor will exhibit different bidding characteristics; some bid consistently high, some bid consistently low, some spread their bids uniformly over a wide range and some may bid within fairly well-defined and narrow limits (Park 1972: 24–7). Differences in level of bid (i.e. consistently high or consistently low) have been termed 'proximity' differences (Skitmore 1981b), said to reflect the relative efficiency (McCaffer 1976a) or 'competitive advantage' of competitors. Competitive advantage, according to Fuerst (1977), includes differences between the methods used, the efficiency and availability of equipment, ownership of supply sources, proximity to home office or sites of current contracts, and managerial skill in performing the work. Both policy-dictated mark-up decisions and competitive advantage have been modelled as random variables (Mercer and Russell 1969; Fuerst 1977).

Several researchers have modelled individual bids, starting with Friedman (1956) and including Taylor (1963) and Morin and Clough (1969). The approaches are similar to that of modelling competitors collectively in that competitors' bid/cost estimate ratios are obtained and probability density functions fitted to the ensuing frequency distributions (Friedman 1956; Taylor 1963; Benjamin 1972, for instance). Beeston (1982) has suggested using D ratios, in a similar manner to Sasieni, Yaspan and Friedman, where D = {(lowest bid) − estimated cost)/estimated cost} expressed as a percentage. Morin and Clough (1969), on the other hand, have used the relative frequencies of competitors' bid/cost estimate to own bid/cost estimate ratios.

While all of the distribution parameters postulated for collective models necessarily apply to individual bidders, some modellers have proposed probability distributions specifically for the individual case. Griesmer et al. (1967) assume bidders draw from a Uniform distribution unique to each, and Winkler and Brookes (1980) have proposed models in which differing amounts of information (i.e. different variances) exist between bidders. Capen et al. (1971), Curtis and Maines (1973) and Fuerst (1977) have attempted to derive parameter estimates for each bidder by simulation techniques. Weverbergh (1982) has used a multivariate technique to estimate parameters of coalition bidding for oil leases, assuming the winning bid to be a constant. Skitmore (1982) has proposed a multivariate approach to a part of the parameter estimation problem, involving the solution of two sets of simultaneous equations to determine the variances and the relative means of the log transformation of bid values. This approach was later developed into an iterative technique for the analysis of some live data (Skitmore 1986). Multivariate methods, however, often rely on the assumption of independence between bidders.

The independence assumption

Most modellers since Friedman (1956) assume that errors in an individual bidder's cost estimates are independent of errors in previous cost estimates (within bidders) and also independent of errors in other bidders' cost estimates (between bidders). This assumption has also been generously applied to bids within and between bidders and also the true cost or actual cost/cost estimate and bid/cost estimate ratios. True or actual cost/estimated cost interactions have already been discussed. The way in which competitors behave in bidding may be influenced by several factors. These factors are considered to be those associated with the project decision environment. The effects of collusion are treated separately.

The project decision environment

Several models have been proposed which incorporate features of the project-generating environment in order to utilise any error trends within bidders. Park (1980), for instance, has suggested that models of competitors' bids should incorporate the effects of changes in market conditions and Whittaker (1970), in using a discounted cash-flow technique for the time element, has adjusted the assumption that past bidding behaviour of competitors is a good indicator of future behaviour to take account of the state of the market. Carr and Sandahl (1978) have used multiple regression analysis (MRA) to predict the lowest bid of any competitor by incorporating a variable representing the 'economic environment'. Neufville *et al.* (1977) have found 'economic conditions' to be an important factor affecting bidding behaviour.

Project characteristics have also been recommended as predictor variables (Christenson 1965; Broemser 1968; Benjamin 1972; Neufville *et al.* 1977; Sugrue 1977; Carr and Sandahl 1978; Morin and Clough 1969). Relationships with the class of construction have been postulated (Shaffer and Micheau 1971; Cooke 1981), Morin and Clough (1969) finding the ratios of bids by one contractor to cost estimates by another contractor to have a mean of 1.133, 1.232 and 1.333 for three classes of work. The influence of project size on bidding behaviour has been analysed by McCaffer (1976a), who found no correlations, Harvey (1979), whose MRA attempt to predict low bid/engineers' estimate ratios from variables including job size and Lange (1973) who found a sharp drop in his SECLOW quantities (the percentage difference between the lowest and the second lowest bidders) associated with the size of 451 Massachusetts projects. An analysis by Neufville *et al.* (1977) also found the size of project to be important. Pelto (1971) has fitted a complicated function to bidding data (for oil tracts) involving project location, a variable also used in Harvey's MRA. Surprisingly no studies have been documented using the client as a predictor variable.

Several writers have considered the effect of competitors. The number of bidders has been associated with the distribution of bids by McCaffer (1976a) (inconclusively) and Pelto (1971) in his model. Benjamin (1969) and Harvey (1979) have also used the number of bidders as a predictor variable in their MRAs, although Broemser (1968), in a similar study, found the number of bidders to be of no statistical significance in his regression model for predicting the distribution of low bids. Carr and Sandahl (1978) include the 'make-up of competitors' in their MRA to predict low bids.

172

A further discussion on the effect of the number and identity of bidders is provided later in this section.

Several researchers have considered the implications of each bidder adopting similar (non-random) strategies (Rothkopf 1969; Oren and Rothkopf 1975; Banerjee and Ghosh 1969, for instance). While some results of theoretical importance have been obtained, they only apply under certain restrictive assumptions. Some of these assumptions are of significance in the construction bidding situation for, as has been observed, when considering a competitor's reaction to a bidder's new strategy, the degree of reaction will probably depend on the number of institutional factors not represented by the model, including the speed and certainty with which competitors can discern a policy change and the extent to which the competitors in one auction are likely to be the same as those in the succeeding auctions (Oren and Rothkopf 1975: 1088).

Some evidence also exists which indicates that likely outcomes have a bearing on competitors' behaviour. In Sheldon's (1982) investigations in the process plant industry, nine managers stated that each contract was unique, hence information relating to past contracts would only be of use if each firm offered homogeneous equipment and technologies, and if contracts were undertaken at similar sites in similar conditions. The conclusion of most firms was that evidence on past bidding patterns was too difficult to quantify. It is interesting to note, however, that whatever information was available was used by these organisations. Sugrue (1977) has also examined the effect of union labour on the distribution of low bid/cost estimate ratios for his sixty-eight road projects. No differences were found between the unionised and non-unionised projects in this respect.

The degrading effects of time have been accommodated in Morin and Clough's (1969) model by weighting the more recent data. A similar weighting was also applied to the bids of those competitors who most frequently competed for the same projects.

The association of bids with aspects of the decision environment has clearly been of interest to researchers in the field. The use of multivariate analyses would seem to be particularly appropriate in examining potential correlations between bids and likely character-istics of the project-generating and outcome environments. Little consensus is apparent as yet on the impact of any of the predictor variables employed except perhaps project size, which has received frequent attention. Further work on this aspect of the problem would appear to be desirable. Indeed, one of the most important directions for future research in the competitive bidding area is in the development of satisfactory multivariate statistical models to predict the behaviour of the competition in the bidding situation (Benjamin 1972: 328).

Collusion

All of the models consulted rely on the assumption that no collaboration takes place between the bidders. However, as Mitchell (1977) has pointed out, in any real-life bidding situation, there are many complicating factors, not least the possibility of collusion.

Sheldon (1982) has examined the aspect of collusion in some detail. In view of the uncertainty of competitive bidding and the degree of interdependence between firms engendered by such uncertainty, Sheldon holds that bidding may be conducted a priori through collusive agreements. He considers that such agreements would be an attractive means of maintaining a steady flow of work and achieving higher joint, risk-adjusted, discounted profits. Little evidence of collusive agreements seems to be available, however, which is perhaps to be expected. Sheldon's view of the process plant industry is that the variety of process areas in contracting and also periodic excess capacity would be a destabilising factor in any such agreements. Barriers to entry of the industry are also discussed but it is concluded that the ability of firms to actually raise bid prices in excess of an average cost is a function of the buyer's sensitivity to price and nonprice factors in a bid, rather than a function of the barriers to entry, and hence the ability of firms to actually limit prices is curtailed by the buyer's power. Insofar as the construction industry is concerned, collusive bidding seems even less likely than in the process plant industry as barriers to entry are far less severe and the proliferation of projects is extensive, especially small projects. Collusion, if practised at all in the construction industry, must surely be restricted to a very limited number of specialised projects.

A more realistic proposition is that correlations exist between bidders due to some commonality between companies. Common training, experience and information (Winkler and Brookes 1980), particularly in a localised construction context (Stark and Mayer 1971), support the view that positive correlations seem to be more appropriate than negative correlations (Winkler and Brookes 1980). The very mechanism of the data-generating process, where

174

cost estimates are drawn independently, providing a basis for assessing competitors' bids, implies a dependence of some kind (Weverbergh 1981).

Flanagan and Norman's (1982) analysis of bids entered by three construction companies for thirty-nine county council projects found a discernible trend between specific contractors when bidding in competition, and that this trend can be expected to vary with different types of work, with work of different value ranges, or as a result of varying workloads of the contractors. An empirical analysis of sixty-eight USA road contracts, on the other hand, found no evidence of any correlation between bidders (Sugrue 1977).

Non-serious and unrealistic bids

Whittaker (1970), as a result of his interviews with several construction companies, reported that the management concerned stated that all bids were 'serious and competitive' and these were contracts that the company would have liked to win. McCaffer (1976a), however, who has some considerable experience in this field, has warned that some allowance may be needed for unrealistic bids in modelling competitors' bids.

One type of non-serious bid is known as the 'cover price', where the bidder enters a bid the value of which is advised by a competitor. The Institute of Quantity Surveyors (IQS) Sussex Branch (1979), in an opinion survey involving a few individuals earning their living in preparing bills of quantities, estimates, managing contracts and business, found that cover prices are taken notwithstanding attempts to prevent the practice, adding that the responses showed a marked unanimity. The report concluded, however, that the cover prices did not distort market prices. Daniels (1978), in describing the work of the Builders' Conference, revealed that bidders admitted to the use of cover prices because of the cost of bidding, the high risk of losing, not wishing to offend and the short period allowed for building preparation. Moyles (1973) has suggested that, because of these constraints, contractors will usually give detailed attention only to desirable contracts, the remainder being prepared in a more approximate manner with a risk allowance to cover for unforeseen circumstances and for the less accurate method of estimating. Indeed, discussions at a conference entitled 'Estimating, the Way Ahead' (1979), organised by the *Building Trades Journal*, openly revealed the practice of taking such cover prices, discussing alternative methods of acquiring such prices.

The methods adopted by researchers in discounting these non-bona-fide bids have been inconsistent. Southwell's attempts (1971) to model bid sets simply excludes non serious bids without further comment. Franks (1970), in comparing the variability of students' estimates with bids obtained for several 'live' projects, arbitrarily excludes the upper of 20 per cent of bids as being probably non-serious. Morrison and Stevens (1980) have considered excluding the highest two bids in each set, while Whittaker's analysis (1970) of 153 contracts excluded all bids exceeding the average bid by a factor of 6 and any obviously abnormal sets (for instance, where one bid was more than 21 per cent higher than the next highest bid) were eliminated. Whittaker also imposed an additional restriction by including only the bids which satisfied the condition

$$(\text{highest bid} - \text{lowest bid})/\text{mean bid} \quad \leqslant 24\%$$

Pim (1974), on the other hand, along with the majority of bidding strategists, does not advocate rejecting bids that look 'wrong', although he suggests excluding bids his own firm know to be wrong because of arithmetical or judgemental errors.

McCaffer (1976a) claims to have discovered the presence of outliers during the performance of the Anderson–Darling test, due to the formation of unexpectedly long tails in the analysis. Since his data appeared to have been drawn from a general Normal distribution, a test developed by Grubbs (1950) is recommended. The test, however, has been criticised as inappropriate in this case, as the sample sizes are too small and that the presence of outliers is more likely to be indicative of a wrongly assumed shape parameter than an 'unrealistic' bid (Skitmore 1981a).

Johnston (1978), far from eliminating suspect bids, considers them to be of great importance and, in calculating skewness, has suggested a possible correlation with the industry's workload. Analysis by Skitmore (1981a) of a different set of data has rejected Johnston's findings.

A further reason for retaining the so-called 'unrealistic' bids is that some companies have been found to have quite distinct bidding behaviour, and what appears to be an unrealistic bid may be a genuine one in some cases. In any event, non-serious bidders are not likely to have any effect on low-bid models (Weverbergh 1981; Beeston 1983). It is concluded, therefore, that, in the absence of any reliable predictor of known non-serious bids, it would be advisable to retain all bids in the model.

Data limitations

A major criticism of models of competitors' bidding behaviour is based on the difficulty in obtaining the necessary data. Friedman's (1956) model is particularly susceptible to this criticism, demanding, as it does, the collection of bid/cost estimate ratios against each competitor in order to construct a frequency distribution of sufficient dimensions to enable a probability density function to be fitted. Such a quantity of data does not seem to be generally available in the construction industry (Grinyer and Whittaker 1973), a difficulty considered by some to bring into question the entire applicability of bidding models in the industry (Cooke 1981: 61). The situation deteriorates further when considering combinations of specified competitors due to the reduced amount of data available (Beeston 1983) to assess the joint probability distribution of each possible sub-set of competitors, 2^n for n competitors (Christenson 1965). Added to this are the typical characteristics of the construction bidding situation in that past histories of bidding behaviour are relatively short and only a small number of potential competitors participate in a particular contract (Weverbergh 1981). It is not surprising to find that the experience of the contractor studies seems to indicate that it is of little value to try and estimate the distribution of the bid–cost ratios of known competitors as there are relatively few competitors who are bid against often enough to provide sufficient information to estimate these distributions with any confidence (Benjamin 1972: 328). A further difficulty that has been encountered is that not all (if any) competitors may be known for a project.

Data difficulties and unknown competitors have been anticipated by Friedman's (1956) collective competitors model, termed 'the average bidder', where all competitors are assumed to behave in a similar manner, that is, their bids are considered to be drawn from identical distributions. The majority of empirical studies rely on the collective competitors model, the individual competitor model being restricted to competitors encountered most frequently ('key' competitors), mainly due to the extreme difficulties involved in obtaining stable parameter estimates for individual competitors (see Capen *et al.* 1971; Curtis and Maines 1973; Fuerst 1977, for instance).

Apart from resorting to modelling the distribution of low bids, with the accompanying loss of information, only two approaches appear to be feasible. The first is to use the collective competitor model on the assumption that competing bidders do behave in a similar manner, and the second is to adopt a multivariable approach along the lines of Weverbergh (1982) and Skitmore (1986). There are some grounds for accepting the first approach to be reasonable for although for some companies quite distinct bidding behaviour in terms of mean and spread are found, pooling of companies into 'average competitors' does not seem to be a major cause of bias: for many companies, behaviour is sufficiently similar (Weverbergh 1982: 26). In the context of the bidding problem, it would seem that differences in spread are of more concern than differences in mean (Weverbergh 1982: 62). Insofar as the second approach is concerned, data can be collected on all contracts irrespective of whether the collector enters a bid or not, thereby reducing the informational problems of the univariate approach normally employed. Success is not guaranteed, however, for naive approaches based on pairwise independence and assuming univariate analyses are inevitably quite unreliable. Even using multivariate methods, differences in bidding behaviour are not easy to detect (Weverbergh 1982).

Project acquisition

The allocation of projects by potential clients depends on the client's allocation criteria which may include such factors as price, speed, quality, reliability, flexibility and control. These criteria determine the global procurement methods chosen (such as traditional, design and build, or management contract), the construction companies to be involved, and the value of the project. It is generally assumed that the price of the project is the client's main interest and, in the majority of cases, this is reflected in the competitive traditional approach where the lowest bidder is awarded the project. Such an approach is not the universal practice, however. There are instances of projects being awarded to construction companies offering shorter durations or, directly or indirectly, greater reliability, better quality and greater financial security. On some occasions the second or even third lowest bidder has been known to acquire the project. One reason for this is the view that the lowest bidder may have entered a 'suicidally' low bid due to, perhaps, some gross deficiency in his cost estimate. Cauwelaert and Heynig's (1978) 'Belgian' solution proposes a method of identifying such low bids in order to avoid allocating projects to these bidders.

Simmonds (1968a) has proposed a method of modelling the various features offered by the company in its attempt to acquire a new project in terms of mark-up or mark-up equivalent. By this method, non-price features relative to competitors are evaluated subjectively for their likely effect on project acquisition.

Very little evidence appears to be available on the impact of non-price features and the allocation of project to bidders other than those entering the lowest bid. Benjamin's (1969) analysis of 125 construction projects found only one case of a project being awarded to anyone other than the lowest bidder.

Factors affecting the likelihood of entering the lowest bid

The competitive pressures in the construction industry, it has been said, are probably more intense than any other industry (Park 1972: 24.1). In the presence of such competition it is not altogether surprising to find that judging from the attitudes of some companies, competitive bidding does not result in competition based upon costs or profit margins, but actually produces a lottery in which the inherent uncertainty of the process decides the winner (Whittaker 1970). Indeed, McCaffer (1976a) has found substantial evidence that existing bidding processes are little more than random. Pim's (1974) analysis of the number of projects awarded to four construction companies indicates that the average number of projects acquired is generally the reciprocal of the average number of bidders competing, the proportion that would be expected to be won by 'chance' (Table 7.4).

Table 7.4 Frequency of low bids

Company	No. of Projects	No. of bids	Bids per project	% win by chance	% actually won
A	41	249	6.1	16.4	17.0
B	36	183	7.0	14.2	15.4
C	19	88	4.6	21.6	21.1
D	35	202	5.8	21.6	17.1

Source: Pim (1974: 541).

This would suggest an extremely simple model in which the probability P of entering the lowest bid is the reciprocal of n, the total number of bidders. The value of n, however, may not be known with certainty but may, as has been discussed earlier, itself be modelled by a probability density function, say $f(n)$.

Research by Broemser (1968), however, indicates that n is not significantly correlated with P, although many consider n to be a very important factor (Park 1962, for instance).

Empirical attempts to link other factors with P have also met with limited success. Gates (1967) and McCaffer (1976a), for instance, have examined (inconclusively) the influence of project size, and Broemser's (1968) MRA using several predictor variables was unable to explain most of the variance, concluding that he expected most of the remaining variance, i.e. the standard error of 5.18 per cent, was due to the difference between cost estimates.

A great deal of attention has centred at the theoretical level on the actions of individual competitors, information about which has been regarded as 'critical' (Griesmer *et al*. 1967). Most models implicitly require the analyst to develop probability distributions for any competitor's bid (Neufville *et al*. 1977), which means that the model builder is faced with the problem of explicating probability laws for opposing bids (Weverbergh 1981). Carr (1982) has shown that differences in assumptions of the spreads of opposing bids can have significant effects on results, although asymmetric information (different spreads) produces a 'very messy' theory (Klein 1976). Edelmann (1965) and Flanagan and Norman (1982) have, nevertheless, derived a matrix of award probabilities for each bidder.

In recognition of the informational difficulties, Park (1966) has suggested considering individual competitors when six or less are present and Morin and Clough (1969) have used the 'key' competitor analysis for those competitors encountered in at least 40 per cent of bidding situations.

The most popular factor that has been associated with P is the difference between the bid and cost estimate, commonly termed the 'mark-up', as this represents the underlying assumption of bidding theory in that for each marginal change of mark-up there is a corresponding change in the probability (P) of success (Cooke 1981: 61).

The probability (P) of entering the lowest bid as a function of mark-up

It has been assumed that a company may estimate the prior probability of P for a 'particular bid', this probability being determined from the company's expectations of its competitors' bids. It follows, therefore, that P will vary continuously with the amount bid which may be varied almost continuously (Benjamin 1969). Edelmann's (1965) model relies on the intuitive assessment of the value of P as a function of the bid. An alternative approach has been to fit a curve to the percentage cumulative observed rate of bidding success for a given cost plus a percentage mark-up (Benson 1970). Friedman (1956) has suggested that a value for P for a particular project can be estimated by combining the probabilities of underbidding each individual competitor. Friedman's model has been described many times, probably the most cogent description being that of Fuerst (1976):

Assume for a letting under consideration that the bid of each competitor, C_i, $i = 1, \ldots, n$, is independently drawn from g_i ($b_i \mid c$) – a probability density function of the bid of C_i, conditional upon the actual cost, c. Also, any competitor winning the contract is assumed to have the same actual cost. Therefore

$$P(C_1 \text{wins}) = \int_{b_1=0}^{\infty} g_1(b_1) \int_{b_2=b_1}^{\infty} g_2(b_2) \ldots \int_{b_n=b_1}^{\infty} g_n(b_n) db_n \ldots db_2, db_1$$

in which, for notational ease, g_i (b_i) has been written for g_i ($b_i \mid c$)

(Fuerst 1976: 174)

If bidder C_1's bid is replaced by cost estimate c_1, plus a mark-up m, then the above becomes

$$P(C_1 \text{wins} \mid m) = \int_{c_1+m=0}^{\infty} f_1(c_1) + m. \int_{b_1=c_1+m}^{\infty} g_2(b_2) \ldots \int_{b_n=c_1+m}^{\infty} g_n(b_n) db_n \ldots db_2, dc_1$$

Friedman then advocates obtaining f_1 (c_1) and g_i (b_i) empirically, based on observations from past lettings, from the frequency distributions of actual cost/cost estimate and bid/cost estimate ratios respectively. However, as Fuerst (and others) observe, both a cost estimate and a competitor's bid should be considered random variables, and the density function of the ratio of two random variables is almost always complexly related to the density functions of the individual random variables. A further problem that occurs with the use of ratios is that, if the ratio of bids and cost estimates is to be considered as truly independent of the bids and cost estimates, then the ratio must always be constant, as proved by Rothkopf (1980).

Three alternative approaches appear to be available in circumventing these problems. One approach adopted by Grinyer and Whittaker (1973) assumes that the ratio of bids to average bids, for any project, forms a Uniform density function and then estimating, via a combination of managerial judgement and past data, the value of the mean of the density function for each contract to be bid. Grinyer and Whittaker's assumption of Uniformly distributed bids has, however, been rejected by McCaffer (1976a) on methodological grounds, as previously mentioned. McCaffer has also questioned the accuracy of prediction of the mean bid by this approach.

The second approach has been to utilise the distribution of low bids, irrespective of the identity of the bidders, by compiling a frequency distribution of low bid/cost estimate ratios. This approach, while overcoming the problems to some extent, suffers from informational loss, as already discussed. It has, however, been claimed to be increasingly beneficial as individual competitors' distributions differ (Weverbergh 1981: 19). This must clearly depend on the predictability of the identity of the individual competitors. Estimates of P based on the low bid distribution are likely to be rather poor in the absence of a consistently keen, but absent, competitor, for instance.

A third approach avoids the use of ratios entirely in estimating function parameters by a multivariate technique (Skitmore 1986). The advantage of this approach is that it avoids the usual problems associated with ratios by dealing with the log values of the bid and cost estimate variables, thus enabling these variables to be handled separately. Some aspects of this approach are examined in the Appendix.

A further difficulty that arises with the Friedman model is that bids, as has been discussed, are not expected to be independent, for several reasons. No models have been proposed, however, to deal with this problem in situations where more than two bidders are involved.

Two theoretical conclusions are of interest concerning the Friedman model. First, where symmetric information exists (identical functions) for all competitors, a value of P can be estimated by order statistics (Curtis and Maines 1973; McCaffer 1976a; Klein 1976; Mitchell 1977, for instance); and secondly, it has been shown that, under certain restrictive conditions, the expected value of the winning bid is surely equal to the true value of the contract (Wilson 1979; Milgrom 1981, for instance).

Summary and conclusions

This chapter has examined in some detail the possibility of simplifying some aspects of the project selection decision by means of statistical models. The frequency distribution of the size of the project opportunities has been found to be Exponential in one case and Log–Log–Normal in another, and the work content of the projects modelled as a series of random variables. A Poisson model has been proposed to model the distribution of the number of competitors involved and several linear models have been devised to predict the number of competitors. A linear model and a predictive technique termed the multidistribution model (MD) have been used to predict the identity of competitors and further models have been developed which purport to give the probability of certain competitors being present in a project-bidding situation.

Actual and estimated costs have been extensively modelled stochastically, the degree of independence between these two variables being a major debate. Individual aspects of costs and estimated costs have been considered amenable to statistical modelling, including labour, materials, subcontractors, quantity-related costs, weather and seasons, costs of estimating and additional costs. Many proposals have been reviewed defining the nature of cost distributions and these are summarised in Table 7.2.

Relatively little attention has been paid to modelling project income in a statistical manner, except that a Beta distribution has been applied to cash flows.

The bidding behaviour of competitors, both collectively and individually, has been the subject of many statistical models, the distributional characteristics of which are summarised in Table 7.3. Some possible effects of market conditions have been noted. The distribution of low bids in relation to cost estimates has also been treated in a similar manner, a Normal probability density function often being considered appropriate. An interesting result arising from the analysis of three sets of published data indicates the expected value of low bid/cost estimate ratios to be approximately unity.

The behaviour of individual competitors has been modelled separately in some cases. The assumption that the behaviour of bidders is independent of events, including the actions of competitors, 'economic conditions', type and possibly size of project and location, has been questioned as being an oversimplification although little evidence appears to be available to determine the significance of this. The use of MRA has been recommended in identifying correlations of these events with individual bids.

The possibility of collusion has also been discussed and is considered to be rarely practised in the construction industry. It is thought, however, that a subverted form of collusion may exist because of commonalities between companies. Non-serious and unrealistic bids have also been considered for possible separate treatment with the conclusion that, in the absence of any identification procedures, such bids may be more fruitfully retained in any general analysis.

Data limitations appear to be severe except for collective competitors, low bids and certain key competitors. A multivariate technique, however, has been proposed which may alleviate the problem.

Project allocation has been considered to depend on many possible client-controlled factors and a method has been reviewed which aggregates these factors into a mark-up adjustment.

The effect of the mark-up on the probability (P) of entering the lowest bid has been found to be contained in a model first proposed by Friedman (1956). The model essentially requires some knowledge of the probability distribution of bids for each competitor and the probability distribution of actual/estimated costs of the decision-maker's organisation. The problems associated with bid/estimated cost and actual/estimated cost ratios indicate that an alternative approach may be required. The use of collective and low bid models has been considered and the multivariate approach again identified as a possible suitable alternative.

Statistical models would appear to be reasonable approximations of many aspects of the project decision environment, if only because of the volume of studies reported, only a sample of which have been reviewed in this chapter. Perhaps the most important aspect of the entire project decision system is whether a project is acquired or not, as this event will have a considerable impact on the state of the outcome environment, both initially and particularly over a period of time. The likelihood of project acquisition would seem, as has been seen, to be a strong candidate for modelling in a statistical manner in terms of the probability of entering the lowest bid for the project. An estimate of this probability, if it can be obtained with sufficient accuracy, could then be applied to the model states previously outlined by introducing a probabilistic element to those states of the model that have hitherto been regarded as conditional upon acquisition.

Appendix

1 Probability of entering the lowest bid

Let x_i represent a possible bid by the ith bidder for a project then, if the competition is modelled as the joint distribution of two or more variables, the probability that x_1 is the lowest bid is given by

$$\Pr\left(x_1 < x_i \text{ for all } i, \, i \neq 1\right) =$$

$$\int_{x_1=-\infty}^{\infty} \int_{x_2=x_1}^{\infty} \int_{x_3=x_1}^{\infty} \cdots \int_{x_n=x_1}^{\infty} f\left(x_1, \, x_2, \, x_3, \ldots, \, x_n\right) \, dx_n \cdots dx_3 \, dx_2 \, dx_1 \tag{1}$$

If the above, for instance, is a multivariate normal distribution, then

$$f(x_1, x_2, x_3, \ldots, x_n) =$$

$$dF = (2\pi)^{-1/2 \, (n)} \left|V^{-1}\right| \exp\left\{-\tfrac{1}{2} \left(\boldsymbol{x} - \boldsymbol{\mu_x}\right) V^{-1} \left(\boldsymbol{x} - \boldsymbol{\mu_x}\right)\right\} \Pi dx \tag{2}$$

(Kendall and Stuart 1963)

where $\boldsymbol{x}$ is the vector of $x_1, x_2, x_3, \ldots, x_n$
$\boldsymbol{\mu_x}$ is the vector of means for $x_1, x_2, x_3, \ldots, x_n$
$\boldsymbol{V}$ is the variance/co-variance matrix, e.g.:

$$\boldsymbol{V} = \begin{pmatrix} \sigma^2_1 & p\sigma_1\sigma_2 \\ p\sigma_1\sigma_2 & \sigma^2_2 \end{pmatrix} \text{ for the bivariate normal distribution}$$

Now assuming that the non-diagonal elements of $\boldsymbol{V}$ are zero, i.e. the variables are *independent* if normally distributed, it follows from (1) that

$$\Pr (x_1 < x_i \text{ for all } i, i \neq 1) =$$

$$\int_{-\infty}^{\infty} f_1 (x_1) . \left\{ \prod_{i=2}^{n} \int_{x_i=x_1}^{\infty} f_i (x_i) dx_i \right\} dx_1 \qquad (3)$$

In the case of the uniform (rectangular) distribution, it follows that

$$\Pr (x_1 < x_i, i \neq 1) = \int_{a_1}^{b_1} (b_1 - a_1)^{-1} \left\{ \prod_{i=2}^{n} \int_{x_i=x_1}^{b_i} (b_i - a_i)^{-1} dx_i \right\} dx_1 \qquad (4)$$

Similarly, in the case of the Normal distribution

$$\Pr (x_1 < x_i, i \neq 1) =$$

$$\int_{-\infty}^{\infty} \{(2\pi)^{1/2}\}^{-1} \exp (-\tfrac{1}{2}x^2_1) \left\{ \prod_{i=2}^{n} \int_{x_i = (\sigma_1 x_1 + \mu_1 - \mu_i) \sigma_i^{-1}}^{\infty} \{(2\pi)^{1/2}\}^{-1} \exp(-\tfrac{1}{2}x^2_i) dx_i \right\} dx_1 \qquad (5)$$

written in standard form.

And for the special case where $f_1 (x_1) = f_2 (x_2) = \ldots = f_n(x_n)$

$$\Pr (x_1 < x_i, i \neq 1) = n^{-1} \qquad (6)$$

It can be seen, therefore, for the case of the Normal distribution (Eqn 5), estimates of the parameters μ_i and σ_i are needed. These estimates, it is proposed, can be obtained by means of multivariate analysis as described below.

2 The distribution of bids values entered by each bidder

Skitmore (1982) has proposed the model

$$\ln (x_{ij}) = y_{ij} \ni Y_{ij} \sim f (\alpha_i + \beta_j, \sigma^2_i) \qquad (7)$$

where x_{ij} is bidder i's bid for project j ($i = 1, 2, \ldots, r$; $j = 1, 2, \ldots, c$) and x_{1j} is another bidder l's bid for project j ($l = 1, 2, \ldots, c$; $l \neq i$). Then, assuming bids are independent, estimates of the parameters in (7) may be obtained from

$$\bar{y}_i - \bar{y}_l \simeq \alpha_i - \alpha_i$$
$$s^2{}_i \simeq \sigma^2{}_i$$

by solving the two sets of equations:

$$E[Y_1] - E[Y_1] = \bar{z}_{11}$$
$$E[Y_1] - E[Y_2] = \bar{z}_{12}$$

$$\cdot \qquad \cdot$$
$$\cdot \qquad \cdot$$
$$\cdot \qquad \cdot$$

$$E[Y_1] - E[Y_r] = \bar{z}_{1r}$$

$$\cdot$$
$$\cdot$$
$$\cdot$$

$$E[Y_r] - E[Y_r] = \bar{z}_{rr}, \text{ and} \qquad\qquad (8)$$

$$\mathrm{Var}[Y_1] + \mathrm{Var}[Y_1] = s^2{}_{11}$$
$$\mathrm{Var}[Y_1] + \mathrm{Var}[Y_2] = s^2{}_{12}$$

$$\cdot \qquad \cdot$$
$$\cdot \qquad \cdot$$
$$\cdot \qquad \cdot$$

$$\mathrm{Var}[Y_1] + \mathrm{Var}[Y_r] = s^2{}_{1r}$$

$$\cdot \qquad \cdot$$
$$\cdot \qquad \cdot$$

$$\mathrm{Var}[Y_r] + \mathrm{Var}[Y_r] = s^2{}_{rr} \qquad\qquad (9)$$

where
$$z_{ilj} = (y_{ij} - y_{lj})$$

$$z_{il} = \frac{1}{n_{il}} \sum_{j=1}^{c} \sigma_{ilj} \, z_{ilj}$$

$$s^2{}_{il} = \frac{1}{(n_{il} - 1)} \sum_{j=i}^{c} \sigma_{ilj} \, (z_{ilj} - z_{il})^2$$

$$n_{il} = \sum_{j=1}^{c} \sigma_{ilj}$$

187

$\sigma_{ilj} = 1$ when bidders i and l both enter bids for project j, O otherwise

The problem can, theoretically, be solved by the standard regression procedure as follows.

Letting the event that bidder i bids against bidder l to be denoted by

$$W = \begin{pmatrix} 11 & 21 & \ldots & i1 & \ldots & r1 \\ 12 & 22 & \ldots & i2 & \ldots & r2 \\ \cdot & \cdot & & \cdot & & \cdot \\ \cdot & \cdot & & \cdot & & \cdot \\ 1l & 2l & \ldots & il & \ldots & rl \\ \cdot & \cdot & & \cdot & & \cdot \\ \cdot & \cdot & & \cdot & & \cdot \\ 1r & 2r & \ldots & ir & \ldots & rr \end{pmatrix}$$

which is indexed by:

$k = 1$ for W^{12},	$k = 2$ for W^{13},	$k = l - 1$ for W^{1l},	$k = r - 1$ for W^{1r}
$k = r$ for W^{23},	$k = r + 1$ for W^{24},	$k = r + l - 3$ for W^{2l},	$k = 2r - 3$ for W^{2r}
$k = 2r - 2$ for W^{34},	$k = 2r - 1$ for W^{35},	$k = 2r + l - 6$ for W^{3l},	$k = 3r - 6$ for W^{3r}

$$k = \left\{ (i-1)r - \sum_{p=1}^{i-1} p \right\} + 1 \text{ for } W^{i,i+1} \ldots k = \left\{ (i-1)r - \sum_{p=1}^{i-1} p \right\} + 1 \text{ for } W^{il}$$

$$k = ir - \sum_{p=1}^{i} p \text{ for } W^{ir}$$

$$n = k = \left\{ (r-1)r - \sum_{p=1}^{r} p \right\} \text{ for } W^{r-1,r}$$

Then if

$X_{kij} = 1$ when the event indexed by k occurs, which includes the lower numbered bidder i, on contract j, and

$X_{kij} = -1$ when the event indexed by k occurs, which includes the higher numbered bidder i, on contract j, otherwise

$X_{kij} = 0$

and z_{kj} is the difference in bids between the two bidders when
   event k occurs on contract j

The normal equations are

$$b_1X_{111} + b_2X_{121} + b_3X_{131} + \ldots + b_rX_{1r1} = z_{11}$$
$$b_1X_{211} + b_2X_{221} + b_3X_{231} + \ldots + b_rX_{2r1} = z_{21}$$

$$b_1X_{k11} + b_2X_{k21} + b_3X_{k31} + \ldots + b_rX_{kr1} = z_{k1}$$

$$b_1X_{m11} + b_2X_{m21} + b_3X_{m31} + \ldots + b_rX_{mr1} = z_{m1}$$
....
$$b_1X_{112} + b_2X_{122} + b_3X_{132} + \ldots + b_rX_{1r2} = z_{12}$$
$$b_1X_{212} + b_2X_{222} + b_3X_{232} + \ldots + b_rX_{2r2} = z_{22}$$

$$b_1X_{k12} + b_2X_{k22} + b_3X_{k32} + \ldots + b_rX_{kr2} = z_{k2}$$

$$b_1X_{m12} + b_2X_{m22} + b_3X_{m32} + \ldots + b_rX_{mr1} = z_{m2}$$
....

....
$$b_1X_{11c} + b_2X_{12c} + b_3X_{13c} + \ldots + b_rX_{1rc} = z_{1c}$$
$$b_1X_{21c} + b_2X_{22c} + b_3X_{23c} + \ldots + b_rX_{2rc} = z_{2c}$$

$$b_1X_{k1c} + b_2X_{k2c} + b_3X_{k3c} + \ldots + b_rX_{krc} = z_{kc}$$

$$b_1X_{m1c} + b_2X_{m2c} + b_3X_{m3c} + \ldots + b_rX_{mrc} = z_{mc}$$

Estimates of $E[Y_1]$, $E[Y_2]$, ... will therefore be provided by the vector

$$B = C^{-1} D$$

where

$$B = \begin{pmatrix} b_1 \\ b_2 \\ \cdot \\ \cdot \\ \cdot \\ b_r \end{pmatrix} \qquad D = \begin{pmatrix} \sum\limits_k^m \sum\limits_j^c X_{k1j}\, z_{kj} \\ \sum\limits_k \sum\limits_j X_{k2j}\, z_{kj} \\ \cdot \\ \cdot \\ \cdot \\ \sum\limits_k \sum\limits_j X_{krj}\, Z_{kj} \end{pmatrix}$$

$$C = \begin{pmatrix} \sum\limits_k^m \sum\limits_j^c X^2_{k1j} & \sum\limits_k \sum\limits_j X_{k1j} X_{k2j} & \ldots & \sum\limits_k \sum\limits_j X_{k1j} X_{krj} \\ \sum\limits_k \sum\limits_j X_{k2j} X_{k1j} & \sum\limits_k \sum\limits_j X^2_{k2j} & \ldots & \sum\limits_k \sum\limits_j X_{k2j} X_{krj} \\ \cdot & \cdot & & \cdot \\ \cdot & \cdot & & \cdot \\ \cdot & \cdot & & \cdot \\ \sum\limits_k \sum\limits_j X_{krj} X_{k1j} & \sum\limits_k \sum\limits_j X_{krj} X_{k2j} & \ldots & \sum\limits_k \sum\limits_j X_{krj}^2 \end{pmatrix} \quad (10)$$

And the variance of b_1 is estimated by

$$\text{Var } b_1 = \frac{S^2}{N - r}\, c^{ii}$$

where $S^2 = \sum\limits_k^m \sum\limits_j^c \{z_{kj} - (b_1 X_{k1j} + b_2 X_{k2j} + \ldots + b_r X_{krj})\}^2$

and N is the total number of paired observations.

The major difficulty with this approach is in the sparseness of the matrix system. In each row (in Eqn 10) there are $r-2$ empty cells. Afifi and Elashoff (1966) have reviewed the literature on the problem of handling multivariate data with observations missing for some or all of the variables under study, noting that the estimation problems can often be simplified if the missing data follows certain patterns. Hocking and Smith (1968) have used estimates of parameters from one part of a (multivariate normal) data structure to insert into the other parts prior to using an iterative procedure. Elman (1982) has considered the use of direct and iterative methods of solving large sparse non-symmetric systems of linear equations, finding difficulties with direct methods due to the factoring process generating many more non-zeros than the coefficient matrix, thereby increasing the computational storage size needed. A further problem is that the number of arithmetic operations could become excessive. His general conclusion is that '. . . although progress has been made in the development of orderings for the unknowns that decrease the complexity of directness for solving sparse problems . . . many large sparse problems cannot be solved by direct methods on present day computers'.

The type and structure of data normally available for building projects suggests that Elman's view is likely to be particularly pertinent in the bidding situation. The extreme sparseness of bidding data, in the proportion cr to $c(r - 2)$, produces results severely distorted by computational rounding errors. An iterative procedure has been found to be a more appropriate approach.

3 The iterative procedure

The model, from Eqn (7), is

$$y_{ij} = \alpha_i + \beta_j + \epsilon_{ij} \tag{11}$$

where ϵ_{ij} is $f(o, \sigma^2_i)$

(note that $y_{ij} - y_{lj} = \alpha_i - \alpha_l + \epsilon_{ij} - \epsilon_{il}$, where $\epsilon_{ij} - \epsilon_{il}$ is $f(o, \sigma^2_i + \sigma^2_l)$ and that, although appropriate for differences, Eqn (11) retains more information).

Assuming $f(o, \sigma^2_i)$ is $N(o, \sigma^2_i)$

y_{ij} has a pdf $\dfrac{1}{\sigma^2_i} \exp\left\{ - \dfrac{1}{2\sigma^2_i} (y_{ij} - \alpha_i - \beta_j)^2 \right\}$

The log-likelihood is

$$\ln L = - \sum_{i=1}^{r} (n_i/2)\ln \sigma^2_i - 1/2 \sum_{i=1}^{r} (1/\sigma^2_i) \sum_{j=1}^{c} \delta_{ij} (y_{ij} - \alpha_i - \beta_j)^2$$

191

where Kroneka's $\delta_{ij} = 1$ if bidder i bids for project j
$\qquad\qquad\qquad = 1$ if bidder i does not bid for project j

$n_i = \sum\limits_{j=1}^{c} \delta_{ij}$ = number of bids made by bidder i

The MLL over α's, β's and σ^2 is

$$\frac{\delta \ln L}{\delta \beta j} = \sum\limits_{i=1}^{r} \delta_{ij}(\gamma_{ij} - \alpha_i - \beta_j)/\sigma^2_i = 0$$

$$\lozenge \quad \beta_j = \sum\limits_{i=1}^{r} \delta_{ij}(\gamma_{ij} - \alpha_i)/n_i \qquad\qquad (12)$$

$$\frac{\delta \ln L}{\delta \alpha i} = (1/\sigma^2_i) \sum\limits_{j=1}^{c} \delta_{ij}(\gamma_{ij} - \alpha_i - \beta_j) = 0$$

$$\lozenge \quad \alpha_i = \sum\limits_{j=1}^{c} \delta_{ij}(\gamma_{ij} - \beta_j)/n_i \qquad\qquad (13)$$

$$\frac{\delta \ln L}{\delta \sigma^2_i} = \frac{-n_i}{2\sigma^2_i} + \frac{1}{2\sigma^{4i}} \sum\limits_{j=1}^{c} \delta_{ij}(\gamma_{ij} - \alpha_i - \beta_j)^2$$

$$\lozenge \quad \sigma^2_i = \frac{1}{n_i} \sum\limits_{j=1}^{c} \delta_{ij}(\gamma_{ij} - \alpha_i - \beta_j)^2$$

The procedure is to initialise all $\alpha_i = 0$ and iterate equations (12) and (13) to convergence. The estimates of σ^2_i may be adjusted for bias by the approximation

$$\sigma^{2\prime}_i = \sigma^2_i \left\{ \frac{n_i}{(n_i - 1)\ \dfrac{(1 - C - 1)}{(\ \ \overline{N - r})}} \right\}$$

where $N = \sum\limits_{j=1}^{c} n_i$, the total number of observations

Once-only bidders ($n_i = 1$) can be assigned an 'average' variance estimate

$$s^2_i = \sum\limits_{j} \sum\limits_{i} \delta_{ij}(\gamma_{ij} - \beta_j - \alpha_i)^2/(N - c - r + 1)$$

References

Ackoff, R I and Sasieni, M 1968 *Competitive problems of operations research.* John Wiley, New York, ch. 13.

Adam, J H 1965 *Longman concise dictionary of business English.* Longman York Press, ISBN 0 582 84221 2.

Adams, J S 1963 Towards an understanding of inequality. *Journal of Abnormal and Social Psychology* **67**: 422–36.

Adler, I 1963 *Probability and statistics for everyman.* Dobson Books Ltd.

Adrian, J J 1973 Estimating and building. In *Quantitative methods in construction management.* American Elsevier Publishing Co, ch. 8. ISBN 0 444 00134 4.

Afifi, A A and Elashoff, R M (1966) Missing observations in multi variate statistics: 1 review of the literature. *American Statistical Association Journal* **61**: 595–606.

Agnew, R A 1972 Sequential bid selection by stochastic approximation. *Naval Research Logistics Quarterly* **19**: 137–43.

Aguilar, I F J 1967 *Scanning the business environment.* Macmillan, New York.

AICBOR (Associated Industrial Consultants Limited and Business Operations Research Limited) 1967 *Report of the joint consulting team on serial contracting for road construction.* Ministry of Transport.

Alderfer, C P 1972 *Existence, relatedness and growth: human needs in organisational settings.* Free Press, New York.

Alexander, A B 1970 *What price estimating accuracy?* Paper 534, Metal Fabricating Institute, Rockford, Illinois.

Allison, G T 1971 *The essence of a decision: explaining the Cuban missile crisis.* Little Brook, Boston.

Alpert, M and Raiffa, H 1969 *A progress report on the training of probability assessors.* Harvard University Graduate School of Business Administration.

Andrew, J 1973 What is our business, and what should it be? *Building Technology and Management* **11**(9): 18.

Andrews, K R 1980 *The concept of corporate strategy* 2nd edn. R D Irwin.

Ansoff, H I 1965 *Corporate strategy.* Penguin.

Ansoff, H I 1979 *Strategic management.* Macmillan. ISBN 0 333 19686 4.

Ansoff, H I 1984 *Implanting strategic management.* Prentice-Hall International. ISBN 0 13 451808 X.

Argenti, J 1974 *Systematic corporate planning.* Nelson.

Argyris, C 1957 *Personality and organisation*. Harper and Row, New York.

Argyris, C 1960 *Understanding organisation behavior*. Dorsey Press.

Aris, R 1978 *Mathematical modelling techniques*. Pitman.

Armstrong, K 1972 *The development and appraisal of a computerised estimating system*. MSc thesis, Loughborough University of Technology.

Arps, J J 1965 A strategy for sealed bidding. *Journal of Petroleum Technology* **17**: 1033–9.

Ashworth, A 1977 *Regression analysis for building contractors. An assessment of its potential*. MSc thesis, Loughborough University of Technology.

Ashworth, A and Skitmore, R M 1983 *Accuracy in estimating*. Occasional paper 27, Chartered Institute of Building. ISBN 0 906600 57 X.

Atkins, K J 1975 *Bidding, finance and cash flow in the construction industry*. PhD thesis, University of Bradford.

Atkinson, J W 1957 Motivational determinants of risk-taking behavior. *Psychological Review* **64**: 359–72.

Bacarreza, R R 1973 *The construction project mark up decision under conditions of uncertainty*. PhD dissertation, Stanford University.

Bahrami H 1981 *Design of corporate planning systems*. PhD thesis, University of Aston in Birmingham.

Ball, R J 1977 Education for top management. *Building Technology and Management* **15**(2): 4–5.

Banerjee, B P and Ghosh, P K 1969 A problem of sequential competitive bidding. In Rao, H S, Jaiswal, N K and Ghosal, A (eds) *Advancing Frontiers in Operational Research*. Hindustan Publishing Company, Delhi.

Barnard, R H 1981 A strategic appraisal system for small firms. *Building Technology and Management* Sept.: 21–4.

Barnes, N M L 1971 *The design and use of experimental bills of quantities for civil engineering contracts*. PhD thesis, University of Manchester Institute of Science and Technology.

Barnes, N M L 1974 Financial control of construction. In Wearne, S H (ed.) *Control of civil engineering projects*, ch. 5. Edward Arnold.

Barnes, N M L and Lau, K T 1974 Bidding strategies and company performance in process plant contracting. In *Transactions*. Third International Cost Engineering Symposium, Association of Cost Engineers.

Battalio, R C, Dwyer, G P and Kagel, J H 1986 Tests of some alternative theories of individual choice behaviour. In Slottje, D J and Rhodes G F (eds) *Advances in economics, volume 5, innovations in quantitative economics: essays in honor of Robert L. Basmann*, pp. 3–30 JAI Press Inc. ISBN 0 89232 686 7.

Becker, G S 1962 Irrational behaviour and economic theory: a comment. *Journal of Political Economy* **71**: 505–10.

Beckmann, M J 1974 A note on cost estimation and the optimal bidding strategy. *Operations Research* **22**: 510–13.

Beeston, D T 1982 Estimating market variance. In Brandon, P S (ed.) *Building cost techniques: new directions*. E and F N Spon, pp. 265–77. ISBN 0 419 12940 5.

Beeston, D T 1974 One statisticians view of estimating. Cost Study No. 3 RICS, Building Cost Information Service.

Beeston, D T 1983 *Statistical methods for building price data*. E and F N Spon. ISBN 0 419 12270 2.

Benes, J and Diepeveen, W J 1985 Flexible planning in construction firms. *Construction Management and Economics* **3**: 25–31.

Bengtsson, S 1985 Organisation and management of construction. *Building Technology and Management* Nov.: 32–4.

Benjamin, N B H 1969 *Competitive bidding for building construction contracts.* PhD dissertation, Stanford University.

Benjamin, N B H 1972 Competitive bidding: the probability of winning. *Journal of the Construction Division, Proceedings of the American Society of Civil Engineers* **98**(CO2): 313–30.

Benjamin, N B H and Meador, R C 1979 Comparison of Friedman's and Gates' competitive bidding models. *Journal of the Construction Division ASCE* **105**(CO1): 25–40.

Bennett, J and Barnes M 1979 Six factors which influence bills. Outline of a theory of measurement. *Chartered Quantity Surveyor* **2**(3): 53–6.

Bennett, J and Fine, B 1980 *Measurement in complexity in construction projects.* SRC Research Report GR/A/1342.4 (Final Report). Department of Construction Management, University of Reading.

Bennett, J and Ormerod, R N 1984 Simulation applied to construction projects. *Construction Management and Economics* **2**: 225–63.

Benson, P H 1970 Selecting price quotations for an industrial firm's sale of individual contract projects. *Operations Research* **18**: 1220–4.

Bishoff, E E 1976 *Aspects of project selection.* MSc thesis, University College of Swansea, University of Wales.

Blake, R R, Avis, W E and Morton, J S 1966 *Corporation Darwinism: an evolutionary perspective on organizing work in the dynamic corporation.* Gulf Publishing Co., Houston.

Bonder, C S 1979 Changing the future of operations research. *Operations Research* 27: 209–24.

Booth, A E 1981 *The design of management information systems to handle uncertainty and complexity: a critical review of current practice.* MPhil thesis, North East London Polytechnic.

Brech, E F L 1975 *Construction management in principle and practice.* Longman.

Brehmer, B 1984 The role of judgement in small-group conflict and decision making, In Stephenson, G M and Davis, J H (eds) *Progress in Applied Social Psychology* 2nd edn, pp. 163–83. John Wiley.

Broemser, G M 1968 *Competitive bidding in the construction industry.* PhD dissertation, Stanford University.

Brown, D M 1974 *A comparative study of four building organisations in relation to their environment.* MSc thesis, University of Bath.

Brown, K C 1966 *A theoretical and statistical study of decision making under uncertainty – competitive bidding for leases of offshore petroleum tracts.* PhD dissertation, Southern Methodist University, Dallas.

Bruner, J 1957 On perceptual readiness. *Psychological Review* **64**: 123–52.

Brunswik, E 1952 *The conceptual framework of psychology.* University of Chicago Press.

Budd, A 1978 *The politics of economic planning.* Fontana/Collins.

Bullock, A and Stallybrass, O 1977 *The Fontana dictionary of modern thought.* Fontana/Collins.

Bunn, D W 1975 *The resolution of uncertainty in decision and policy analysis.* PhD thesis, University of London.

Burton, F M 1972 *A regional economic model of the construction industry.* PhD thesis, University of Pittsburgh.

Calvert, R E 1981 *Introduction to building management* 4th edn. Butterworth. ISBN 0 408 00520 3.

Cameron, I 1980 *To the farthest ends of the earth: the history of the Royal Geographical Society 1830–1980.* Macdonald. ISBN 0 354 04478 8.

Campbell, A, Bloom, M and Groome, C 1974 Demand management and the construction industries now and in the future. *Building Technology and Management* 12(9): 16–21.

Campbell, D T 1969 Reforms as experiment. *American Psychologist* 24: 409–29.

Campbell, J B and Pritchard, R D 1976 Motivation theory in industrial and organisational psychology. In Dunnette, M D (ed.) *Handbook of Industrial and Organisational Psychology.* Rand McNally, Chicago.

Cannon, J 1978 Demand forecasting. *Building Technology and Management* Jan.: 13–14.

Capen, E C, Clapp, R V and Campbell, W M 1971 Competitive bidding in high risk situations. *Journal of Petroleum Technology* June: 641–53.

Carr, R I 1982 General bidding model. *Journal of the Construction Division, Proceedings of the American Society of Civil Engineers* 108(CO4): 639–50.

Carr, R I 1983 Impact of number of bidders on competition. *Journal of Construction Engineering and Management, Proceedings of the American Society of Civil Engineers* 109(1): 61–73.

Carr, R I and Sandahl, J W 1978 Bidding strategy using multiple regression. *Journal of the Construction Division, American Society of Civil Engineers* 104(CO1): 15–26.

Case K E 1972 Consideration of variability in cost engineering. *IEEE Transactions on Engineering Management* 19(4).

Casey, B J and Shaffer, L R 1964 *An evaluation of some competitive bid strategy models for contractors.* Report no. 4, Department of Civil Engineering, University of Illinois.

Cauwelaert, F V and Heynig, E 1978 Correction of bidding errors: the Belgian solution. *Journal of the Construction Division, American Society of Civil Engineers* 105(CO1): 13–23.

Chandler, A D 1962 *Strategy and structure: chapters in the history of American enterprize.* MIT Press, Cambridge, Mass.

Chapman, L J and Chapman, J P 1967 Genesis of popular but erroneous psychodiagnostic observations. *Journal of Abnormal Psychology* 72 193–204.

Cheetham, D W 1980 Management by objectives – the philosophies and techniques with reference to a case study of its application within a building contracting company. *Proceedings* vol. 16, 8th CIB Triennial Congress, Oslo.

Christenson, C 1965 *Strategic aspects of competitive bidding for corporate securities,* pp. 72–89. Boston Division of Research, Graduate School of Business Administration, Harvard University.

Clark, F D and Lorenzoni, A B 1985 *Applied cost engineering* 2nd edn. Marcell Dekker Inc, New York.

Condon, J H and Thompson, K 1982 Belle chess hardware. In Clarke,

M R B (ed.) *Advances in computer chess*, pp. 45–54. Pergamon Press, New York.

Cooke, B 1981 *Contract planning and contractual procedures*. Macmillan. ISBN 0 333 30720 8.

Cotgrove, S 1980 *Risk, value, conflict and political legitimacy*, ch. 7.

Crawford, P B 1970 Texas offshore bidding patterns. *Journal of Petroleum Technology* **22**: 283–9.

Curtis, F J and Maines, P W 1973 Closed competitive bidding. *OMEGA* **1**(5): 613–19.

Cusack, M M 1981 *Time cost models: their use in decision making in the construction industry with particular reference to the use of the micro-computer*. PhD thesis, University of Bath.

Cyert, R M and Marsh, J G 1963 *A behavioural theory of the firm*. Prentice-Hall.

Daniels, R 1978 Keeping tabs on tenders. *Building* 30 June: 49.

Dickenson, G A 1979 *Utility theory and attitudes towards risk in management decision making*. MLitt thesis, University of Glasgow.

Diekmann, J E, Mayer, R H and Stark, R M (1982) Coping with uncertainty in unit price contracting. *Journal of the Construction Division, Proceedings of the American Society of Civil Engineers* **108**(CO3): 379–89.

Diekmann, J and Nelson, M 1981 Construction claim causes and resolution studied. *Journal of Construction Engineering & Management, American Society of Civil Engineers* March.

Diepeveen, W J 1985 *Options for Contracting Firms*. International Council for Building Research, Studies and Documentation.

Diepeveen, W J and Benes, J 1978 A model for corporate planning in the construction firm. *Proceedings* vol. 2: pp. 111–81. CIB W–65 2nd Symposium on Organisation and Management of Construction, Haifa, Israel, 31 Oct–2 Nov. International Council for Building Research.

Diepeveen, W J, Benes, J and Schat, I 1985 Innovation and product development. CIB-W65 Workshop, Zermatt, Switzerland (working paper).

Dougherty, EL and Nozaki, M 1975 Determining optimum bid fraction. *Journal of Petroleum Technology* March: 349–56.

Dressel, G 1965 *Organisation and management of a construction company*, trans. A B Philips. Maclaren.

Dressel, G c.1980 *Company concept: basis for a target-oriented company policy*. Leaflet 63, ifA–Leonberg, West Germany.

Dror, Y 1964 Muddling through: science or inertia. *Public Administration Review* **24**(3): 1953–7.

Drucker, P F 1955 *The practise of management*. Mercury.

Drucker, P F 1959 Long-range planning: challenge to Management Science. *Management Science* **5**(3).

Duff, A R 1976 Control of costs allowances for uncertainty. *Building Technology and Management* July/August: 19, 45.

Edelmann, F 1965 Art and science of competitive bidding. *Harvard Business Review* **43** July/August: 53–66.

Edwards, J P and Harris, D J 1977 Planning in a state of turbulence. *Long Range Planning* June.

Einhorn, H J and Hogarth, R M 1978 Confidence in judgement: persistence of the illusion of validity. *Psychological Review* **85**: 395–416.

Elman, H C 1982 *Iterative methods for large sparse nonsymmetric systems of linear equations*. PhD thesis, Yale University.

Emond, L J 1971 Analytical strategy for the competitive price setter. *Cost and Management* Sept–Oct: 6–11.

Erikson, C A and Boyer, Leroy T 1976 Estimating – state of the art. *Journal of the Construction Division, American Society of Civil Engineers* **102**(CO3): 455–64

Etzioni, A 1967 Mixed scanning: a third approach to decision making. *Public Administration Review* **27** Dec: 385–92.

Ewing, D W 1968 *The practise of planning*. Collier Macmillan.

Fellows, R F and Langford, D A 1980 Decision theory and tendering. *Building Technology and Management* Oct: 36–9.

Fellows, R F, Langford, D A, Newcombe, R and Urry, S A 1983 *Construction management in practice*. Construction Press, ISBN 0 582 30522 5.

Filer, R K 1986 People and productivity: effort supply as viewed by economists and psychologists. In Gilad, B and Kaish, S (eds) *Handbook of Behavioural Economics Vol A Behavioural Microeconomics*, pp. 261–87. JAI Press Inc. ISBN 0 89232 700 6.

Fine, B 1970 Simulation technique challenges management. *Construction Progress* 14 July: 3–4.

Fine, B 1974 Tendering strategy. *Building* 25 Oct: 115–21.

Fine, B and Hackemar, G 1970 Estimating and bidding strategy. *Building Technology and Management* Sept.: 8–9.

Flanagan, R 1980 *Tender price and time prediction of construction work*. DPhil thesis, University of Aston in Birmingham.

Flanagan, R and Norman, G 1982 An examination of the tendering pattern of individual building contractors. *Building Technology and Management* Apr.: 25–8.

Flanagan, R and Norman, G 1985 Sealed bid auctions: an application to the building industry. *Construction Management and Economics* **3**: 145–61.

Foster, P R 1974 *Long range planning and the construction industry*. MSc thesis, University of Bath.

Franks, J 1970 An exercise in cost (price?) estimating. *Building* 12 June: 133–4.

Frazer, R W 1981 *Facing uncertainty in more than one independent variable: the behaviour of firms and implications for policy*. DPhil thesis, University of Oxford.

Freeson, R 1977 Minister's view of our industry in the next few years. *Building Technology and Management* **15**(1): 11–12.

Friedlander, F 1965 Comparative work value systems. *Personnel Psychology* **18**: 1–20.

Friedman, L 1956 A competitive bidding strategy. *Operations Research* **1**(4): 104–12.

Fryer, B G 1977 *The development of managers in the construction industry*. MSc thesis, University of Salford.

Fryer, B G 1985 *The practice of construction management*. Collins. ISBN 0 00 383030 6.

Fuerst, M 1976 Bidding models: truths and comments. *Journal of the Construction Division, American Society of Civil Engineers* **102**(CO1): 169–77.

Fuerst, M 1977 Theory for competitive bidding. *Journal of the Construction Division, American Society of Civil Engineers* **103**(CO1): 139–52.

Galbraith, J 1973 *Designing complex organizations*. Addison-Wesley.

Gates, M 1960 Statistical and economic analysis of a bidding trend. *Journal of the Construction Division, American Society of Civil Engineers* **86**(CO3): 13–35.

Gates, M 1967 Bidding strategies and probabilities. *Journal of the Construction Division, American Society of Civil Engineers* **93**(CO1): 75–107.

Gates, M 1971 Bidding contingencies and probabilities. *Journal of the Construction Division, American Society of Civil Engineers* **97**(CO2): 277–303.

Georgescu-Roegen, N 1966 *Analytical economics: issues and problems*. Harvard University Press.

Gerth, H H and Mills, C W 1958 *From Max Weber: essays in sociology*. Oxford University Press.

Gilchrist, W 1984 *Statistical modelling* Wiley. ISBN 0 471 90380 9.

Gill, P M 1968 *Systems management techniques for builders and contractors*. McGraw-Hill.

Goodlad, J B 1974 *Accounting for construction and management: an introduction*. Heinemann ISBN 0 434 90680–8.

Gottinger, H W 1983 *Coping with complexity: perspectives for economics, management and social sciences*. D Reidel Publishing Company. ISBN 90 277 1510 6.

Green, M F 1978 Construction cost forecasting – the potential for using simple probability techniques. *Proceedings*, vol. 1: II, 185–200. CIB–W65 2nd symposium on organisation and management of construction.

Griesmer, J H, Levitan, R E and Subik, M 1967 Towards a study of bidding processes, part 4: games with unknown costs. *Naval Research Logistics Quarterly* **14**: 415–33.

Grinyer, P H 1972 Systematic strategic planning for construction firms. *Building Technology and Management* **10**(2): 8–14.

Grinyer P H and Whittaker, J D 1973 Managerial judgement in a competitive bidding model. *Operational Research Quarterly* **24**(2): 181–91.

Grubbs, F E 1950 Sample criteria for testing outlying observations. *Annals of Maths and Statistics* **21**: 27–58.

Guzzo, R A and Bondy, J S 1983 *A guide to worker productivity experiments in the United States 1976–81*. Pergamon, New York.

Hackemar, G C 1970 Profit and competition: estimating and bidding strategy. *Building Technology and Management* Dec.: 6–7.

Hackett, R D and Guion, R 1985 A re-evaluation of the absenteeism–job satisfaction relationship. *Organisational behaviour and human decision processes* **35**: 340–81.

Hafele, W 1974 A systems approach to energy. *American Scientist* **63**(4): 438–47.

Hammond, K R 1965 New directions in research on conflict resolution. *Journal of Social Issues* **21**: 44–66

Hammond, K R and Brehmer, B 1973 Quasi-rationality and distrust: implications for international conflict. In Rappoport, L and Summers, D A (eds) *Human judgement and social interaction*, pp. 338–91.

Hammond, K R, Stewart, T R, Brehmer, B and Steinmann, D O 1975 Social judgement theory. In Kaplan, M F and Schwartz, S (eds) *Human judgement and decision processes*, pp. 271–312. Academic Press, New York.

Hanssmann, F and Rivett, B H P 1959 Competitive bidding. *Operational Research Quarterly* **10**(1): 49–55.

Harding, P 1985 The construction company and its systems. In Barton, P (ed.) *Information systems in construction management: principles and applications*, ch. 14, pp. 210–22. Batsford. ISBN 0 7134 4790 7.

Harris, F and McCaffer, R 1983 *Modern construction management* 2nd edn. Granada. ISBN 0 246 11818 0.

Harrison, R S 1981 *Estimating and tendering – some aspects of theory and practice*. The Chartered Institute of Building, Estimating Information Service no. 41. ISBN 0308 8073.

Harrison, R S 1982 Tendering policy and strategy. In Burgess, R A (ed.) *Construction projects, their financial policy and control*, ch. 7, pp. 51–61 Construction Press. ISBN 0 86095 876 0.

Harvey, J R 1979 *Competitive bidding on Canadian public construction contracts, stochastic analysis for optimization*. PhD thesis, School of Business Administration, University of Western Ontario.

Herrnstein, R J 1961 Relative and absolute strength of response as a function of frequency of reinforcement. *Journal of the Experimental Analysis of Behavior* **4**: 267–72.

Herrnstein, R J 1970 On the law of effect. *Journal of the Experimental Analysis of Behavior* **13**: 243–66

Hillebrandt, P M 1974 *Economic theory and the construction industry*. Macmillan. ISBN 0 333 14944 0.

Hills, W D 1985 *The connection machine*. The MIT Press. ISBN 0 262 08157 1.

Hocking, R R and Smith, W B 1968 Estimation of parameters in the multivariate normal distribution with missing observations. *American Statistical Association Journal* **63** Mar.: 159–73.

Hogarth, R M 1981 Beyond discrete biases: functional and dysfunctional aspects of judgmental heuristics. *Psychological Bulletin* **90**(2): 197–217.

Holderman, D 1984 Characteristics of an unsuccessful contractor. *American Professional Constructor* Winter: 15–18.

Holstein, C A S von 1971 Two techniques for assessment of subjective probability distributions: and experimental study. *Acta Psychologica* **35**: 478–94.

Hossein, B R 1977 *Risk analysis of tendering policies for capital projects*. PhD thesis, University of Bradford.

Humphreys, G A 1977 *Financial planning and project cost control techniques applied to building management*. MPhil thesis, University of Aston in Birmingham.

Hunt, G 1986 *Survey of computer applications in construction*. Unpublished communication.

Hurwicz, L 1959 Optimality and informational efficiency of resource allocation processes. In *Mathematical Methods in the Social Sciences*, ch. 3. Stanford University Press, Stanford, California.

Ibbs, C W and Crandall, K C 1982 Construction risk: multiattribute approach. *Journal of the Construction Division, Proceedings of the American Society of Civil Engineers* **108**(CO2): 187–200. ISSN 0569 7948/82/0002 0187.

IQS Sussex Branch Committee 1979 Tenders. *The Quantity Surveyor* **37**(7): 384–6.

Ireland, V 1985 The role of managerial actions in the cost, time and quality performance of high-rise commercial building projects. *Construction Management and Economics* **3**: 59–87.

Jarman, R J 1978 *Building production in a capitalist economy, the response of a sample of building companies ot changing market conditions.* MSocSc thesis, University of Birmingham.

Jensen, A 1976 *Future prospects of OR.* Paper presented at Euro II Congress, Stockholm, Sweden.

Jepson, W R and Nicholson, M P 1972 *Marketing and Building Management.* Medical and Technical Publishing Co. Ltd. SBN 852–000–46–4.

Johnson, G J and Scholes, K 1984 *Exploring corporate strategy.* Prentice-Hall International. ISBN 0–13–295924–0.

Johnston, R H 1978 *Optimisation of the selective competitive tendering system by the construction client.* Transport and Road Laboratory Report 855 DOG.

Kahn, R 1981 *Work and Health.* Wiley, New York.

Kahneman, D and Tversky, A 1972 Subjective probability: a judgement of representativeness. *Cognitive Psychology* **3**: 430–54.

Kahneman, D and Tversky, A 1973 On the psychology of prediction. *Psychological Review* **80**: 237–51

Kahneman, D and Tversky, A 1979 Prospect theory: an analysis of decision under risk. *Econometrica* **47**: 263–91.

Kangari, R and Boyer, L T 1981 Project selection under risk. *Journal of the Construction Division, American Society of Civil Engineers* **107**(CO4): 597–608.

Keeney, R L and Raiffa, H 1976 *Decisions with multiple objectives: preferences and value trade-offs.* Wiley, New York.

Kelly, G A 1955 *Psychology of personal constructs.* W W Norton.

Kempner, T 1976 *A handbook of management.* Penguin.

Kendall, M G and Stuart, A 1963 Distribution Theory, Charles Griffen *The Advanced Theory of Statistics* **Vol 1**: 349.

King, W R and Cleland, D I 1978 *Strategic planning and policy.* Van Nostrand-Reinhold Co.

Klein, J D 1976 Joint ventures and bidding for offshore oil. In Amihud, Y (ed.) *Bidding and auctioning for procurement and allocation.* New York University Press.

Kmietowicz, Z W and Pearman, A D 1981 *Decision theory and incomplete knowledge.* Gower. ISBN 0 566 00327 9.

Koontz, H and O'Donnell, H 1972 *Principles of management: an analysis of managerial functions* 5th edn. McGraw-Hill.

Kotter, J P 1973 The psychological contract: managing the joining up process. *California Management Review* **15**. 91–9.

Lange, J E 1973 *The bidding process in the construction industry.* PhD thesis, Harvard University, Cambridge, Massachusetts.

Langford, D S and Wong, C W 1979 Towards assessing risk. *Building Technology and Management* Apr.: 21–3.

Lansley, P 1981a *Maintaining the company's workload in a changing market.* The Chartered Institute of Building.

Lansley, P 1981b Corporate planning for the small builder. *Building Technology and Management* Dec.: 7–9, 12.

Lansley, P 1983 *Case studies of the constraints to the application of construction management research*. Department of Construction Management, University of Reading.

Lansley, P, Quince, T and Lea, E 1979 *Flexibility and efficiency in construction management* The final report on a research project with the financial support of the DoE. Building Industry Group, Ashbridge Management Research Unit (unpublished).

Lansley, P, Quince, T and Lea, E 1980 Flexibility and efficiency in construction management. *Building Technology and Management* Dec.: 42–3.

Larew, R E 1976 *A quantitative approach to estimating and pricing in a construction company*. PhD thesis, University of Iowa.

Leech, D J and Earthrowl, D L 1972 Predicting design costs. *Aeronautical Journal* **76**: 575–7

Leech, D J and Jenkins, D J 1978 Simulating the work of a tendering technical company. *Journal of the Operational Research Society* **29**(12): 1203–8.

Levinson, H C 1953 Experiences in commercial operations research. *Operations Research* **1**: 220–39.

Liddle, C 1979 Process Engineering – the QS role. *Chartered Quantity Surveyor* **2**(3): 58–60.

Lindblom, C E 1959 The science of muddling through. *Public Administration Review* **19**(2): 79–88.

McCaffer, R 1976a *Contractor's bidding behaviour and tender price prediction*. PhD thesis, Loughborough University of Technology.

McCaffer, R 1976b The effect of estimating accuracies. *The Project Manager* **1**(5): 3–5.

McCaffer, R and Pettitt, A N 1976 Distribution of bids for buildings and road contracts. *Operational Research Quarterly* **27**(4i): 835–43.

McCall, F E 1977 Pricing for profits. *World Construction* **30**(5): 65, 68, 70–1.

McCrimmon, K R 1973 An overview of multiple objective decision making. In Cochrane, J L and Zeleny, M (eds) *Multiple criteria decision making*. University of South Carolina Press.

McGregor, D 1960 *The human side of enterprise*. McGraw-Hill.

MacKenzie, K I and Harris, F C 1984 Money, the only motivator. *Building Technology and Management* **22**(5)–9.

Majid, S A 1967 *Resource forecasting models for private housing projects*. PhD thesis, University of Manchester Institute of Science and Technology.

Mannerings, R 1970 *A study of factors affecting success in tendering for building works*. MSc thesis, University of Manchester Institute of Science and Technology.

Mansson, K 1985 *Higher productivity through improved working conditions*. CIB-W65 workshop, Zermatt, Switzerland (working paper).

March, J G 1978 Bounded rationality, ambiguity, and the engineering of choice. *Bell Journal of Economics* **9**: 587–608.

Maslow, A H 1954 *Motivation and Personality*. Harper and Row, New York.

Mercer, A and Russell, J I T 1969 Recurrent competitive bidding. *Operational Research Quarterly* **20**(2): 209–21.

Merkhofer, M W 1977 The value of information given flexibility. *Management Science* **23**: 716–27.

Milgrom, P R 1981 Rational expectations, information acquisition and competitive bidding. *Econometrica* **49**(4): 921–43.

Mintzberg, H 1975 *Policy as a field of management theory.* Aix-en-Provence (working paper).

Mintzberg, H 1979 *The structuring of organisations.* Prentice-Hall.

Mitchell, M S 1977 The probability of being the lowest bidder. *Applied Statistics* **2**(2): 191–4.

Mood, A M 1983 *Introduction to policy analysis.* Edward Arnold, ISBN 0 7131 3473 9.

Moore, A B 1984 *Marketing management in construction: a guide for contractors.* Butterworth. ISBN 0 408 01196 3.

Morin, T L and Clough, R H 1969 OPBID: competitive bidding strategy model. *Journal of the Construction Division, Proceedings of the American Society of Civil Engineers* **95**(CO1): 85–106.

Morrison, N 1984 The accuracy of quantity surveyors' cost estimating. *Construction Management and Economics* **2**(1): 57–75.

Morrison, N and Stevens, S 1980 *Construction cost data base.* 2nd annual report of research project by Dept of Construction Management, University of Reading, for Property Services Agency, Directorate of Quantity Surveying Services, DoE.

Moss, S J 1981 *An economic theory of business strategy: an essay in dynamics without equilibrium.* M Robertson, Oxford. ISBN 0 85520 386 2.

Moyles, B F 1973 *An analysis of the contractor's estimating process.* MSc thesis, Loughborough University of Technology.

Murray, A H 1938 *Explorations in personality.* Oxford University Press.

Murray, J A 1978 *Towards a contingency model of strategic decision.* ESSEC, CERCY conference, April (working paper).

Murray, M 1980 *The interaction of the theory of corporate planning and the microeconomic theory of the firm in the development of corporate planning models.* MSc thesis, University of Bath.

Nadler, D A, Hackman, J R and Lawler, E E 1979 *Managing organizational behavior.* Little Brown and Co, Boston.

Naert, P A and Weverbergh, M 1978 Cost uncertainty in competitive bidding models. *Journal of the Operational Research Society* **29**(4): 361–72.

Neale, R H (1985) Principal factors in the design and practical implementation of computer-based contract control systems. In Barton, P (ed.) *Information systems in construction management,* ch. 7. Batsford. ISBN 0 7134 4790 7.

Neil, J 1978 *Construction cost estimating concepts and their application.* PhD dissertation, Texas A & M University.

Neo, R B 1976 *International construction contracting.* PhD thesis, Heriot Watt University.

Neufville, R D de, Hani, E N and Lesage, Y 1977 Bidding model: effects of bidders' risk aversion. *Journal of the Construction Division, Proceedings of the American Society of Civil Engineers* **103**(CO1): 57–70.

Neumann, J von 1969 Probabilistic logics and the synthesis of reliable organisms from unreliable components. In Shannon, C E (ed.) *Automata Studies.* Princeton University Press.

Newcombe, R 1976 *The evolution and structure of the construction firm.* MSc thesis, University College, London.

Niss, J F 1965 *Custom production, theory and practise, with special emphasis on the goals and pricing procedures of the contract construction industry*. PhD(Ec) thesis, University of Illinois.

Oren, S S and Rothkopf, M H 1975 Optimal bidding in sequential auctions. *Operations Research* **23**(6): 1080–90.

Ortega-Reichert, A 1968 *Models for competitive bidding under uncertainty*. Technical Report 103, Department of Operations Research, Stanford University.

Otway, H and Pahner, P 1980 Risk assessment. In Dowie, J and Lefrere, P (eds) *Risk and Chance*, ch. 8, pp. 148–60. Open University Press.

Pais, A 1982 *Subtle is the Lord . . . the science and life of Albert Einstein*. Oxford University Press. ISBN 0 19 853907 X.

Park, W R 1962 How low to bid to get both job and profit. *Engineering News Record* **168**: 38–40.

Park, W R 1966 *The strategy of contracting for profit*. Prentice-Hall.

Park, W R 1972 *Cost Engineering Analysis*. J Wiley, New York.

Park, W R 1980 Comparison of Friedman's and Gates' competitive bidding models – discussion. *Journal of the Construction Division, Proceedings of the American Society of Civil Engineers* **106**(CO2): 225–6.

Parry-Lewis, J 1968 *Bidding cycles and Britain's growth*. Macmillan.

Peirce, C S 1980 Collected papers. Hartshorn, C and Weiss, P (eds), cited in Bork, A Randomness and the twentieth century. In Dowie, J and Lefrere, P (eds) *Risk and chance*. Oxford University Press.

Pelto, C R 1971 The statistical structure of bidding for oil and mineral rights. *Journal of the American Statistical Association* **66**: 456–60.

Peters, T J and Waterman, R H J 1982 *In search of excellence*. Harper and Row. ISBN 0 06 015042 4.

Pim, J C 1974 Competitive tendering and bidding strategy. *National Builder* **55**(11): 541–5; **56**(2): 56–7; **56**(10): 361–5; **57**(3): 68–70.

Porter, L W and Lawler, EE 1968 *Managerial attitudes and performance*. Dorsey Press.

Porter, L W, Lawler, E L and Hackman, J R 1975 *Behavior in organisations*. McGraw Hill.

Porter, M E 1980 *Competitive strategy*. The Free Press. ISBN 0 02 925360 8.

Portsmouth Polytechnic, Department of Surveying 1974 *Acceptable levels of risk*. RICS/NFBTE Standard Method of Measurement Development Unit.

Prosper, J 1984 The right type of training. *Building Technology and Management*. May: 24.

Pye, R 1978 A formal decision theoretic approach to flexibility and robustness. *JORSA* **29**: 215–27.

Raiffa, H 1968 *Decision analysis*. Addison-Wesley.

Rajab, Z T S 1981 *An investigation into the nature and extent of corporate planning in construction companies*. MSc thesis, Heriot Watt University.

Rickwood, A K 1972 *An investigation into the tenability of bidding theory and techniques, and proposals for a bidding game*. MSc thesis, Loughborough University of Technology.

Rockeach, M 1973 *The nature of human values*. The Free Press, New York.

Ronen, J 1973 Effects of some probability displays on choices. *Organizational Behavior and Human Performance* **9**: 1-50.

Rosenhead, J V *et al.* 1972 Robustness and optimality as criteria for strategic decisions. *Operations Research Quarterly* **23**: 413–31.

Rothkopf, M H 1969 A model of rational competitive bidding. *Management Science* **15**(7): 362–73.

Rothkopf, M H 1980 On multiplicative bidding strategies. *Operations Research* **28**(3): 1, 570–7.

Rubey, H and Milner, W W 1966 *Construction and professional management*, pp. 229–65. Macmillan.

Rutland, P 1984 What determines success? *Building Technology and Management* **22**(9): 17.

Sasieni, M, Yaspan, A and Friedman, L 1959 *Operations research: methods and problems*, ch. 7. J Wiley, New York.

SEBI *c.*1965 *Study*. A report submitted by the University of Manchester Institute of Science and Technology to the Ministry of Public Buildings and Works (in Jepson and Nicholson 1972: 29).

Shackle, G L S 1952 *Expectations in economics*. Cambridge University Press.

Shaffer, L R and Micheau, T W 1971 Bidding with competitive strategy models. *Journal of the Construction Division, Proceedings of the American Society of Civil Engineers* **97**(CO1): 113–26.

Shaffer, L R and Micheau, T W 1973 Discussion – bidding with competitive strategy models. *Journal of the Construction Division, Proceedings of the American Society of Civil Engineers* **99**(CO1): 205–6.

Sheldon, I M 1982 *Competitive bidding and objectives of the firm, with reference to the UK process plant contracting industry*. Occasional paper 8210. Dept of Management Science, The University of Manchester Institute of Science and Technology.

Sidwell, A 1984 Management of opportunities. *Building Technology and Management* **22**(6): 21–2.

Simmonds, K 1968a Competitive bidding: deciding the best conditions for non-price features. *Operational Research Quarterly* **19**(1): 5–14.

Simmonds, K 1968b Adjusting bias in cost estimates: viewpoints. *Operational Research Quarterly* **19**(1): 325.

Simon, H A 1955 A behavioral model of rational choice. *Quarterly Journal of Economics* **69**: 99–118.

Simon, H A 1957 *Administrative behavior: a study of decision making processes in administrative organizations*. The Free Press.

Simon, H A 1959 *American Economic Review* **49**: 253–80.

Skitmore, R M 1981a *Bidding dispersion – an investigation into a method of measuring the accuracy of building cost estimates*. MSc thesis, University of Salford.

Skitmore, R M 1981b Why do tenders vary? *Chartered Quantity Surveyor* **4**: 128–9.

Skitmore, R M 1982 A bidding model. In Brandon, P S (ed.) *Building Cost Techniques: New Directives*, pp. 278–89. E and F N Spon. ISBN 0 419 12940 5.

Skitmore, R M 1985 *The influence of professional expertise in construction price forecasts*. Dept of Civil Engineering, University of Salford. ISBN 0 901025 09 7.

Skitmore, R M 1986 *A model of the construction project selection and bidding decision*. PhD thesis, The University of Salford.

Slovic, P, Fischoff, B and Lichtenstein, S 1977 Behavioral decision theory. *Annual Review of Psychology* **28**: 1–39.

Slovic, P and Lichtenstein, S 1971 Comparison of Bayesian and regression approaches to the study of information processing in judgement. *Organizational Behavior and Human Performance* **6**: 649–744.

Smart, P M 1976 *Design budget allocation and project selection.* PhD thesis, University of Wales.

Smith, G 1981 Tendering procedures scrutinised – Essex costs the alternatives. *Chartered Quantity Surveyor* **June** 356–7.

Smith, J G 1985 *Business strategy.* Blackwell, ISBN 0 631 13986 9.

Smith, T and Case, J H 1975 Nash equilibria in sealed bid auctions. *Management Science* **22**: 487–97.

South, L E 1979 *Construction companies and demand fluctuations.* MSc thesis, Loughborough University of Technology.

Southwell, J 1971 *Building cost forecasting.* Selected papers on a systematic approach to forecasting building costs presented to the Quantity Surveyors (Research and Information) Committee. Royal Institution of Chartered Surveyors.

Sowa, J F 1984 *Conceptual structures: information processing in mind and machine.* Addison-Wesley. ISBN 0 201 14472 7.

Spiegelhalter, D J 1983 Diagnostic tests of distributional shape. *Biometrika* **70**(2): 401–9.

Spooner, J E 1971 Bidding with competitive strategy models – discussion. *Journal of the Construction Division, Proceedings of the American Society of Cost Engineers* 97(CO1): 345.

Spooner, J E 1974 Probabilistic estimating. *Journal of the Construction Division, Proceedings of the American Society of Cost Engineers* **100**(CO1): 65–77.

Stacey, N 1979 Estimates of uncertainty. *Building* Oct.: 63–4.

Staddon, J E R 1979 Operant behavior as adaptation to constraint. *Journal of Experimental Psychology: General* **108**: 48–67.

Stark, R M 1976 An estimating technology for unbalancing bid proposals. In *Bidding and auctioning procedures and allocations*, ch. 3, pp. 21–34.

Stark, R M and Mayer R H 1971 Some multi-contract decision-theoretic competitive bidding models. *Operations Research* **19**: 469–83.

Steinbrunner. 1974 *The cybernetic theory of decision.* Princeton University Press, New Jersey.

Sugrue, P K 1977 *The design and evaluation of three competitive bidding models for application in the construction industry.* PhD thesis, University of Massachusetts.

Sugrue, P K 1980 An optimum bid approximation model. *Journal of the Construction Division, Proceedings of the American Society of Civil Engineers* **106**(CO4): 499–505.

Tavistock Institute of Human Relations 1966 *Interdependence and uncertainty: a study of the building industry.* Tavistock Publications.

Taylor, N 1963 A bidding model for timber purchasing. *Research program in marketing*, pp. 28–44. Special publication of Institute of Building and Economic Research, Graduate School of Business Administration, University of California at Berkeley.

Thompson, P 1981 *Organization and economics of construction*. McGraw-Hill, ISBN 0 07 084122 5.

Tjosvold, D 1985 Power and social context in superior-subordinate interaction. *Organizational behaviour and human decision processes* **35**: 281–93.

Toffler, A 1971 *Future shock*. Pan Publications.

Tomer, J F 1986 Productivity and organizational behavior: where human capital theory fails. In Gilad, B and Kaish, S (eds) *Handbook of behavioral economics*, vol. 5, pp. 233–55. JAI Press.

Tversky, A and Kahneman, D 1971 Belief in the law of small numbers. *Psychological Bulletin* **76**: 105–10.

Tversky, A and Kahneman, D 1974 Judgement under uncertainty: heuristics and biases. *Science* **185**: 1124–31.

Vergara, A J 1977 *Probabilistic estimating and applications of portfolio theory in construction*. PhD dissertation, University of Illinois.

Vergara, A J and Boyer, L T 1974 Probabilistic approach to estimating and cost control. *Journal of the Construction Division, Proceedings of the American Society of Civil Engineers* **100**(CO4): 543–52.

Vickrey, W 1961 Counterspeculation auctions and competitive sealed transfers. *Journal of Finance* **16**: 8–37.

Vroom, V 1964 *Work and motivation*. Wiley, New York.

Wade, R L and Harris, B 1976 LOMARK: a bidding strategy. *Journal of the Construction Division, Proceedings of the American Society of Civil Engineers* **102**(CO1): 197–211.

Wagner, H M 1971 The ABC of OR. *Operations Research* Oct.: 1259–81.

Weverbergh, M 1977 *Competitive bidding – games, decision making and cost uncertainty*. Doctoral thesis, Universitaire Faculteiten Sint-Ignatius te Antwerpen UFSIA/78*03141.

Weverbergh, M 1978 *The Gates-Friedman controversy: a critical review*. Working paper 78–1 April. Centrum voor Bedrijfseconomie en Bedrijfseconometrie Universiteir Antwerpen – UFSIA.

Weverbergh, M 1981 *Competitive bidding models: an overview*. Working paper 81–72 Aug. Centrum voor Bedrijfseconomie en Bedrijfseconometrie Universiteit Antwerpen – UFSIA.

Weverbergh, M 1982 *Competitive bidding: estimating the joint distribution of bids*. Working paper 82–79 Dec. Centrum voor Bedrijfseconomie en Bedrijfseconometrie Universiteit Antwerpen – UFSIA.

Whittaker, J D 1970 *A study of competitive bidding with particular reference to the construction industry*. PhD thesis, City University, London.

Willenbrock, J H 1972 *A comparative study of expected monetary value and expected utility value bidding strategy models*. PhD thesis, The Pennsylvania State University.

Wilson, A 1982 Experiments in probabilistic cost modelling. In Brandon, P S (ed.) *Building cost techniques: new directions*, pp. 169–80. E and F N Spon. ISBN 0 419 12940 5.

Wilson, A J 1979 *Need-important and need-satisfaction for construction operatives*. MSc thesis, Loughborough University of Technology.

Wilson, R 1979 A bidding model of perfect competition. *Review of Economic Studies* **44**: 511–18.

Winkler, R L 1967 Assessment of prior distributions in Bayesian analysis. *Journal of the American Statistical Association* **62**: 776–800.

Winkler, R L and Brookes, D G 1980 Competitive bidding with dependent value estimates. *Operations Research* **28**(3): 1603–13.

Winterfeldt, D von and Edwards, W 1986 *Decision analysis and behavioral research*. Cambridge University Press. ISBN 0 521 27308 X.

Wolf, C and Kalley, G S 1983 Risk management in cost engineering – application of utility theory. In *Transactions* American Association of Cost Engineers. 27th Annual Meeting Philadelphia, Pennsylvania. ISBN 0 930284 17 8.

Wong, C 1978 *Bidding strategy in the building industry*. MSc thesis, Brunel University.

Woodward, J F 1975 *Quantitative methods in construction management and design*. Macmillan. SBN 333–17720–7.

Young, M 1978 *Analysis of the relationship between model-building and decision-making*. PhD thesis, University of Oxford.

Zinn, D C, Lesso, W G and Givens, G R 1975 OILSIM – a simulation model for evaluating alternative bidding strategies. Dec. Paper presented at 96th Annual Meeting of the ASME.

Index

209